Horizontalism and Historicity in Argentina
Cultural Dialogues of the Post-Crisis Era

# LEGENDA

LEGENDA is the Modern Humanities Research Association's book imprint for new research in the Humanities. Founded in 1995 by Malcolm Bowie and others within the University of Oxford, Legenda has always been a collaborative publishing enterprise, directly governed by scholars. The Modern Humanities Research Association (MHRA) joined this collaboration in 1998, became half-owner in 2004, in partnership with Maney Publishing and then Routledge, and has since 2016 been sole owner. Titles range from medieval texts to contemporary cinema and form a widely comparative view of the modern humanities, including works on Arabic, Catalan, English, French, German, Greek, Italian, Portuguese, Russian, Spanish, and Yiddish literature. Editorial boards and committees of more than 60 leading academic specialists work in collaboration with bodies such as the Society for French Studies, the British Comparative Literature Association and the Association of Hispanists of Great Britain & Ireland.

The MHRA encourages and promotes advanced study and research in the field of the modern humanities, especially modern European languages and literature, including English, and also cinema. It aims to break down the barriers between scholars working in different disciplines and to maintain the unity of humanistic scholarship. The Association fulfils this purpose through the publication of journals, bibliographies, monographs, critical editions, and the MHRA Style Guide, and by making grants in support of research. Membership is open to all who work in the Humanities, whether independent or in a University post, and the participation of younger colleagues entering the field is especially welcomed.

ALSO PUBLISHED BY THE ASSOCIATION

*Critical Texts*
*Tudor and Stuart Translations* • *New Translations* • *European Translations*
*MHRA Library of Medieval Welsh Literature*

*MHRA Bibliographies*
*Publications of the Modern Humanities Research Association*

*The Annual Bibliography of English Language & Literature*
*Austrian Studies*
*Modern Language Review*
*Portuguese Studies*
*The Slavonic and East European Review*
*Working Papers in the Humanities*
*The Yearbook of English Studies*

www.mhra.org.uk
www.legendabooks.com

# STUDIES IN HISPANIC AND LUSOPHONE CULTURES

*Studies in Hispanic and Lusophone Cultures* are selected and edited by the Association of Hispanists of Great Britain & Ireland. The series seeks to publish the best new research in all areas of the literature, thought, history, culture, film, and languages of Spain, Spanish America, and the Portuguese-speaking world.

The Association of Hispanists of Great Britain & Ireland is a professional association which represents a very diverse discipline, in terms of both geographical coverage and objects of study. Its website showcases new work by members, and publicises jobs, conferences and grants in the field.

*Founding Editor*
Trevor Dadson

*Editorial Committee*
Chair: Professor Catherine Davies (University of London)
Professor Stephanie Dennison (University of Leeds)
Professor Sally Faulkner (University of Exeter)
Professor Andrew Ginger
(New College of Humanities at Northeastern University)
Professor James Mandrell (Brandeis University, USA)
Professor Hilary Owen (University of Manchester/University of Oxford)
Professor Philip Swanson (University of Sheffield)
Professor Jonathan Thacker (Exeter College, University of Oxford)

*Managing Editor*
Dr Graham Nelson
41 Wellington Square, Oxford OX1 2JF, UK

www.legendabooks.com/series/shlc

# STUDIES IN HISPANIC AND LUSOPHONE CULTURES

20. *(Un)veiling Bodies: A Trajectory of Chilean Post-Dictatorship Documentary*, by Elizabeth Ramírez-Soto
21. *Photographing the Unseen Mexico: Maya Goded's Socially Engaged Documentaries*, by Dominika Gasiorowski
22. *The Rise of Spanish American Poetry 1500-1700*, edited by Rodrigo Cacho Casal and Imogen Choi
23. *José Saramago: History, Utopia, and the Necessity of Error*, by Mark Sabine
24. *The Cultural Legacy of María Zambrano*, edited by Xon de Ros and Daniela Omlor
25. *Cortázar and Music*, by Nicholas Roberts
26. *Bodies of Disorder: Gender and Degeneration in Baroja and Blasco Ibáñez*, by Katharine Murphy
27. *The Art of Cervantes in Don Quixote: Critical Essays*, edited by Stephen Boyd, Trudi L. Darby and Terence O'Reilly
28. *The Modern Spanish Canon: Visibility, Cultural Capital and the Academy*, edited by Stuart Davis and Maite Usoz de la Fuente
29. *The Novels of Carmen Laforet: An Aesthetics of Relief*, by Caragh Wells
30. *Humanizing Childhood in Early Twentieth-Century Spain*, by Anna Kathryn Kendrick
31. *Gómez Manrique, Statesman and Poet*, by Gisèle Earle
32. *No Country for Nonconforming Women: Feminine Conceptions of Lusophone Africa*, by Maria Tavares
33. *Form and Reform in Eighteenth-Century Spain*, by Carla Almanza-Gálvez
34. *Women and Nationhood in Restoration Spain 1874–1931*, by Rocío Rødtjer
35. *Francisca Wood and Nineteenth-Century Periodical Culture*, by Cláudia Pazos Alonso
36. *Pepetela and the MPLA: The Ethical Evolution of a Revolutionary Writer*, by Phillip Rothwell
37. *Queer Genealogies in Transnational Barcelona*, by Natasha Tanna
38. *Hispanic Baroque Ekphrasis: Góngora, Camargo, Sor Juana*, by Luis Castellví Laukamp
39. *Contemporary Galician Women Writers*, by Catherine Barbour
40. *The Marvellous and the Miraculous in María de Zayas*, by Sander Berg
41. *Twentieth-Century Sephardic Authors from the Former Yugoslavia*, by Željko Jovanović
42. *From Doubt to Unbelief: Forms of Scepticism in the Iberian World*, edited by Mercedes García-Arenal and Stefania Pastore
43. *Franco's Female Prisoners: Writing No / Bodies*, by Holly J. Foss
44. *Memory and Utopia: The Poetry of José Ángel Valente*, by Manus O'Dwyer
45. *Quim Monzó and Contemporary Catalan Culture (1975–2018)*, by Guillem Colom-Montero
46. *Horizontalism and Historicity in Argentina: Cultural Dialogues of the Post-Crisis Era*, by Brigid Lynch
47. *The Visualization of a Nation: Tàpies and Catalonia*, by Emily Jenkins
48. *Naturalism Against Nature: Kinship and Degeneracy in Fin-de-siècle Portugal and Brazil*, by David J. Bailey
49. *Queering Lorca's Duende: Desire, Death, Intermediality*, by Miguel García

# Horizontalism and Historicity in Argentina

*Cultural Dialogues of the Post-Crisis Era*

Brigid Lynch

Studies in Hispanic and Lusophone Cultures 46
Modern Humanities Research Association
2021

*Published by Legenda*
*an imprint of the Modern Humanities Research Association*
*Salisbury House, Station Road, Cambridge* CB1 2LA

*ISBN 978-1-78188-464-5 (HB)*
*ISBN 978-1-78188-468-3 (PB)*

*First published 2021*

*All rights reserved. No part of this publication may be reproduced or disseminated or transmitted in any form or by any means, electronic, mechanical, photocopying, recording or otherwise, or stored in any retrieval system, or otherwise used in any manner whatsoever without written permission of the copyright owner, except in accordance with the provisions of the Copyright, Designs and Patents Act 1988, or under the terms of a licence permitting restricted copying issued in the UK by the Copyright Licensing Agency Ltd, Saffron House, 6–10 Kirby Street, London* EC1N 8TS, *England, or in the USA by the Copyright Clearance Center, 222 Rosewood Drive, Danvers MA 01923. Application for the written permission of the copyright owner to reproduce any part of this publication must be made by email to legenda@mhra.org.uk.*

*Disclaimer: Statements of fact and opinion contained in this book are those of the author and not of the editors or the Modern Humanities Research Association. The publisher makes no representation, express or implied, in respect of the accuracy of the material in this book and cannot accept any legal responsibility or liability for any errors or omissions that may be made.*

*Trademark notice: Product or corporate names may be trademarks or registered trademarks, and are used only for identification and explanation without intent to infringe.*

*© Modern Humanities Research Association 2021*

*Copy-Editor: Dr Ellen Jones*

# CONTENTS

| | | |
|---|---|---|
| | *Acknowledgements* | ix |
| | Introduction | 1 |
| 1 | After the *Argentinazo* — Historicity, *Horizontalidad* and a New 'Structure of Feeling' | 11 |
| 2 | A Spectre Calls: Hauntology as Historicity | 40 |
| 3 | The Map and the Territory: Space and Place in Post-Crisis Buenos Aires | 66 |
| 4 | Back in Time for Dinner: Living History on the Small Screen | 98 |
| 5 | Vile Bodies: The Grotesqueries of History | 126 |
| | Afterword | 151 |
| | *Bibliography* | 155 |
| | *Index* | 167 |

# ACKNOWLEDGEMENTS

This book began life as a PhD thesis at the University of St Andrews and its transformation, from research to thesis to book, would not have been possible without the kindness and encouragement of a broad community of people. This community is diverse and disparate, and therein lies it strength. From university classrooms in St Andrews to a chilly PH in the microcentro of Buenos Aires, via living rooms and kitchens in Edinburgh and Lanark and in many pubs and cafes in between, I found advice and support from this community. Here, I think, it might be timely to mention that the civic motto of the area where I live in North Edinburgh, generally known as the 'People's Republic' of Leith, is 'Persevere'. Perseverance, as anyone who has ever sat before a computer screen in the wee small hours of the morning knows, is key to writing. As I see it, the potential for perseverance comes not through individual force of will alone, but in conjunction with the collective support and solidarity of a community. My ability to see this project through to its end, in the book that you are now reading, comes from the support I have received from this community along the way.

At the University of St Andrews, special thanks must go to my supervisor, Dr Eleni Kefala. Without her guidance and support, this book would not exist. At the Department of Spanish, I am also grateful to Professors Bernard Bentley and Gustavo San Roman for their encouragement. Dr Javier Letrán helped me to think more deeply about late capitalism and its discontents and was always a cheering presence during my PhD. Professor Will Fowler was always helpful and kind. Professor Catherine O'Leary, the Director of the Cultural Identity and Memory Studies Institute at St Andrews, has been extremely supportive of my work, especially in the challenging post-PhD phase and I am very grateful to her for this. Indeed, the community of scholars at the Institute has and continues to be a source of valuable and considered feedback, for which I am very thankful. Professor Nikki Hitchcott provided me with some crucial advice as I began to develop this project as a book. In the academic community outside St Andrews, Professor Philip Swanson has been extremely generous with his time and support. I also owe a debt of thanks to Dr Lauren Rea, whose perceptive and insightful comments on my work helped me to assert my own voice in the writing that bridged the gap between my thesis and this book.

The doctoral thesis that eventually became this book was made possible through a three-year Santander PhD scholarship from the School of Modern Languages at the University of St Andrews. A Santander Mobility grant helped to fund a period of research in Buenos Aires, as did awards from the Society of Latin American Studies (SLAS) Postgraduate Travel Bursary Fund and the D.J. Gifford Travel Fund.

Financial support from the University of St Andrews Postgraduate Discretionary Fund enabled me to complete the final year of my research, as did the additional funding I received in 2018 from both the Sutherland Page Trust and the May Wong Smith Trust. In addition, I owe special thanks to the team at Student Services, and to Joyce Lapeyre in particular, for their assistance during the final year of my project. At the Association of Hispanists of Great Britain and Ireland (AHGBI), my thanks go to Professor Claire Taylor and Dr Martín Veiga. At Legenda, I am grateful to Dr Graham Nelson for his support throughout the publication process, and to Dr Ellen Jones for her insightful editing of my original text. Cheryl Hunston's help with the index was also invaluable.

My friends Guadalupe Arias, Karen Brown, Isabelle Gribomont, Julia Hieske and Karunika Kardak helped me to get through the daily grind of this doctoral project. Kirsty Boardman was also a most encouraging ally and friend, not least during bleak winter train journeys between Edinburgh and St Andrews. In Edinburgh, Blair Sadler, Michael Black and Craig Paterson have provided high quality non-PhD-related chat. Nicola Law helped me to escape the exigencies of my research project with interesting excursions to the new towns of Scotland. In Buenos Aires, my thanks to the writers and activists of Mu, the monthly magazine produced by the autonomous media collective lavaca. There, Claudia Acuña offered valuable insight into the magazine's origins, and Julieta Colomer was generous with both her time and her friendship. I am also grateful to the Fundación Tomás Eloy Martínez for granting me access to their wonderful archive. At Calle Libertad, Matías and Cande were the best of hosts and Artsey, Gii, Indu and Alex helped me through some difficult times with their good company.

My greatest thanks go to my family. It is due to the support and encouragement of my parents Michael and Maureen Lynch, and their belief in the transformative potential of free education, that my undertaking of a PhD project was, all along, the only path I wished to follow. Deborah, Jody, Daniel and Isabella have helped me in ways too numerous to mention here. James and Rachael merit a special mention for their technological and artistic expertise. Dr Patricia Dennison taught me the exigencies of historical research and referencing with good humour and patience. My uncle Martin Hilland was always incredibly enthusiastic about my research, and he is much missed. And last, but by no means least, thanks must go to the inspirational women in my family: Maureen, Margaret, Anna, Margaret Devlin, Cathy, Helen and Maisie. First and foremost, history is personal, and it is from these personal histories that I draw strength and inspiration.

B.L., January 2021

# INTRODUCTION

At the time of writing, in the heady political climate of 2020, the term 'crisis' has itself undergone something of a crisis of meaning, so ubiquitous has it become in contemporary discourse around the parlous and increasingly uncertain state of the polity at both a national and global level. In the third decade of the twenty-first century, moments of crisis have become something akin to background noise, a shifting and spectacular media wallpaper of epoch-defining economic shocks and socio-political catastrophes that pervade our lived experience of the world. Such 'normalization of crisis'[1] has long been identified as integral to the success of the neoliberal economic model, a system that, as David Harvey has asserted, is characterized by 'periodic episodes of growth interspersed with phases of creative destruction, usually registered as severe financial crises'.[2] Yet, as he clarifies, the impact of such fiscal catastrophes reverberates far beyond the trading floors of the world's great financial centres, penetrating the realms of 'labour, social relations, welfare provisions [...], ways of life, attachments to the land, habits of the heart, ways of thought, and the like'.[3] Drawing upon the writings of Karl Marx, Harvey's concept of 'creative destruction' enunciates the ruinous potential which, he asserts, is inherent within contemporary capitalism. It is, he suggests, precisely through the cyclical crises which the praxis of neoliberalism engenders that the discourse of the free market has grown and thrived, permeating public consciousness as the only viable form of resolution and, more perniciously, the natural state of being.[4] As Margaret Thatcher, one of neoliberalism's foremost advocates, presciently declared in the early 1980s, 'economics is the method, but the object is to change the heart and soul'.[5]

As the grand narrative to emerge from the post-ideological ruins of the late twentieth century, an age ostensibly defined by 'an incredulity towards meta-narratives',[6] neoliberalism and its attendant crises has progressed from the economic plane to the ontological, assuming the hegemonic role of a common-sense 'cultural logic' that governs our relations with the world in which we live.[7] Yet, paradoxically, it is also in these episodes of crisis, so crucial to the advancement of the neoliberal worldview, that the greatest opportunity for transformation exists. In December 2001, Argentina faced total economic collapse, burdened by huge debt default, the devaluation of the national currency and a historic decline in GDP levels of almost twenty per cent over the three-year period since 1998.[8] The causes were complex, but as Christopher Wylde propounds, were rooted as much in politics as in economics; they resided in factors such as 'the institutional weakness of both the Argentine state apparatus as a result of decades of dictatorship, neoliberal reforms in the 1990s, and of the Alianza government'.[9] Furthermore, whilst popular discontent was widespread throughout December 2001, fuelled in no small measure by the technocratic restrictions of the *corralito* –– government legislation which effectively froze all bank-held savings and curtailed the cash withdrawal of US dollars –– it was the explicitly political declaration of a national state of siege on the nineteenth of that month which precipitated the mass protests that would bring down a succession of four presidents in the two weeks that followed. In limiting the civil rights of the populace in a democratic era, President De la Rúa's decree mobilized memories of both a recent dictatorial past and the societal inequities wrought by the neoliberal economic model implemented since the transition to democracy. Moreover, beyond the legacy of the 1976–1983 dictatorship, the government's draconian response to the crisis raised fundamental questions for many Argentines as to the legitimacy of a socio-economic order that had acted as midwife to no fewer than six military coups during the twentieth century.[10] In this way, as scholars such as Maristella Svampa and Joanna Page have argued, the Crisis of 2001 was unique in the 'denaturalizing effect' it had upon the Argentine popular consciousness, in that it facilitated an interrogation of the common sense of present-day existence, particularly when viewed through the prism of the past.[11]

Ana Cecilia Dinerstein goes further, identifying the events of December 19th and 20th as a temporal and epistemic 'hinge' within the popular imaginary, as citizens reclaimed the public spaces of the *polis* through the praxis of direct democracy in order to demand a renegotiation of their existing relationship with the institutions of state and market.[12] Facilitated by the spontaneous public mobilizations of December 2001, this hinge, she contends, unleashed 'a surplus or excess that has no grammar in the logic of state power',[13] and, as such, could not be contained by a return to the status quo ante. Citing Molly Ann Rothenberg's theories of excess, Dinerstein contends that the *Argentinazo* 'carried certain continuity with the past, but as an "event" it "[brought] something new into the world that change[d] the determinants and significance of the very terms by which we had previously comprehended the situation"'.[14] In other words, in its epiphanic potential, the Crisis enabled new perspectives on the past, present and future, fracturing the validity of the neoliberal consensus and eliciting alternative modes of thinking around the relationship between *citizens, state and market*. In this sense, the events of December 2001 signalled the emergence of an alternative 'structure of feeling', a notion which, in coining the term, Raymond Williams described as 'a particular sense of life, a particular community of experience hardly needing expression, through which the characteristics of our way of life [...] are in some way passed, giving them a particular and characteristic colour'.[15]

The variant hues of the structure of feeling that came to prominence through the turbulent events of late 2001 coalesced around a profound dissatisfaction with the current reality of a democracy enfeebled: first by the repeated interventions of the armed forces in the political life of the nation throughout the twentieth century; and subsequently by a neoliberal economic project that had failed to deliver greater socio-economic equality. With the galvanizing slogan '¡Que se vayan todos!' [They all must go!], the multitude that assembled on the streets of Buenos Aires during the *Argentinazo*, although varied in class, political orientation and economic status, articulated a repudiation of the polity and its recent history which was underpinned by the desire for an alternative future. New approaches were required not only to make sense of the present but also to forge alternative ways of living in the times ahead. Consequently, in the post-Crisis period a revitalized sense of historicity became a crucial mobilizing impetus, along with the innovative and iconoclastic praxis of *horizontalidad*, a non-verticalist model of social and political organization previously employed by activist groups such as the unemployed *piqueteros* and the nascent human rights group H.I.J.O.S (Hijos por la identidad y la justicia contra el olvido y el silencio).[16]

Therefore, it is the purpose of this book to identify the two discursive forces of historicity and *horizontalidad* as central to the new 'structure of feeling' which emerged following the 2001 Crisis in Argentina, and to analyse their iterations across the cultural realm. Comprising five case studies that range from literary fiction to film, journalism, photography and television drama, the rationale of this study is grounded in the specificities of William's concept of the structure of feeling and his catholic approach to culture as a 'body of intellectual and imaginative work, in which, in a detailed way, human thought and experience are variously recorded'.[17] Here, it is worth quoting his argument at length:

> The abstraction of art has been its promotion or relegation to an area of special experience (emotion, beauty, phantasy, the imagination, the unconscious), which art in practice has never confined itself to, ranging in fact from the most ordinary daily activities to exceptional crisis and intensities, and using a range of meanings from the words of the street and common popular stories to strange systems and images which it has yet been able to make common property[18]

It is Williams's assertion that, through the imposition of artificial taxonomies of perception and criticism, art has traditionally been isolated from common experience. Such classifications not only degrade the potential of traditional art forms, isolating the totems of the cultural canon from lived experience, but also deny the legitimacy of popular cultural narratives. Therefore, for Williams, in order to engage fully with the communal sense of life of any given period, it is crucial to move beyond the antiquated Modernist dichotomy of high and low art, towards a consideration of what he describes as 'the documentary culture, from poems to buildings and dress fashions'.[19] These cultural forms, along with numerous other possible examples, are artefacts that reflect both the dominant ideologies of their era, and how life is experienced within a community. It is for this reason, following Williams's holistic approach, that this study analyses examples of historicity and *horizontalidad* from a range of media modalities, observing how these two discourses intersect and diverge within the specific narratives of the texts chosen.

This study also has a second purpose, and it is one closely imbricated with how the corpus of texts it examines were selected, in that it seeks to articulate how works of culture enable us to construct connections between our own everyday lives and the lives of others, particularly in an era where new and ever more destabilizing forms of crisis manifest themselves with what seems like unparalleled frequency. This book is both the product of a recent doctoral research project and the fruit of a decade of interest in this topic before that, spent away from academia. I first visited Argentina in 2002, around six months after the events of the *Argentinazo*, and I have returned on many subsequent occasions since. But the works of culture which I analyse in the following five chapters were all largely encountered *away* from Argentina, mainly in the Scottish capital city of Edinburgh, where I lived and worked during that ten-year period. Some texts I actively sought out; others presented themselves to me in a series of mundane yet fortuitous encounters. After all, as Williams wrote in a 1958 essay, 'culture is ordinary', and we interact with culture in hundreds of different ways every day.[20] For example, in Chapter Two, I discuss the work *El cantor de tango* by Tomás Eloy Martínez, a novel which I first discovered in a review of its English translation, *The Tango Singer*, in the freesheet newspaper *Metro*, glancing absentmindedly through the paper on the bus journey home from work. Two films that appear in Chapters One and Three, *Los aparecidos* and *Elefante blanco*, I watched on cold winter evenings spent at the Edinburgh Filmhouse. I first heard the author Carlos Gamerro, discussed in Chapter Five, talk about his work on a marginally, but not much, warmer summer afternoon at the Edinburgh Book Festival. These initial encounters, and other similar experiences that followed, helped me to construct a series of connections between my own lived experience and the representations of life present in these texts. While some of these connections fostered positive comparisons, and others highlighted discontinuities of geography, social relations, and political activism, all opened up new ways of thinking about being in the world. Simply put, engaging with these works of culture, then and now, opened up new vistas of understanding and of solidarity for me on both a personal and an intellectual level. As David Featherstone asserts, the notion that solidarity only flourishes through likeness and common experience is not only false, but it also 'obscures the importance of solidarities in constructing relations between places, activists, diverse social groups' and 'the active creation of new ways of relating'.[21] In times of crisis, culture offers us more than distraction and escapism, although these too are important attributes; it demands new ways of seeing and engaging with the world we live in, and promotes resistance and solidarity in the encroaching darkness of our contemporary present. It is in this spirit that this book was written, and it is this spirit which it seeks to promote.

In the light of the two-fold purpose of the monograph, the chapters which follow comprise a series of rich and varied case studies which examine different and often, initially at least, apparently disparate, cultural texts alongside one another. Chapter One explores the theoretical specificities of historicity and *horizontalidad* within the Argentine context. Firstly, it scrutinizes how revitalized perceptions of the past gained popular currency from 2001 onwards, as comparisons were inevitably drawn between the state terrorism of the last military dictatorship and the social and economic violence which the subsequent neoliberal turn had wrought upon the Argentine body politic. Secondly, it examines the theoretical tenets of horizontalism and the origins of the movement in the second half of the Menemist decade of the

1990s. In its analysis, the chapter considers *horizontalidad* with reference to the works of scholars such as Raul Zibechi, Marina Sitrin, and *lavaca,* an autonomous media collective based in Buenos Aires. Particular attention is paid to Sitrin's notion of horizontalism as 'politica afectiva', a form of affective politics grounded in mutual respect and cooperation, as opposed to the pragmatism and ambition of conventional democratic realpolitik. Finally, in considering the syncretic journalistic narratives of the monthly magazine *Mu*, the chapter explores how this publication, first produced by *lavaca* in 2006, weaves together the discourses of historicity and horizontalism through its narrative modalities and aesthetic motifs.

Having identified the contextual specificities of both discourses, in Chapter Two, 'A Spectre Calls', we move to an analysis of a literary text set during the period of the *Argentinazo* itself, in the 2004 novel *El cantor de tango* [The Tango Singer] by Tomás Eloy Martínez. The novel narrates the efforts of American graduate student Bruno Cadogan to meet the enigmatic, aged tango singer Julio Cardel, whose impromptu street performances around the urban labyrinth of Buenos Aires resonate with historicist meaning. Interpreting the text as work of urban hauntology, the chapter explores Buenos Aires as a Benjaminian crime scene, in the spirit of Ricardo Piglia's assertion that the whole of Argentine history can be read as one long detective story. Jacques Derrida's concept of hauntology, as interpreted by the contemporary British theorists Owen Hatherley and Mark Fisher, is also employed to interrogate both the material and textual spectres that populate the Buenos Aires of *El cantor de tango*, in its palimpsestic depiction of a city haunted by words and deeds. In keeping with the notion that the spectral is indicative of both presence and absence, this chapter interrogates a lacuna of meaning at the heart of the novel, in its apparent disavowal of the transformational potential of the 2001 Crisis.

In contrast, in Chapter Three, entitled 'The Map and the Territory', two alternative interpretations of the spatial potential of historicity and horizontalism are considered. Where *El cantor de tango* is primarily sited within the geographical and ontological terrain of Buenos Aires 'proper', Martín Oesterheld's documentary *La multitud* [The Crowd] and Pablo Trapero's feature film *Elefante blanco* [White Elephant] venture further afield, exploring the suburban territories of the *conurbano bonaerense* in the post-Crisis era.[22] Utilising Fredric Jameson's notion of 'cognitive mapping' and David Harvey's subsequent interpretation of the concept, the chapter traces the spatio-temporal imaginaries present within each film's depictions of the liminal spaces of Villa Lugano, a district bordering the capital and its urban hinterland of greater Buenos Aires. Both films are concerned with the materiality of place, in the historicist relics of the suburban, and highlight the network of discontinuities which exists between material cartographies, the popular urban imaginary and the physical reality of the city's periphery. However, as this chapter demonstrates, it is only within Trapero's mainstream feature film that these uncovered dislocations between map and territory move beyond historicist lament towards the construction of a new subjectivity of urban citizenship. In *Elefante blanco*, Trapero seeks to re-chart the subaltern space of Ciudad Oculta, a *villa miseria* on the outskirts of Buenos Aires, guiding the viewer through the ruined zones of state and market, and on to a third unexplored territory, akin to Chantal Mouffe's description of a 'space of agonism' where past, present and future subjectivities collide in the construction of what I describe as an enclave of pragmatic utopianism.[23] In combining an investigation of the history of cinematic depictions of the *villa miseria* with analysis of the spatio-temporal specificities of *Elefante blanco*, Chapter Three elucidates the significance of both films in post-Crisis cultural production.

Chapter Four, 'Back in time for Dinner', considers manifestations of historicity and horizontalism within television drama, in an analysis of the 2010 mini-series *Lo que el tiempo nos dejó*, produced to coincide with the national bicentenary celebrations organised by the federal government of Cristina Fernández de Kirchner. Broadcast by the television channel Telefe, with the popular historian Felipe Pigna acting as historical consultant, this collection of six one-hour long dramas retold significant events from the Argentine twentieth century from the perspective of the ordinary citizens involved. Within the series archival news footage, iconic popular music and the affective artefacts of a carefully curated *mise en scène* are married with the melodramatic impetus of the *telenovela* and the cinematic affiliations of commemorative televisual history. This chapter scrutinizes the series as an iteration of Raphael Samuel's notion of 'living history', a popular historiography that privileges the material minutiae of the past, such as consumer artefacts, outmoded clothing and popular music, over the hierarchical orthodoxies of academic history. It is a form of historicist discourse which links the everyday of history with how we live now, inviting us to 'pretend we are at home in the past' and, in doing so, engendering a genealogy of meaning between past and present lived experience. With reference to 'El pañol', an artistic installation by Marcelo Brodsky from 1999, Chapter Four explores the haptic materiality of *Lo que el tiempo nos dejó* and its foregrounding of the environs of home and workplace as sites of historical significance. Combining tropes of historicity and horizontalism in its depiction of national history, the prominence and popularity of the television series illustrate how thoroughly both discourses had permeated the popular cultural imaginary in the decade after the 2001 Crisis.

'Vile Bodies', the fifth and final chapter, examines the 2004 satirical novel *La aventura de los bustos de Eva* [The Adventures of the Busts of Eva Peron] by Carlos Gamerro. Set in 1975 against the backdrop of social unrest and political violence, Gamerro's text is a bawdy romp of a novel that narrates the efforts of a hapless business executive to satisfy the outlandish ransom demands of the leftist urban guerrillas who have kidnapped his employer. In its visceral physicality and frequent grotesquery, the novel destabilizes sacralized notions of the past, interrogating the legacy of the armed struggle prosecuted by the Argentine radical left in the 1960s and 1970s. With reference to Mikhail Bahktin's writings on the grotesque and Frances Connelly's subsequent analysis of the form's horizontalist potential, this chapter explores the ways in which Gamerro's text ruptures established boundaries of historicist representation and articulates an alternative version of this brutal period in Argentine history.

The afterword reflects on how the dialogic relations between historicity and *horizontalidad* manifest themselves in each of the five case studies featured. Moreover, it gathers together certain observations, and attempts to garner some conclusions in the light of the evolving social and political circumstances in Argentina at the time of writing.

In accordance with the intermedial approach of this book, the texts selected as case studies span the cultural spectrum. Furthermore, since the purpose of the study is to break new ground in its examination of the cultural legacy of the 2001 crisis, several of the works included are, to date, little-studied and so offer fertile potential for interpretation and analysis. For example, whilst both Eloy Martínez and Gamerro are prominent Argentine authors, the texts analysed here are broadly considered as the minor works of their *oeuvre* and consequently, have been neglected as the focus of academic study. Conversely, the box office success and widespread distribution of Trapero's feature film *Elefante blanco* has, as Chapter Three explains, contributed to its dismissal by critics as a glossy and superficial narrative of life within a Buenos Aires *villa miseria*. Two works featured are notable for their chronological significance within the post-Crisis period. The monthly magazine *Mu* has its origins in a series of ad-hoc email bulletins written by independent journalists who witnessed first-hand the events of the *Argentinazo* in December 2001. Produced almost a decade later, the television mini-series *Lo que el tiempo nos dejó* offers valuable insight into the evolution of historicity and horizontalism as a structure of feeling and the transformation of both discursive forces from emergent subjectivities to hegemonic modes of viewing the world.

However, the texts considered in the chapters that follow have been chosen as much for their collective heterogeneity as for their individual significance. In the multiple narratives of historicity and *horizontalidad* that feature within this study, discordance and disharmony exist alongside congruity and cohesion. Different stories, with different attendant values and aspirations, are encoded in each individual text, and it is from this discursive tension within the works themselves and the corpus as a whole that new meanings can be gleaned. In narrating the epistemic foundations of historicity and *horizontalidad*, Chapter One focuses on both discourses equally. Chapter Two is dominated by narratives of historicity and their hauntological potential. In Chapter Three, *horizontalidad* and historicity both feature whilst in Chapter Four the latter discourse is once again at the forefront of this analysis of historical television drama. Finally, Chapter Five returns to an examination of both discourses in its consideration of the egalitarian impulse of the grotesque, within the historicist prism of Gamerro's novel *Las aventuras de los bustos de Eva*. This varied focus reflects the ebb and flow of historicity and horizontalism in the wider social context throughout the post-Crisis period. For, as Williams points out, culture is never static. It is an entity that is constantly in flux, reflecting the evolving relationships 'between elements in a whole way of life'.[24] For example, although historicity flourished under successive Kirchner administrations, the impact of horizontalism as a political project began to dwindle following the 2003 elections, leading several commentators, most prominently among them Beatriz Sarlo, to dismiss the movement as a failed enterprise.[25] Yet, whilst in structural and institutional terms at least, horizontalism did not effect significant political or economic change, failing to penetrate governmental or commercial spheres to any notable degree, the utopian potential that the movement had articulated continued to influence the popular cultural imaginary. Thus, it is in the dialogic relations between historicity and *horizontalidad*, and in the fractures as well as the interconnections between their varied narratives, that this monograph seeks meaning.

By way of a final illustration, it is useful to refer to a recent theatrical interpretation of the events of the *Argentinazo*. On Saturday 28 May 2017, almost sixteen years after the events of December 2001, a unique historical re-enactment was staged at the Centro Cultural San Martín in central Buenos Aires. Conceived and directed by the Argentine dramatist Lola Arias, *Audición para una manifestación* [Audition for a Demonstration] was a work of radical theatre that sought to (re)perform certain events from those two turbulent days.[26] With a duration of approximately five hours, the production featured no professional actors, and was instead performed by members of the public who had responded to advertisements placed in local newspapers and across social media. Whilst many of these volunteers had witnessed or taken part in the events around which the production centred, direct experience did not constitute a pre-condition of participation. Upon registering an interest, participants selected their preferred role from a range of options that included 'una persona en la multitud, un político que da un discurso, un policía que se bate contra la multitud' [a person in the crowd, a politician giving a speech, a police officer beating back the crowd].[27] After completing a questionnaire on their memories, personal experiences or perceptions of the *Argentinazo*, the 'actors' were then provided with appropriate costumes and make-up, and filmed auditioning for their roles before a panel composed of Arias and several other artists. Positioned against a backdrop of media images of the demonstrations, and prompted by questions from the panel, participants performed their chosen roles. These images were then transmitted to a large screen in the theatre, before an audience of spectators.

In this work of innovative and inclusive dramaturgy, news footage, photographic images and material objects were employed to re-stage the 2001 Crisis. For those who witnessed the events at first-hand, participation in the production as actors or audience members activated memories of the *Argentinazo* whilst generating new perspectives on their experiences. For the participants who had no direct experience of the popular uprising, the horizontalist ethos of the production and its improvisational approach provided a unique opportunity to engage physically and affectively with history. Likening the production to a 'time machine', the director described her project as presenting both participants and spectators with the opportunity 'to think the unthinkable, to make possible things that are not within the range of our possibilities [...] because if you create a new perception of reality, you are also creating a new reality'.[28]

*Audición para una manifestación* sought to historicize the events of December 2001 whilst maintaining the horizontalist ethos that characterized the popular insurrection. Equally, it highlighted the potential of plurality and contestation, both in fostering alternative perceptions of the 2001 Crisis and in extricating broader meaning from its events. In the chapters which follow, we shall trace the discursive warp and weft of historicity and horizontalism throughout the post-Crisis period in order to gain a greater understanding of the change in the structure of feeling precipitated by the *Argentinazo*. However, before we begin to consider the similarities and the tensions between individual narratives, it is first apposite to examine the origins of each discourse and some theoretical foundations.

### Notes to the Introduction

1. Mark Fisher, *Capitalist Realism* (Winchester: Zero Books, 2008), p. 1.
2. David Harvey, 'Neoliberalism as Creative Destruction', *The Annals of the American Academy of Political and Social Science*, 610 (2007), pp. 22–44 (p. 34).
3. Ibid.
4. Harvey, 'Neoliberalism as Creative Destruction'.
5. Interview of May 1982, cited in Michael Biddiss, 'Thatcherism: Concepts and Interpretations', in *Thatcherism: Personality and Politics*, ed. by Kenneth Minogue and Michael Biddiss (Basingstoke: Macmillan, 1987), pp. 1–20 (p. 2).
6. Jean Francois Lyotard, *The Postmodern Condition: A Report on Knowledge* (Minneapolis: University of Minnesota Press, 1984).
7. This theory was first advanced in detail by Fredric Jameson, in his work *Postmodernism, or The Cultural Logic of Late Capitalism* (Durham, NC: Duke University Press, 1991).
8. For a comprehensive summary of the social and economic instability Argentina faced in late 2001, see *Argentina Since the 2001 Crisis*, ed. by Cara Levey, Daniel Ozarow and Christopher Wylde (Basingstoke: Palgrave Macmillan, 2014).
9. Christopher Wylde, 'Continuity and Change in the Interpretation of Upheaval: Re-examining the Argentine Crisis of 2001–02' in *Argentina since the 2001 Crisis*, ed. by Levey et al, pp. 23–43, (p. 40). The Alianza government was a coalition comprising representatives from the Unión Cívica Radical (UCR) and the Frente País Solidario (Frepaso). Led by Fernando de la Rúa, the Alianza won the 1999 presidential elections. For further details, see Sebastián P. Salvia, 'La caída de la Alianza. Neoliberalismo, conflicto social y crisis política en Argentina', *Colombia Internacional*, 84 (2015), 107–38.
10. During the period from 1930 to 1983, there were six coup d'états in Argentina, each followed by a period of military government. The first took place in 1931, when democratically-elected President Hipólito Yrigoyen was ousted by the armed forces. Subsequent coups took place in 1943, 1955, 1962, 1966 and 1976. For a comprehensive exploration of this turbulent period in Argentine history, see David Rock, *Argentina, 1516–1982: From Spanish Colonization to the Falklands War* (London: Tauris, 1986).
11. See Maristella Svampa, 'Revisiting Argentina 2001–2013: From "¡Que se vayan todos!" to the Peronist decade', in *Argentina Since the 2001 Crisis*, pp. 155–76, and Joanna Page, *Crisis and Capitalism in Contemporary Argentine Cinema* (Durham, NC: Duke University Press, 2009), p. 6.
12. Ana Cecilia Dinerstein, 'Disagreement and Hope: The Hidden Transcripts in the Grammar of Political Recovery in PostCrisis Argentina', in *Argentina Since the 2001 Crisis*, pp. 115–33 (p. 116).
13. Ibid., p. 117.
14. Ibid.
15. Raymond Williams, *The Long Revolution* (Cardigan: Parthian, 2011), p. 68.
16. The term *piqueteros* refers to the organized groups of activists who construct roadblocks and picket lines to protest against economic inequality and its impact on the poor and the unemployed. H.I.J.O.S is the acronym used by the human rights group formed in the mid-1990s by the children of those who were disappeared during the military dictatorship of 1976–1983.
17. Williams, *Long Revolution*, p. 61.
18. Ibid., p. 60.

19. Williams, *Long Revolution*, p. 70.
20. Raymond Williams, 'Culture is Ordinary', in *Raymond Williams on Culture and Society: Essential Writings*, ed. by Jim McGuigan (London: Sage Publications, 2014), pp. 1–18 (p. 2).
21. David Featherstone, *Solidarity: Hidden Histories and Geographies of Internationalism* (London: Zero Books, 2012), p. 5.
22. The *conurbano bonaerense* is the term widely used to refer to Greater Buenos Aires, the area which surrounds the autonomous city of Buenos Aires.
23. *Villa miseria*, or the plural *villas miseria*, refer to the city's informal settlements variously known in English as shanty towns or slums.
24. Williams, *Long Revolution*, p. 67.
25. For a summary of the criticisms levelled at the horizontalist project following the elections of 2003, see James Scorer, *City in Common: Culture and Community in Buenos Aires* (Albany: State University of New York Press, 2016), pp. 17–18.
26. For further information, see the description of the project on Lola Arias' website: <http://lolaarias.com/proyectos/audicion-para-una-manifestacion/?lang=es> [accessed 12 August 2017].
27. Arias, *Audición para una manifestación*.
28. Interview with Lola Arias, from the video 'Audition for a Demonstration, Berlin, with English subtitles' from the webpage <http://lolaarias.com/proyectos/audicion-para-una-manifestacion/?lang=es> [accessed 12 August 2017].

CHAPTER 1

# After the *Argentinazo* — Historicity, *Horizontalidad* and a New 'Structure of Feeling'

> We swim in the past as fish do in water and cannot escape from it.
> ERIC HOBSBAWM

Firstly, what is historicity? It is perhaps useful to begin with some definitions. The Oxford English dictionary defines historicity as denoting 'the historical genuineness of an event' or, more succinctly, 'historical authenticity'. Issues of historiographical veracity are central to this conceptualization of the term. Accordingly, we can describe historicity as the irruption of the historical record in the present. Our pasts, both collective and individual, inevitably inform our perceptions of everyday lived experience, shaping national and personal subjectivities. Indeed, asserting the ubiquity of history, Eric Hobsbawm states that 'to be a member of any human community is to situate oneself with regard to one's (its) past, if only by rejecting it'.[1] He continues, asserting that 'the problem for historians is to analyse the nature of this "sense of the past" in society and to trace its changes and transformations'.[2] There is a tension apparent, then, between the lexical definition of historicity and its uses within society, since 'a sense of the past' is a fluid and heterogeneous entity which percolates through and beyond the clearly demarcated boundaries of historical fact. As Elizabeth Jelin suggests, while historians may establish and disseminate veridical and verifiable historical facts, 'the significance of past events is never constant or immutable; their meanings are never established once and for all'.[3]

The events of the *Argentinazo* precipitated a seismic transformation in how the historical record was interrogated, interpreted and mobilized, as a popular impetus grew for 'alternative ways of citing a historical past that could connect with current forms of oppression'.[4] Hence, a new collective sensibility emerged across Argentine society post-2001, a rupture in the fabric of historicity that was facilitated in no small part by a blooming of horizontalist subjectivities, as the innovative theories and praxis of the autonomous social movements gained popularity as a form of collective organization against the social and economic precarity caused by the Crisis. In this context, alternative definitions of historicity were fomented, generating innovative and disruptive narratives of the past that did not conform to the specificities of the hegemonic historical record. This chapter will begin by establishing some apposite definitions of this revitalized historicity, along with the emergent horizontality which accompanied it, identifying the specificities of each discourse in the context of the post-Crisis era. It will then chart certain epistemic interrelations between these two discursive forces, in their articulations of a common meaning between the injustices of the past, the inequities of the present, and the potentialities of an alternative future. Finally, we will then examine several journalistic narratives within the monthly magazine *Mu*, a publication first produced by the autonomous media collective *lavaca* in 2006. In the discursive syncretism of its narrative and aesthetic motifs, the journalism of *Mu* provides a specific iteration of the dialogic relations between historicity and horizontalism.

Thus, to begin, it is pertinent to look beyond our original definition of historicity. Referring to theoretical articulations of this sense of the past, the *OED* adds a subsequent coda, further describing historicity as 'the theory that social and cultural phenomena are determined by history'. Therefore, the ontology of historicity is closely intertwined with the theoretical exigencies of historical materialism and the writings of its foundational thinker, Karl Marx. In his 1852 essay 'The Eighteenth Brumaire of Louis Bonaparte', Marx contends that:

> Men make their own history, but they do not make it as they please; they do not make it under self-selected circumstances, but under circumstances existing already, given and transmitted from the past. The tradition of all dead generations weighs like a nightmare on the brains of the living.[5]

According to Marx's analysis, all human existence and its potential for transformation is, to a greater or lesser extent, governed by public and private narratives of history. Our comprehension of both the realities of the present and the potentialities of the future are determined by how we view the past. From the early 1980s onwards, Fredric Jameson utilized Marx's notions in his formulation of a new definition of historicity for the postmodern age, an epoch which he suggested had 'forgotten how to think historically in the first place'.[6] As the cultural helpmeet of late capitalism, the postmodern cultural turn is, according to Jameson, a 'degraded landscape of schlock and kitsch',[7] where the past is either present solely in its commodified version, as pastiche, retro or heritage, or absent entirely. The former is evident in the kitsch consumer miscellanea of the neoliberal marketplace, objects packaged with the patina of past historical moments; a colour, typeface or image that evokes the chronological specificity currently *en vogue*. As fetishized commodities, the purpose of such products is not to evoke any meaningful engagement with the past but rather to market and sell slivers of history, stripped of meaning and context. For Jameson, true historicity is:

> neither a representation of the past nor a representation of the future (although its various forms *use* such representations): it can first and foremost be defined as a perception of the present as history; that is as a relationship to the present which somehow defamiliarizes it and allows us that distance from immediacy which is at length characterized as historical perspective.[8]

There is a latent utopianism underlying this assertion, for if the present can be read historically, alternative futures can be constructed beyond the strictures of late capitalism. Jameson's approach posits historicity as crucial to a critical understanding of our lived existence, both 'in our relationship to public History and in the new forms of our private temporality'.⁹ For, whilst true historicity encodes an emancipatory potential, the simulacra of the past which he warns against strip history of its multiple meanings and homogenize its narratives. In post-dictatorship societies, where neoliberal reform was first enacted alongside state repression, official historical narratives of the past often discard the complexities of history and align the practice of forgetting with the pursuit of modernity. As Idelber Avelar asserts, the free market of late capitalism in Latin America must 'impose forgetting not only because it needs to erase the reminiscence of its barbaric origins but also because it is proper to the market to live in a perpetual present'.¹⁰ Thus, within such official narratives disseminated by state and market, historicity and memory work are characterized as oppositional to the collective progress of the nation, in that such a focus on the past inhibits an embracing of modernity in the present.

In his 1977 work *Marxism and Literature*, Raymond Williams outlines the difference between these hegemonic narratives of historicity propagated by the state and its institutions, and the alternative historical discourses that circulate within society. He defines the former as 'official consciousness', 'received and produced fixed forms' of thought and knowledge that emanate from within the establishment. The antithetical discourse to these institutional narratives is what Williams terms 'practical consciousness', a state of thinking and feeling that is 'what is actually being lived; and not only what it is thought is being lived'. Unlike those of the 'official consciousness', the alternative histories of the 'practical consciousness' are not static narratives but fluid sketches of the past, subject to the influence of social and political forces that rework and retrace their discursive outlines. Moreover, the free circulation of alternative histories within the 'practical consciousness' is always at risk from hegemonic narratives of the past, which either contest the validity of these more organic, popular histories or, alternatively, seek to appropriate and subsume these divergent stories in order to bind them to a single official, homogenous history. According to Williams, it is in the tension between these oppositional discourses that the potential exists for a new 'structure of feeling' to emerge. In its inchoate form, he describes this conflict as 'often an unease, a stress, a displacement, a latency: the moment of conscious comparison not yet come, often not even coming'.¹¹ Yet if it does emerge, it grows in strength and potency to become 'a particular sense of life',¹² a force which finds its full expression in the cultural realm. The evolution of new subjectivities is often the signifier of a generational change in perceptions of the past, in which 'the new generation responds in its own ways to the unique world it is inheriting, taking up many continuities, [...] yet feeling its whole life in certain ways differently, and shaping its creative response into a new structure of feeling'.¹³

In Argentina after the Crisis of 2001, one such 'structure of feeling' emerged, resonant with alterity in both how the past was conceptualized and in the cultural forms used to engage with it. To explore how this came about, it is useful to consider a cinematic text that encodes the antagonisms between the old and new structures of feeling pre and post-2001. In the summer of 2008, amongst the selected

Fig. 1.1. Promotional poster for the 2007 film *Aparecidos*, directed by Paco Cabezas. Image: www.imdb.com

offerings at the annual Edinburgh Film Festival was a little-known genre film entitled *Aparecidos* [*The Appeared*] (Fig. 1.1).

Written and directed by the Spanish film-maker Paco Cabezas, the film had premiered the previous year at the Sitges Film Festival and was now doing the rounds of the European festival circuit. Capitalizing on the contemporaneous trend within horror cinema for explicit depictions of violence and injury which the critic David Edelstein, in 2006, dubbed 'torture porn',[14] *Aparecidos* contains graphic and bloody scenes of physical abuse, albeit within a supernatural milieu. Advertised with the trepidatory tagline 'hay muertos que no olvidan' [there are dead people who do not forget], the film narrates the return of two siblings to the country of their birth in order to visit their estranged dying father. Brother and sister Malena and Pablo, who moved to Spain with their mother twenty years previously, travel to Argentina to see the father, of whom they remember very little. Semi-comatose and on the verge of death, he is unable to communicate with his children or respond to any of their questions about the past in what is for them a foreign country. However, concealed in his pristine vintage Ford Falcon, they find a yellowing diary that proffers some clues to their fractured family history and they set out to investigate further, driving to their childhood home in Patagonia in search of answers. What quickly becomes apparent is that this is not a typical road trip movie, nor a post-dictatorship tale of exile and re-discovery. Through the information contained in the diary and visitations by a series of ghostly apparitions whose torture and murder are re-enacted before their eyes, the children discover that their father was himself an enthusiastic *represor*; a member of the Argentine military who participated in the abductions and executions of suspected 'subversives' during the military dictatorship of 1976–1983. From his death bed, he continues to violate and abuse, only this time around he inflicts his sadism and brutality upon his own children, particularly Pablo, who, it transpires, is the stolen child of a *desaparecida*.[15] Somewhat apocryphally described as 'a gory, tense and stylish horror film that demonstrates why Argentina is one of the hippest film producing countries in the world',[16] *Aparecidos* is, save for its 'gorno' inclinations, an unremarkable film that exoticizes the trauma and violence of Southern Cone state terrorism for the European gaze. A Spanish production, with funding from several regional governments, a Spanish director and predominantly Spanish cast, it is an often wrong-footed and insensitive interrogation of *el Proceso*, in which the Argentine characters are either complicit participants, ignorant bystanders or bloodied victims.[17] By privileging shock and splatter over socio-cultural context, the film dislocates the violence of the dictatorship, obscuring issues of national trauma and rendering the narratives of the disappeared as little more than incidental plot vehicles which propel the attractive protagonists on to their next personal adventure.

Yet, for all its failings, *Aparecidos* does contain one significant scene. Towards the end of the film, having survived their ordeal and thwarted the sadistic impulses of their dying father, the siblings drive through Buenos Aires. They stop at a busy junction, waiting for the road to be cleared after a traffic accident. As they discuss their recent ordeal, ghostly figures appear around the car, clad in white and bearing the effects of violence. The tattered clothing of these apparitions, their unearthly pallor and festering wounds at first evoke the physical characteristics of another generic horror paradigm, the cannibalistic zombie. However, these spectres do not walk abroad in search of human flesh. Neither do they groan and flail their limbs pathetically. Instead they stand motionless and uncomprehending around the busy intersection, surveying their surroundings with an unrelenting and accusatory gaze and apparently unseen by all save Pablo and Malena. Here are the titular *Aparecidos*, the victims of state terrorism whose restless spirits will continue to roam restlessly as long as truth and justice are denied them. The fragility of these spectres, condemned to hover in a purgatorial zone between life and death, recalls their description by Jorge Rafael Videla, leader of the military junta and President of Argentina from 1976 to 1981 who, at a 1979 press conference infamously dismissed the issue of the missing as 'a mystery, a *desaparecido*, a nonentity, it is not here: they are neither dead nor alive, they are disappeared'.[18] But for Malena and Pablo, these figures are no longer invisible. The siblings' arduous quest for the dark truth of their family's history has enabled them to see the ghosts of the past within the present and thus to recognize the impunity and injustice which still persist. As the camera retreats towards an elevated wide shot of the crossroads, the scene grows progressively darker, but the white silhouettes of the ghostly figures persist, until the image resembles a photographic negative. The inference is clear: as long as silence and impunity thrive within the body politic, these spectres will haunt the landscape, trapped between past and present.

While the scene is a striking if somewhat clumsy evocation of the urban spectralities engendered by the violence of state terrorism, it is, in chronological terms, hopelessly outdated. The phantasmagoric lamentations of *Aparecidos* evoke something akin to the discourse of forgetting that prevailed during the transition to democracy and the early years of Carlos Menem's presidency, a period which saw the imposition of juridically-sanctioned impunity and multiple pardons for the *represores* of the last dictatorship. Resolute in his commitment to a future unburdened by historicity, in 1989 Menem himself employed the notion of haunting as rhetorical leitmotif, declaring: 'the Argentine people [...] are working for their future and not burying themselves in the past. Together [...] we will find a specific and definitive remedy to our unhealed wounds. We will not awaken the ghosts of discord; we will pacify the spirits'.[19] During the early years of the transition to democracy, a degree of justice for the victims of the dictatorship was achieved through both the 1984 report of the Comisión Nacional para la Desaparición de Personas (CONADEP), and the trial of the military junta in 1985, although all those convicted would later receive a full presidential pardon in 1989/1990.[20] But it was through the findings of the CONADEP report that the hegemonic narrative of the recent past would emerge, and effectively facilitate a generalized atmosphere of forgetting. In the prologue, commission president Ernesto Sábato asserted that 'during the 1970s, Argentina was torn by terror from both the extreme right and the far left'.[21] In equating the state-sponsored terrorism of *el Proceso* with the armed struggle of leftist guerrilla groups such as the Montoneros, Sábato's prologue formulated a narrative that absolved the majority of Argentines from culpability and which Susana Kaiser characterizes as 'the keystone in what has passed as a historical explanation for the "dirty war"'.[22] In essence, the CONADEP prologue portrayed a vision of Argentine society during the dictatorship as an innocent bystander, caught between the 'two demons' of revolutionary violence and the repression of such activity by the armed forces.[23] In its depoliticized portrait of the victims of this conflict, such as the archetypal *desaparecido/a*, the theory of the 'two demons' discarded the complexities of socio-historical context. As Hugo Vezzetti avers, in this approach the CONADEP report 'devolvía hacia atrás un certificado de inocencia a la sociedad frente al desastre y la degradación a la que la República se había visto sometida' [retroactively applied a certificate of innocence to society in the face of the disaster and degradation to which the Republic had visibly been subjected].[24]

Therefore, the exculpatory logic of the 'two demons' theory would, throughout the decade that followed, come to implant itself in the public consciousness as the hegemonic discourse of the recent past. The popularity of the CONADEP report should not be understated; within weeks of its publication, *Nunca Más* topped the bestseller lists in a nation of avid readers.[25] Subsequent legislation such as the 'Punto Final' and 'Obediencia Debida' laws of 1986 and 1987 respectively, and the pardons granted by Menem in 1989 and 1990 further consolidated this official narrative of forgetting.[26] In effect, the past was erased from the discourse of state and a tabula rasa erected upon which a modern, forward-looking nation could be fashioned. These events, and the official narrative which they exemplified, signalled the advent of what Jameson terms a 'waning of our historicity, of our lived possibility of experiencing history in some active way'.[27] In this sense, the ghosts of *Aparecidos* are the metonymic remnants of a past that is denied historicity, and ignored by the 'official consciousness' of the present. However, in the two decades that followed, it became increasingly clear that such ahistorical endeavours were not only futile but extremely damaging to the body politic. By 2008, the year of the film's release, Argentina was in the grip of what various commentators have termed an 'explosion of memory',[28] in which narratives of the past, and most prominently the recent past of the last dictatorship, had become fully woven into the fabric of the present. As Cecilia Sosa asserts, following the election of Peronist presidential candidate Néstor Kirchner in 2003, and the new incumbent's publicly articulated commitment to an 'unprecedented and belligerent human rights politics, [...], memory became mandatory'.[29] In particular, historicist narratives of the disappeared now manifested themselves everywhere, from literature to non-fiction, from television chat shows to documentaries. Put simply, the ghosts of the past were no longer unseen. In the temporal disarticulations of *Aparecidos*, the difference between what had been the hegemonic narrative of forgetting and the contemporary reality is clearly enunciated.

How then had a revitalized historicity emerged as the dominant 'structure of feeling' in Argentina by the end of the first decade of the twenty-first century? In its spatial articulations of historicity and the central role of the two siblings within the film, *Aparecidos* offers some clues. It is only Malena and Pablo who can see the apparitions at the crossroads because, through the sadism inflicted upon them by their father, they have experienced a similar violence. But the ghosts remain invisible to everyone else. Here, there is a parallel between vision and cognition: if we cannot see the remnants of the past and recognize them as historicist traces, we are oblivious to history. Before 2001, in Buenos Aires and across Argentina, much of the physical infrastructure of the last dictatorship remained unmarked, save for certain emblematic sites at which relatives of the missing would paste posters and artworks decrying the human rights abuses perpetrated there. One of the largest and most notorious prisons of *el Proceso*, the Escuela Mecánica de la Armada [Navy Mechanics School] in the wealthy suburb of Núñez, was still in use as a naval training school.[30] However, from 2002 onwards, the non-governmental organization Memoria Abierta [Open Memory] began to publish information booklets detailing the locations of dictatorship-era 'sites of repression'[31] in Buenos Aires. The aim of the project was to 'reveal the suppressed history buried in every location where the last military dictatorship focused its reign of terror, in order to transform these hidden spaces into outlets for remembrance'.[32] Seven years later, in September 2009, the list of memory sites had grown so extensive that the group published a comprehensive guidebook to these memorial spaces, entitled *Memorias en la Ciudad: Señales del Terrorismo de Estado en Buenos Aires* (*Memories of Buenos Aires: Signs of State Terrorism in Argentina*).[33] This text documents two hundred and forty sites of memory across forty eight districts of the capital, including former clandestine detention centres, squares and parks now rededicated to disappeared members of the community and the former homes and workplaces of victims of state terrorism. Many of the larger memorials featured are the fruit of collaborative

Fig. 1.2. A commemorative *baldosa* in the San Telmo district, Buenos Aires. Image: Brigid Lynch.

efforts between governmental institutions at both federal and municipal levels, civic bodies and human rights organizations, in spaces such as the coastal Parque de la Memoria and the former ESMA, which was finally handed over to the city government by the navy in 2004.[34] By documenting the topographical signifiers of state terrorism and the reclamation of these sites by the human rights community, Memoria Abierta revealed their existence to an unseeing public, tearing down the cloak of oblivion in which these locations had previously been shrouded.

Landmark sites such as the former ESMA exemplified the transformation in official narratives of historicity brought about by successive Kirchner administrations, which 'assum[ed] mourning as a national commitment'.[35] Other smaller memorial spaces documented in the guide were the work of autonomous neighbourhood associations and memory groups such as H.I.J.O.S. The work of such collectives, in the creation of brightly decorated *baldosas* or paving stones at sites of personal significance in the life of the disappeared person, was particularly representative of a popular and idiosyncratic reclamation of historicity (Fig. 1.2).

At the inauguration of a *baldosa*, autonomous groups of activists would join with neighbours and family and friends to decorate a paving stone outlining the biographical details of the disappeared person, embellishing these ad-hoc memorials with vividly-coloured paints and tiles. In doing so, they sought to recuperate the identities of the missing, remembering the *desaparecidos* as they were in life and not merely as a victim of state terrorism. In physically inscribing the identities of the missing upon the urban landscape, literally under the feet of the city's inhabitants, these unofficial memorials re-asserted the rights of the disappeared as individuals, rather than the uniform, nameless and dishevelled ghosts of *Aparecidos*. Moreover, through the *baldosa* initiative and other similar urban memory projects, the past was rendered visible in the everyday public spaces of the city, outside hegemonic commemorative spaces and events.

Such 'unofficial' collective memory work, described by Vincent Druliolle as 'micro-memory projects',[36] and the autonomous groups which organize these informal commemorations are emblematic of the revitalised narratives of historicity that emerged following the *Argentinazo*.

Indeed, the formation of H.I.J.O.S. was central to the evolution of a new sensibility around issues of memory and historicity in Argentine society. Founded in 1996, the group quickly expanded to become a nationwide network of the now-adult children whose parents were disappeared, murdered or forced to flee Argentina during the dictatorship. Many of those who came together within H.I.J.O.S. were already seasoned veterans of human rights activism, having grown up in families whose members included Madres or Abuelas of the Plaza de Mayo.[37] As they reached adulthood, many of these young people began to problematize the 'two demons' consensus, questioning the lacuna of meaning between public narratives of memory and their own personal histories. Francesca Lessa describes these changing sensibilities as a natural process, asserting that 'memory does not preserve a single, conclusive account of what happened, but rather what is remembered changes with evolutions in ideas, interests, identities and visions of the future'.[38] So, the coming of age of the children of the disappeared signalled the advent of a new alternative historicist discourse, one which explicitly challenged the legitimacy of a status quo that was increasingly unfit for purpose. As fictional members of this generation, the siblings at the centre of *Aparecidos* do in some limited way reflect the change in subjectivities towards issues of historicity and memory.

For many within H.I.J.O.S., their activism was predicated upon the need to formulate their own relations with the past, rather than to passively consume and perpetuate the versions constructed by their grandparents or other members of the 'witness generation'.[39] For others, their involvement with the group represented an opportunity to reclaim the radical political activism of their parents, and to question the validity of their parents' choices and use of violence. Employing innovative methods of activism, H.I.J.O.S. revitalized the landscape of historicity in Argentina, raising awareness of past crimes in the face of continued judicial impunity and employing art, film and other media to articulate the absence of the past within contemporary neoliberal society. Their most powerful tool was the *escrache*, a form of collective shaming of unpunished former repressors in the midst of their own communities.[40] As Julieta Colomer, a photographer and member of H.I.J.O.S., states:

> Fue el escrache lo que nos permitió apropiarnos del espacio público para reinventarlo. Caminar el barrio activando diálogos en centros culturales, sociedades de fomento, asambleas de vecinos, escuelas, plazas donde hacer teatro callejero, pintar murales en algún que otro paredón, repartir volantes puerta por puerta. Fue la excusa para encontrarnos, conversar cara a cara con los vecinos y así, recuperar los lazos solidarios desarticulados durante la dictadura. Recomponer el vínculo entre la sociedad y los desaparecidos, recuperando sus memorias, sus historias, sus militancias.[41]
>
> [The *escrache* allowed us to occupy the public space in order to re-invent it: walking around the neighbourhood speaking out in cultural centres, neighbourhood associations and schools, meeting in squares where we could perform open theatre, painting on this or that wall or delivering flyers door to door. It was also an excuse to meet each other, to talk face to face with the neighbors and recover the bonds of solidarity, broken during the dictatorship.

> Rebuilding the bond between the disappeared and society, recovering memories of them, their stories and political trajectories.]

The pivotal role of H.I.J.O.S. in transforming historicist discourse before the *Argentinazo* of 2001 cannot be underestimated. The work of the 'canonical' human rights groups, such as the Madres and Abuelas of the Plaza de Mayo and the Centro de Estudios Legales y Sociales (CELS) had focussed on investigation, and the gathering of evidence and testimonial accounts, in order to uncover the truth behind the disappearances of their loved ones.[42] They sought justice through legal means, through the courts and other institutions of state that had failed them so egregiously during the dictatorship. Sosa refers to the discursive identity of these human rights groups as that of a 'wounded family' whose members 'evoked their biological ties to the missing to put forward their claims for justice'.[43] As she asserts, throughout the twenty years that followed the dictatorship, this 'broken lineage had been the guardian of a national grief, and its entitlement was founded on blood'.[44] The moral inviolability of this bloodline, and the role it enshrined for the Madres and other groups as the custodians of the recent past, gave rise to a certain cleavage within Argentine society between the *afectados* of *el Proceso* and those without an affective or biological connection to its victims.[45] Historicity and memory had become the traumatic vocation of those directly affected by state terrorism.

The activities of H.I.J.O.S. punctured the certitude of the bloodline narrative. In their sustained attempts to engage with the wider community, H.I.J.O.S. converted the private pain of the *afectados* into collective excoriations of impunity, actively seeking the collaboration of society at large, so that 'cada vez sean más quienes elijan no mirar para otro lado' [each time more people choose not to look away].[46] Through the *escrache*, these activists sought to galvanize into action neighbourhood residents who had been, often unwillingly, living alongside former *represores*. Sosa describes the *escrache* as 'a form of "coming out", in which an expanded society was invited to play a part'.[47] Indeed, in 1999, in voting to accept members from outside the community of *afectados*, the organization further demonstrated its commitment to this more inclusive form of historicity.[48] For the purposes of this study, the most pertinent aspect of the theory and praxis espoused by H.I.J.O.S. is their adherence to a horizontalist framework. In their methods of organization and activism, this group is distinct from their forebears in the human rights community. As Marina Sitrin affirms, H.I.J.O.S. 'were not using the language of *horizontalidad* before the rebellion, but the ways in which they organized were much the same'.[49] Consisting of a network of regional groups not subject to any central authority, these activists gather regularly in an assembly to debate and decide collectively on current and future activities. Within the autonomous regional groups, smaller groupings known as commissions are responsible for a range of different projects, such as 'legal matters, siblings, direct action, anthropological investigation, schools, reception, archive, and radio'.[50] The comprehensive nature of this list demonstrates the commitment and professionalism of the organization, amongst whose ranks number artists, photographers, writers, teachers, designers, builders and civil servants. But if we are to examine how the praxis of horizontalism flourished after the crisis of

2001, we must first further examine the specificities of this emergent ideology. In short, what is *horizontalidad*?

The emergence of *horizontalidad* following the *Argentinazo* of 2001 signalled both a rupture from and a contiguity with the affective politics of human rights and collective memory. Unlike the long-established human rights campaign groups such as the Madres and the Abuelas, H.I.J.O.S. consisted of 'network formations, without hierarchy or central power structures',[51] and pursued a form of social justice beyond the judicial realm. Following the economic crisis of 2001, other proponents of horizontalism began to mobilize in initiatives such as the recuperation of workplaces left empty by the flight of capital and investors, barter networks, neighbourhood and inter-district assemblies, and the protests of the *piqueteros* and unemployed workers movements. The word horizontalism is a neologism, coined in the period following the 2001 economic crisis in Argentina to describe the ideology and praxis of a group of autonomous social movements. As one of the earliest chroniclers of this nascent political discourse Mariana Sitrin explains, 'the word horizontalidad was first heard in December 2001, in the days after the popular rebellion in Argentina. No one recalls where it came from or who might have used it first'.[52] She begins by defining horizontalism as rejecting 'imposed values, ideas and decisions',[53] privileging the participation of ordinary citizens in autonomous groups, and seeking to construct new political communities in both the local and national sense, outside the hegemonic apparatus of state.

Whilst Sitrin is an adept chronicler of the origins and development of the horizontalist movement in Argentina, it is in the work of theorists such as Raúl Zibechi that a broader exploration of the ontological specificities of *horizontalidad* can be found. In his 2012 work, *Territories of Resistance*, Zibechi identifies seven commonalities present amongst the varied horizontalist movements at work throughout Latin America, from the Zapatistas in Mexico, to the autonomous social movements in Argentina. Amongst these seven commonalities, Zibechi lists and describes the 'changing role of women'; 'the formation of their own intellectuals'; 'a concern for the organization of work and the relationship with nature'; and that the 'self-affirming forms of action through which the new actors make themselves visible and assert their distinctive identities tend to replace the older forms, such as the strike'.[54] Furthermore, he is at pains to underline the autonomous aspirations of such horizontalist movements in that they invoke an independence of thought and action detached not only from the institutions of state and government but also from other leftist groups and parties that may seek to co-opt their activities in the pursuit of power. For Zibechi, territory, in both physical and metaphorical terms, is another important common feature within the autonomous social movements, since it provides the stability and impetus within which activists can begin to gather, discuss and enact theoretical tenets upon a physical space. In Argentina, such territories can be glimpsed in the recuperated factories and businesses of Zanón Ceramics and the Hotel Bauen in Buenos Aires, and in the reclamation of public spaces by the *piqueteros*. Whilst Zibechi considers territory as the most crucial of all seven horizontalist features, arguably his evaluation of the evolving perception of citizenship within *horizontalidad* is of equal importance. Here, it is worth reproducing his summary at length. Of the horizontalist movements, he states:

> They work for the re-valorization of the culture and the affirmation of the identity of their people and social sectors [...]. Their de facto exclusion from citizenship seems to have prompted them to build a fundamentally different world. Understanding that the concept of citizenship has meaning only if some are excluded has been a painful lesson learned over the past decades. Hence the movements tend to press beyond the concept of citizenship, which was useful for two centuries for those who needed to contain and divide the dangerous classes.[55]

Therefore, the autonomous social movements which adhere to a horizontalist ethos seek far more than the dismantling of specific social inequalities through the politics of protest; they work to construct new subjectivities of citizenship, beyond both state and market, and to redefine the body politic itself, eliminating the outdated political taxonomies of the traditional left. Following the events of the 19 and 20 December 2001, such an approach to lived experience gained new currency in Argentina, as communities began to work together to ameliorate the harsh economic reality with which they were confronted. Before analysing one specific cultural manifestation of *horizontalidad* in the output of *Mu*, a monthly magazine produced by the *lavaca* collective, it is useful to briefly outline certain key events of the *Argentinazo* in order to highlight just how calamitous the circumstances were. Amongst the seemingly insuperable challenges facing the country were 'the largest debt default in international history (at the time), the abandonment of the ten-year-old currency exchange regime, [...] a general strike, major lootings, as well as the *corralito* –– a government decree that froze savers' deposits in order to prevent capital flight and a run on the banks'.[56] Once again, Argentine civil society appeared to undergo a process of unimpeded disintegration, this time during an era of democracy. Looting accelerated in the impoverished communities of Greater Buenos Aires, accentuating the stark divisions between the *polis* and its hinterland and perpetuating the notion of what Maristella Svampa terms the 'frontera social' [social frontier] that had come to exist between 'la ciudad rica y cosmopolita de Buenos Aires y el conurbano bonaerense, pauperizado y desindustrializado, sede permanente de las llamadas "clases peligrosas"' [the rich and cosmopolitan city of Buenos Aires and its surrounding areas, the pauperized and deindustrialized seat of the so-called "dangerous classes"] .[57] Poverty reached such previously unseen levels amongst certain sectors of the populace that rioting for food became the only viable option for many. Within this crucible of economic and social violence, even those more prosperous citizens were not immune to the quotidian struggle of obtaining hard currency and sourcing provisions before fluctuating inflation levels rendered their cash withdrawals worthless. Clearly, something had to give.

The events of 19 and 20 December 2001 are popularly referred to as the *Argentinazo*. An idiosyncratically Argentine use of the superlative suffix, *-azo* is commonly employed to describe popular uprisings or events of great political significance, such as the *Cordobazo* of 1969 and the *Rodrigazo* of 1975.[58] It has no direct translation in English but has been described by Naomi Klein as 'just what the word sounds like: a chaotic explanation of Argentinian-ness'.[59] As a noun, the *Argentinazo* connotes firstly the geographic diversity of the protests, which took place not only in Buenos Aires but all across the country. It was a national insurrection, although the demonstrations which took place in the capital were those that drew most media attention. Secondly, in linguistic terms, this noun is intrinsically linked to popular conceptions of nationhood and citizenship: its literal meaning is that of the most Argentine of uprisings. Through this designation of the events of late December 2001 as the *Argentinazo*, the protests are invested with a civic and political potential — a rising up of the people against a government without a mandate.

The spark that set the tinderbox of Argentine society aflame came in the form of a presidential decree from the incumbent Fernando de la Rúa on the summer evening of 19 December 2001. In a televised speech just before 11pm, the president declared a state of siege, excoriating the 'enemies of order and of the Republic who are taking advantage to try to sow discord and violence'.[60] As a political response to the socio-economic malaise that beset the country, de la Rúa's decree was disastrous. The restrictions which this measure placed upon civil liberties evoked deep-seated memories of the authoritarian rule of *el Proceso* and raised public anxiety over the fragility of democracy. His edict provoked a righteous indignation in citizens. As Marcela López Levy writes, this 'was the last straw from a president who had proved unable to keep any of his promises and had led the country to the brink of default — by default — with an indecisiveness that protracted the dire economic state of the nation'.[61] The populace, whom the president had hoped to placate with his television address, reacted with belligerent indignation. Beating out an incantatory rhythm on pots and pans, hundreds of thousands of citizens streamed from their homes out onto the streets and public spaces of their towns and cities, in a spontaneous mass repudiation of the state of siege. In Buenos Aires, the crowds made their way to the Plaza de Mayo, the civic heart of the nation's capital, to express their displeasure. Amassing before the Casa Rosada, the seat of government, the crowds sang, chanted and banged their pots and pans in a raucous cacophony of protest (Fig. 1.3).

These demonstrations continued throughout the night of the 19 December and on into the following day, despite increasingly violent attempts by police to contain the uprising. But the crowds were too dense and determined, and comprised a far more diverse group than the usual suspects of popular protest, such as trade unionists, students and political activists. Enervated by the demonstrations they had seen on the television and by the resignation of the minister of the economy Domingo Cavallo in the early hours of the morning, newcomers continued to arrive on 20 December, further bolstering the numbers. As López Levy describes, 'from the early morning on, women in suits, men with briefcases, housewives and grandparents and all sorts of people congregated in the Plaza de Mayo'.[62]

The choice to participate in this spontaneous popular protest did not come without risk, as mounted police and armed officers continued to provoke skirmishes

Fig. 1.3. Scenes of protest in the Plaza de Mayo on 20 December 2001. Image: La Nación

Fig. 1.4. A *baldosa* dedicated to the memory of Gastón Riva, one of five men killed in and around the Plaza de Mayo on 20 December 2001. Image: Brigid Lynch.

through their frustrated attempts to disperse the crowds gathered in the *microcentro*. At around 4pm, a group of armed police officers sought temporary refuge in the foyer of the HSBC building on the Avenida de Mayo, to regroup and reload their weapons. They were spotted by a small group of protestors, who began to throw stones and other missiles at the building, shattering the glass frontage of the bank's lobby. Journalist and author Naomi Klein describes what followed: 'The police and private security guards inside panicked and opened fire. According to evidence heard later in court, in just four seconds a hail of 59 bullets was fired on the packed street outside'.[63] Gustavo Benedetto, a twenty-three-year-old supermarket worker walking by on his way home, was struck in the back of the head by a bullet and died almost instantly. Four other young men were also killed by security forces on 20 December in or around the Plaza de Mayo, augmenting a national death toll of thirty-three (Fig. 1.4).

Yet the use of such repressive force did not dissuade the demonstrators; rather it provoked further defiance, since protestors made a cognitive link between the repressive actions of contemporary law enforcement and the murderous practices of the armed forces during the dictatorship. Furthermore, as several scholars have suggested, the dogged intransigence of the crowds who protested on the 19 and 20 December 2001 can be attributed to something more complex than the economic crisis alone. Olga Onuch poses the question concisely when she asks 'what motivated "ordinary" citizens to risk their lives and form an unlikely and momentary cross-class alliance in the streets?'[64] She suggests that the catalyst for the demonstrations comprised not only 'structural variables like economic crisis and austerity policies'[65] but also a response to 'a political crisis and political triggers as much as, if not *more* than, to the economic crisis and any deprivation it caused'.[66] Essentially. she describes her central argument as 'that "ordinary" Argentines came out to protest on December 19, with the purpose of defending their political rights, and not solely to voice their grievances against an ongoing economic crisis'.[67]

The *lavaca* cooperative has its origins in the violence and impunity of the events of the *Argentinazo*.[68] Given the prominence and media visibility of the protests in and around the Plaza de Mayo, it was the deaths of five young men in the *microcentro* of Buenos Aires, which provoked particular consternation. In an article published on the *lavaca* website on 20 December 2005 entitled '20 de diciembre de 2001: la batalla que nos parió' [20 December 2001: The Battle From Which We Were Born], the initial impetus for the founding of the media collective is clearly laid out:

> Esta nota cuenta la historia de Gustavo Benedetto, Fernando Almirón, Gastón Riva, Diego Lamagna y Luis Alberto Márquez, asesinados el 20 de diciembre de 2001 en Plaza de Mayo. No fue publicada en nuestra página web porque no existía. Fue distribuida por mail a una decena de direcciones con la esperanza de aportar algunos datos que transformaran la información sobre los muertos y heridos aquel 20 de diciembre en algo más que el mero número que daban cuenta los medios comerciales. No sabíamos qué estábamos haciendo, pero sí porqué. Así nació **lavaca**. (emphasis in original) [69]

> [This article tells the stories of Gustavo Benedetto, Fernando Almirón, Gastón Riva, Diego Lamagna and Luis Alberto Márquez, murdered on 20

December 2001 in the Plaza de Mayo. The article was not published on our website because it did not yet exist. It was distributed by email to dozens of recipients with the hope of providing certain facts that might augment the basic numerical information about those who were dead and wounded that 20 December, which appeared in the mainstream commercial media. We didn't know what we were doing, but we did know why we were doing it. And so, **lavaca** was born.]

The article that follows is a virtuoso example of *engagé* investigative reporting which narrates the events of 20 December 2001 in meticulous detail. It incorporates eye-witness accounts from those who found themselves in the vicinity of the Plaza de Mayo on that day, testimonies from the magistrate investigating the violent response of the security forces and the medical professionals who tended to the wounded, and profiles of those killed and injured. In the tradition of Argentine author Rodolfo Walsh, it is a journalistic text which situates the violence in its wider social context, alongside issues such as insecure employment, economic precarity and the social divisions which these factors entrench. It destabilizes the official narrative of events and the divisive rhetoric of criminalization employed by the popular media to describe the more economically-disadvantaged sectors of society. This discriminatory worldview is evident in the comments of a doctor from the Hospital Ramos Mejía, who assures the journalist that the people he treated on the day in question were not 'gente como usted o como yo. [...] No eran de clase media, seguro' [people like you or me, [...]. They weren't middle class people, for sure].[70] His comments are based on the fact that the wounded he treated had tattoos and old cuts and bruises on their bodies, sufficient evidence, in his opinion, to classify these victims as members of a self-interested, violent *lumpen* proletariat with intentions far from altruistic, intent on indulging in looting and senseless violence. Yet, as the *lavaca* text demonstrates in its accounts of those killed and injured in the *microcentro* on December 20, the majority were not engaged in violence. Benedetto, for example, had been unable to work that day due to the looting of the supermarket where he was employed and so had decided to go to the city centre to express his discontent at the social unrest. He was, the article concludes, like many young men from a similar social background, the victim of 'una falta de futuro, la policía y la desocupación. Son parte de la generación del ajuste' [lack of a future, the police and unemployment. They are part of the austerity generation].[71]

*Lavaca's* alternative narrative of the *Argentinazo* would go on to win the prestigious *Premio Rey de España a la Mejor Crónica Periodística*.[72] Its composition reflects the horizontalist theory underpinning the work of the media collective, in that it was written by journalist Claudia Acuña yet its by-line includes the names of Diego Rosemberg, Judith Gociol and Patricia Rojas, who were equally involved in the research, investigation and preparation of the article. For the four participants, this method of working represents 'la metodología habitual de lavaca: todos colaboramos, pero cada uno se hace cargo del seguimiento y el armado de cada parte' [the usual way of working at lavaca: we all collaborate, but each individual takes charge of the preparation and checking of each section].[73] Therefore, the finished product is the result of a collective effort, incorporating a plurality of thought and enterprise. This practice would also become a feature of the magazine *Mu*, the monthly magazine created by *lavaca* in 2006; the members of the collective involved in the production of the magazine would usually be listed on the opening pages of the publication, but the majority of the articles would not be credited to one specific author, unless written by a guest contributor. Indeed, *lavaca*'s name is itself a signifier of collective endeavour, since in Lunfardo argot, the noun *vaca* is defined as 'una apuesta a prorrata' [a pro rata bet or wager] and 'dinero que juegan en común dos o más personas' [money placed as a collective bet by two or more people].[74]

*Mu* first went on sale in kiosks across the country on 3 December 2006 and the opening issue reads as something of a manifesto for the new structure of feeling that the climactic events of December 2001 had helped engender. Its content encompasses a diverse range of issues including the progress of recuperated factories and businesses; community protests against the building of a paper mill in Entre Ríos and increased multinational mining enterprises in the southern province of Chubut; the disappearance of Jorge Julio López, the first *desaparecido* since the transition to democracy; and the progress of the legal case against police officers accused of the murders of the five protestors on 20 December 2001. From its inception, *Mu* incorporated theoretical treatises from a range of academics, philosophers and social scientists, such as Suely Rolnik and Miguel Benasayag, and, in its content, reflected the seven commonalities identified by Zibechi as central to horizontalism.[75] Furthermore, the discourse of *Mu* is idiosyncratic in one other key respect. It seeks to address what Zibechi characterizes as the failure of contemporary theoretical and linguistic constructs to engage with the new reality of existence in Argentina. Dismissing the antiquated rhetoric of the old left movements of the 1960s and 1970s as much as the hegemonic discourse of neoliberalism, he describes how:

> A new language, one that is capable of talking about relationships and movements, must break through the tangle of inherited concepts to analyse structures and organizational frameworks. We need expressions capable of capturing the ephemeral, the flows that are invisible to the vertical, linear eye of our masculine, legalistic, and rational culture. That language does not exist, and thus we must invent it in the heat of the various resistances and collective creations.[76]

This new lexicon that Zibechi demands, through which innovative forms of social relations can be constructed, is omnipresent in the discourse and content of *Mu*. This nascent structure of feeling is grounded in the realities of human relationships within the autonomous social movements and in the way in which protagonists are striving to construct new personal and communal subjectivities upon the ruins of antiquated and dogmatic patterns that characterized previous movements of the left. Sitrin describes this discourse as 'política afectiva', a form of relations 'based in open, direct communication, grounded in trust and love'.[77] It privileges equality of expression, compassion, and dignity and rejects the tribalism of party politics. One example of this appears in the fourth instalment of *Mu*, entitled 'Fiolos' and published on 3 April 2007 (Fig. 1.5).

FIG. 1.5. *Mu*, cover, issue 4, May 2007. Image: *Mu*.

This issue employs the paradigmatic figure of the lunfardo pimp to represent the myriad ways in which, according to the authors, the neoliberal economic system represses and enslaves individuals. The subtitle promises enlightenment as to how 'el sistema fiolo te hace sentir que no te merecés una vida mejor y algunas propuestas que lograron sacárselo de encima con humor, arte o el terapéutico grito: ¡al carajo!'[the pimp system makes you feel like you don't deserve a better life and some proposals for getting rid of it with humour, art or the therapeutic cry: To hell with it!].[78] However, the unashamedly shocking metonymy of the magazine's cover is no sensationalist gimmick; the opening article of the magazine is an interview with Sonia Sánchez, an activist who uses her experiences as a former sex worker to frame an allegorical representation of the exploitative relationship between the state and its citizens. She cites the example of charitable initiatives on the part of government and third sector organizations that provide sex workers with food parcels and an allowance of 7,000 condoms per month yet offer little additional help in the form of opportunities for work or education, in effect sustaining the status quo. Such donations, she asserts, provoke humiliation from those in receipt of the goods and engender a sense of submission, since paltry as the donations are, they are often the difference between eating and going hungry for many women.

Sánchez describes this model of exploitation in order to explore how a similar process is at work within the lives of many citizens in 'la cuestión laboral, con los abusos que se sufren las personas como ciudadanos, usuarios, consumidores, con el recorte de los derechos y de la capacidad de tener su voz, pensamiento, poder de decisión' [the question of employment, in the abuses that people are subjected to as citizens, users, consumers, in the restriction and cutting of people's rights and the capacity to have their own voice, thoughts, power to make decisions].[79] She cites the treatment of the unemployed, of those in precarious and repetitive occupations such as call centre work and families reliant on state handouts to clothe and feed their families. The article continues with comment from Suley Rolnik, a psychotherapist and author whose accompanying essay entitled 'Geopolítica del Rufián' [The Geopolitics of the Pimp] explores similar issues of societal exploitation and enforced obedience. Rolnik propounds the theory that this phenomenon 'abarca la dictadura del consumo, los recursos cada vez más sofisticados de control social y una especie de hipnosis neoliberal' [comprises the dictatorship of consumption, the ever-more sophisticated tools of social control and a form of neoliberal hypnosis].[79] Thus, the text moves from private to public, from the personal experiences of Sánchez to a theoretical exploration of the collective humiliations of those marginalized by late capitalism, relating the issues of exploitation and inequality that effect sex workers to a wider notion of societal depredation in the neoliberal era. Furthermore, it does not privilege the academic discourse of Rolnik over the personal testimony of Sánchez, instead affording both narratives equal weight within the piece. In both discursive motifs, it epitomizes the horizontalist ethos of equality, collectivism and dignity, and the compassion of this *política afectiva*.

There is one other aspect of the discourse produced by *Mu* which is important to explore: that of its engagement with historicity as a force for change in the present. In the article by Sánchez and in Rolnik's essay, certain keywords resonate

Fig. 1.6. *Mu*, cover, issue 8, September 2007. Image: *Mu*.

with historical meaning, referents of an exigent past. For example, terms such as 'la dictadura del consumo' [the dictatorship of consumption] and 'obediencia debida' [due obedience] are pregnant with historicist significance. The former phrase aligns the imposition of social control under the military dictatorship with the organizing principles of free market capitalism. The latter is a rhetorical allusion to the legislation which protected junior military officers from prosecution for crimes committed during *el Proceso*, on the basis that they were following orders from their superiors. Drawing an analogy between the annulment of individual responsibility within the hierarchical military structures and the relinquishment of personal autonomy under the decentralized systems of late capitalism, this term once again asserts an epistemic connection between the injustices of the past and those of the present. Through the use of this historicist idiom the text articulates a palimpsest discourse, constructing layers of meaning and explicitly linking the social and economic violence wrought by late capitalism to the human rights violations of *el Proceso*. This discursive modality, visible from its inception in *Mu*'s output, becomes increasingly vibrant in subsequent issues of the magazine, where aesthetic motifs are also employed to reconnect the past with the present. Issue 8, published on 1 September 2007 and entitled 'San Walsh', features one of the most visually striking exemplars of this journalistic historicity. The cover is dominated by a single image: a portrait of the radical intellectual Rodolfo Walsh, whose seminal non-fiction work *Operación Masacre* was first published fifty years earlier, in 1957 (Fig. 1.6).

In tones of black, yellow and grey, the pixelated image of Walsh stares out defiantly from the confines of the cover page. The image is an artistic reinterpretation of a photograph of the author, in the style of a character from a graphic novel or a work of Pop Art. In an overt nod to the latter, the portrait of Walsh is outlined with bold and dark strokes and its interior densely populated by the ubiquitous Ben-Day dots. Alongside the image, the cover text reads: 'Operación Masacre cumplió 50 años, en plena movida revisionista. Una nueva generación busca respuestas y encuentra de todo: revistas, películas y libros que le rinden un curioso culto' [Operation Massacre celebrates its 50th birthday, in the midst of a revisionist cultural scene. A new generation searches for answers and finds all kinds of things: magazines, films and books that worship a curious cult]. It concludes with the promise: 'Aquí, prendemos unas velas para conjurar el mito' [Here, we light a few candles to exorcise the myth].[81] Thus, the image and accompanying text can be read as a re-examination of Walsh and his legacy as both writer and militant, and in particular his role as chief of intelligence for the leftist guerrilla organization the Montoneros. Here, the Walsh cover is an intermedial nod to the work of Roy Lichtenstein, the seminal North American artist who was in the vanguard of the Pop Art movement which emerged in the 1950s. Sarah Churchwell describes Lichtenstein's art as not 'art trouvé but art retrouvé: refashioned, recovered, reframed [...] blending careful techniques of handwork with the reproduction and screening of found images'.[82] The image and accompanying text can be read, then, as a re-examination, a refashioning, of Walsh, during a period in which the ethics of the armed struggle on the left were the subject of intense debate. This conversion of one of the most well-known photographs of Walsh into a work of Pop Art presents

Fig. 1.7. . *Mu*, cover, issue 21, December 2008. Image: *Mu*.

us with a new visual syncretism of Walsh's legacy, reframing his life and work with a ludic sensibility and formulating a new approach to his importance in the present.

Further historicist motifs are visible in subsequent issues, in an indication of the magazine's continued interaction with new popular narratives of the national past. The cover of issue 21, dated 8 December 2008 (Fig. 1.7), is a photograph of a blindfolded young woman, standing before an H.I.J.O.S. banner during a street protest and is headlined: 'Que nos parió: como nos está marcando la generación H.I.J.O.S.' [That which gave birth to us: How the H.I.J.O.S. generation has impacted us].[83]

The blindfold is a visual reference to a common punishment applied to those kidnapped and held in clandestine detention centres during the dictatorship. To disorientate prisoners, their military captors would keep them blindfolded or hooded at almost all times, a state referred to in the argot of the detention centres as 'tabicado'.[84] It is a disturbing image and one which once again articulates the continuities between the injustices of the past and the present.

The cover of issue 29, published in October 2009 is another example of such discourse (Fig. 1.8). It features a school photograph of sixteen-year-old Luciano Arruga and, in bold enlarged text beneath, the slogan 'algo habrá hecho' [he must have done something].[85] On 31 January 2009, Arruga was intercepted by a police patrol on his way home in Lomas de Mirador, an area of the La Matanza neighbourhood of Greater Buenos Aires. He is known to have been taken to a local police station, but subsequently disappeared. His family were informed that he had been the victim of a road accident but his remains were not returned to them for burial and it was only in October 2014 that his body was discovered in an unmarked grave in a city cemetery.[86] The cover text links his abduction in times of democracy with the victims of state terrorism during the military dictatorship, asserting that 'la desaparición de Luciano Arruga pone en evidencia los mecanismos actuales de la violencia de Estado que tiene como blanco a los adolescentes pobres'[the disappearance of Luciano Arruga highlights the current mechanisms of state violence which target poor adolescent boys].[87] The slogan beneath his photograph is a phrase commonly used during *el Proceso* by the public at large to explain the apparently arbitrary abductions and disappearance of members of the community. Here, it resonates with indignation at the demonization of young men like Luciano in the popular media and calls into question why the human rights of some Argentines are less valid than those of others. In the construction of such narratives, there is a high degree of heteromediality. As observed, references to literary texts endow the exploration of contemporary political issues with complex historicist meaning: visual artwork and photography are overlaid, connecting aesthetic motifs from the past to events in the present; and academic discourse commingles with the testimony of workers and activists. The result is a hybrid journalistic discourse which exemplifies the communicative strategies that Zibechi demands. It encodes a revitalized historicity which is grounded in contemporary struggles against injustice and inequality.

As previously asserted, this was, in no small part, due to the influence and

Fig. 1.8. *Mu*, issue 21, October 2009. Image: *Mu*.

involvement of activists from H.I.J.O.S. whose non-hierarchical praxis and human rights activism created a template for new narratives of the past and present. Similarly, it was the *lavaca* collective that was amongst the first chroniclers of the discourse of lived experience that arose in the wake of the economic chaos of December 2001, in the recuperated factories, the neighbourhood assemblies and in the streets and squares of towns and cities across Argentina. *Mu* combines the discourses of horizontalism and historicity, as horizontalist methods of organizing and producing coincide with the revitalized historicity expounded by H.I.J.O.S. This coalescence of purpose and meaning is expressed in a comment from Emiliano Hueravilo, an activist from the group, in the first issue of *Mu*, as he baldly states: 'Los derechos humanos los viola siempre un Estado, y los viola también cuando hay chicos que se mueren de hambre o personas que no tienen trabajo. Nosotros lo denunciamos' [It is always the state which violates human rights and it also violates them when children are dying of hunger or people are unemployed. We will always condemn this].[88]

Thus, the innovative new discourses of historicity and *horizontalidad* that emerged post-2001 ruptured hegemonic narratives of the Argentine national past, present and future. These discursive forces and their dialogic interactions destabilized the rhetoric of consensus established during the transition to democracy, entrenched as it was in the binary logic of 'the melancholic gaze or the festive celebration of the neoliberal market'.[89] In the activities of H.I.J.O.S. and the *lavaca* media collective, the outlines of a new structure of feeling can be traced, where historicity and horizontalism commingle to articulate 'a perception of the present as history'.[90] In Chapter Two, 'A Spectre Calls', we return to the past with an examination of Tomás Eloy Martínez's 2004 novel *El cantor de tango* [The Tango Singer]. In this text, it is historicity that predominates, and iterations of *horizontalidad* are notable in their absence, raising the question as to whether a sense of the past is sufficient to bring about change in the present.

## Notes to Chapter 1

1. Eric Hobsbawm, *On History* (London: Abacus, 1998), p. 13.
2. Ibid., p. 13.
3. Elizabeth Jelin, *State Repression and the Struggles for Memory* (London: Latin American Bureau, 2003), p. 52.
4. Susana Draper, 'The Question of Awakening in Postdictatorship Times: Reading Walter Benjamin with Diamela Eltit', *Discourse: Benjamin in Winter*, 32 (2010), pp. 87–116 (p. 89).
5. Karl Marx, 'The Eighteenth Brumaire of Louis Bonaparte', in *The Communist Manifesto* (London: Penguin, 2013), p. 85.
6. Santiago Colas, 'The Third World in Jameson's *Postmodernism or the Cultural Logic of Late Capitalism*', *Social Text: Third World and Colonial Issues*, 31/32 (1992), pp. 258–70.
7. Jameson, *Postmodernism*, p. xxiv.
8. Jameson, *Postmodernism*, p. 284.
9. Ibid., p. 6.
10. Idelber Avelar, *The Untimely Present: Postdictatorial Latin American Fiction and the Task of Mourning* (Durham, NC: Duke University Press, 1999), p. 2.
11. Raymond Williams, *Marxism and Literature* (Oxford: Oxford University Press, 1977), p. 130.
12. Raymond Williams, *Long Revolution*, p. 68.

13. Ibid.
14. Steve Jones, 'The Lexicon of Offence: The Meanings of Torture, Porn, and "Torture Porn"', in *Controversial Images: Media Representation on the Edge*, ed. by Feona Attwood, Vincent Campbell, I. Q. Hunter and Sharon Lockyer (London; New York: Palgrave Macmillan, 2013), pp. 186–201, (p. 168). In his article, Jones refers to three other terms commonly used to describe the genre, namely 'blood porn', 'carnography', and 'gorno'.
15. The terms desaparecido/a/as describe those 'disappeared' by the military dictatorship of 1976–1984, in the practice of extra-judicial abduction, imprisonment and ultimately execution adopted by the regime during this period.
16. Edinburgh International Film Festival 2008 website: <http://www.edfilmfest.org.uk/films/2008/the-appeared/full-details#>[accessed 2 June 2016].
17. *El Proceso* is an abbreviation of *El Proceso de Reorganización Nacional* [The Process of National Reorganization], the term used by the military dictatorship of 1976–1983 to describe their governmental project of remodelling Argentine society. It is now widely used within Argentina to refer to this historical period, along with the phrase *la última dictadura cívico-militar* [the last civic-military dictatorship], largely superseding the phrase 'la guerra sucia' [the dirty war].
18. Martin Böhmer, 'An Oresteia for Argentina: Between Fraternity and the Rule of Law' *in Law and Democracy in the Empire of Force*, ed. by Jefferson Powells and James Boyd White (Ann Arbor, MC: University of Michigan Press, 2009), pp. 89–124 (p. 90).
19. Carlos Menem, cited in Francesca Lessa, *Memory and Transitional Justice in Argentina and Uruguay: Against Impunity* (New York: Palgrave Macmillan, 2013), p. 95
20. CONADEP is the acronym in Spanish for the truth commission convoked by President Raul Alfonsín in December 1983. In English, the report was published (without the tilde) as *Nunca Mas: A Report by Argentina's National Commission on Disappeared People* (London: Faber & Faber, 1986). All bibliographic references are taken from the English-language edition, although when referring to the report in the text, I will use the Spanish title, *Nunca Más*. For a full chronology of the salient events during the transition to democracy in Argentina, see Elizabeth Jelin, *State Repression and the Struggles for Memory* (London: Latin American Bureau, 2003), pp. 107–33.
21. *Nunca Mas*, p. 1.
22. Susana Kaiser, *Postmemories of Terror* (Basingstoke: Palgrave Macmillan, 2005), p. 25.
23. Sabato's narrative in the prologue would come to be known as 'la teoría de los dos demonios' [theory of the two demons/evils]. As Emilo Crenzel asserts in his 2011 monograph on the CONADEP report, the introductory text 'projects a past "we" that took no part in the exercise of violence or in state terror, a community of citizens who did not participate in the confrontations that marked Argentine society'. See Emilio Crenzel, *Memory of the Argentina Disappearances: The Political History of Nunca Más* (Abingdon: Routledge, 2017), p. 78.
24. Hugo Vezzetti, *Pasado y presente: guerra, dictadura y sociedad en la argentina* (Buenos Aires: Siglo Ventiuno, 2002), pp. 127–28.
25. Marguerite Feitlowitz, *Lexicon of Terror: Argentina and the Legacies of Torture* (Oxford: Oxford University Press, 2011), p. 15.
26. The so-called 'Punto Final' [Full Stop] legislation set a finite period of time in which any further prosecutions could be brought for crimes committed by the state during *el Proceso*, whilst 'Obediencia Debida' [Due Obedience] awarded immunity from prosecution to all military personnel below the rank of colonel. Carlos Menem, who succeeded Alfonsín as President of the nation in 1989, would, on 29 December 1990, pardon all the military junta members convicted in 1985, along with former guerrillas previously convicted of crimes against the state during the dictatorship. The previous year, on 7 October 1989, Menem signed a presidential decree pardoning all those military officers who had not already been pardoned through the earlier Full Stop and Due Obedience legislation. For further information, see Lessa, *Memory and Transitional Justice*, pp. 57–59.
27. Jameson, *Postmodernism*, p. 21.
28. Emilio Crenzel, 'Present Pasts: Memory(ies) of State Terrorism in the Southern Cone of Latin America', in *The Memory of State Terrorism in the Southern Cone: Argentina, Chile and Uruguay*, ed. by Francesca Lessa and Vincent Druliolle, (New York: Palgrave Macmillan, 2011)), pp. 1–14 (p. 5).

29. Cecilia Sosa, *Queering Acts of Mourning in the Aftermath of Argentina's Dictatorship: Performances of Blood* (Woodbridge: Tamesis, 2014), p. 19.
30. The Escuela Mecánica de la Armada (ESMA) was one of the largest and most notorious clandestine detention centres of the 1976–1983 dictatorship. In Chapter Four, the significance of the site is discussed in more detail.
31. Memoria Abierta, 'Introduction', in *Memories of Buenos Aires: Signs of State Terrorism in Argentina*, ed. by Max Page (Amherst; Boston, MA: University of Massachusetts Press, 2013), pp. xxi–xxii.
32. Ibid., p. xvii.
33. Published in Spanish in 2009, this work was subsequently published in English in 2012. See footnote 31 for full bibliographic details.
34. In 1988, during the government of Carlos Menem, demolition of the ESMA site was proposed. Following great public outcry and a court judgement prohibiting demolition, the project was shelved. In 2004, the site was returned by the navy to the city of Buenos Aires and the process of converting the former prison into a museum and 'space of memory' began. See *Memories of Buenos Aires*, p. 160.
35. Sosa, *Queering Acts of Mourning*, p. 18.
36. Vincent Druliolle, 'Remembering and its Places in Postdictatorship Argentina', in *The Memory of State Terrorism in the Southern Cone: Argentina, Chile, and Uruguay*, ed. by Francesca Lessa and Vincent Druliolle (Palgrave Macmillan: Basingstoke, 2011), pp. 15–41 (p. 17).
37. The Madres de Plaza de Mayo are Argentina's most prominent human rights organization. The group was founded in April 1977 by a group of mothers whose children had been abducted and subsequently disappeared by the military dictatorship. In 1986, following differences as to how to continue their pursuit of justice, the group split into two separate organizations, namely the Asociación Madres Plaza de Mayo and the Madres de Plaza de Mayo — Línea Fundadora. The organization Abuelas de Plaza de Mayo was also founded in 1977, by mothers whose daughters or daughters-in-law were pregnant at the time of their abductions. They continue to search for their missing grandchildren. For a detailed history of the Mothers, see Diana Taylor, *Disappearing Acts: Spectacles of Gender and Nationalism in Argentina's "Dirty War"* (Durham, NC: Duke University Press, 2005).
38. Lessa, *Memory and Transitional Justice*, p. 2.
39. See Kaiser, *Postmemories of Terror*, p. 3, for a general discussion of the founding principles of H.I.J.O.S.
40. *Escrache* is the noun form of the lunfardo verb '*escrachar*', which means to uncover something or someone previously hidden. When H.I.J.O.S. activists discovered the existence of a former repressor in a community, they would spend several weeks raising awareness of his or her presence in the neighbourhood, distributing leaflets with details of the subject's participation in the human rights abuses of the dictatorship. This would culminate in the *escrache* itself, a demonstration with music, song and chanting. Neighbours were encouraged to join the march, which would terminate with protests outside the home or workplace of the repressor.
41. Julieta Colomer, *Escrache: Imágenes de una generación que nos devolvió a la historia* (Buenos Aires: Mónadanomada + el zócalo, 2015), p. 5. The text is also available in English, as *Escrache: Images of a Generation that Brought us Back History* (Buenos Aires: Mónadanomada + el zócalo, 2015), and all translations are from the English-language version.
42. CELS is a human rights organisation founded in 1979 by Angélica and Emilio Mignone, whose daughter Mónica was abducted by the military regime in 1976 and remains disappeared. The organization focuses upon the prosecution of military officers and others who committed human rights violations during *el Proceso*. See Feitlowitz, *Lexicon*, pp. 281–83 for further details.
43. Cecilia Sosa, 'Food, Conviviality and the Work of Mourning, the *Asado* Scandal at Argentina's ex-ESMA', *Journal of Latin American Cultural Studies*, 25:1 (2016), 123–46, (p. 131).
44. Ibid.
45. Jelin uses the general term *afectados* to describe all those directly affected by the years of state terrorism. She includes within this definition the families of the disappeared, the survivors of clandestine detention centres and the former political militants forced to seek external or domestic exile in order to evade capture by state forces. See Elizabeth Jelin, *La lucha por el pasado: como construimos la memoria social* (Buenos Aires: Siglo Veintiuno, 2017), p. 194.

46. Colomer, 'Introducción', in *Escrache*, p .6.
47. Sosa, *Queering Acts of Mourning*, p. 32.
48. Ibid., p. 36.
49. Marina Sitrin, *Everyday Revolutions: Horizontalism and Autonomy in Argentina* (London: Zed Books, 2012), p. 23.
50. Ibid., p. 24. For further details of the horizontalist praxis of H.I.J.O.S, see pp. 17–26.
51. Ibid., p. 23.
52. Marina Sitrin, '*Horizontalidad* and Territory in the Occupy Movements', *Tikkun*, 27:2 (2012), pp. 32–63, (p. 32).
53. Sitrin, *Everyday Revolutions*, p. 65.
54. Raúl Zibechi, *Territories in Resistance: A Cartography of Latin American Social Movements* (Oakland, CA: AK Press, 2012), pp. 14–19.
55. Zibechi, *Territories in Resistance.*, p. 16.
56. Cara Levey, Daniel Ozarow and Daniel Wylde, 'Revisiting the Argentine Crisis a Decade on: Changes and Continuities', in *Argentina Since the 2001Crisis*, pp. 1–22 (p. 5).
57. Maristella Svampa, *Cambio de época* (Buenos Aires: Siglo Veintiuno, 2008), p. 52.
58. The *Cordobazo* was a popular uprising that took place in Cordoba in May 1969, in protest against the repressive measures implemented by the military government of General Onganía. The term *Rodrigazo* is used to describe the economic crisis of June 1975, which was precipitated by the economic reforms of finance minister Celestino Rodrigo. For further details of both incidents, see Rock, *Argentina: 1561–1982*. The suffix is still widely applied to such events, e.g. the *Tarifazo* of 2015, the wide-ranging increase in public service charges implemented by the newly-elected government of Mauricio Macri.
59. Naomi Klein, 'Out of the Ordinary', *The Guardian*, Saturday 25 January 2003, <https://www.theguardian.com/world/2003/jan/25/argentina.weekend7 > [accessed 5 July 2016].
60. Marcela López Levy, *We Are Millions: Neo-Liberalism and New Forms of Political Action in Argentina* (London: Latin American Bureau, 2004), p. 7
61. López Levy, *We Are Millions*.
62. López Levy, *We Are Millions*.
63. Klein, 'Out of the Ordinary'.
64. Olga Onuch, '"It's the Economy, Stupid," Or Is It? The Role of Political Crises in Mass Mobilization: The Case of Argentina in 2001', in *Argentina Since the 2001 Crisis*, pp. 89–114, (p. 90).
65. Ibid., p. 91.
66. Ibid.
67. Ibid., p. 92.
68. The name of the collective is always used without initial capitalization.
69. *lavaca*, '20 de diciembre de 2001: la batalla que nos parió', 20 December2005 <http://www.lavaca.org/notas/20-de-diciembre-de-2001-la-batalla-que-nos-pario> [accessed 7 July 2016].
70. *lavaca*, '20 de diciembre de 2001'.
71. *lavaca*, '20 de diciembre de 2001'.
72. Claudia Acuña, Diego Rosemberg, Judith Gociol and Patricia Rojas, '19 y 20 de diciembre de 2001: Los días en que todo cambio', in *Grandes crónicas periodísticas*, ed. by Graciela Pedraza (Cordoba: Editorial Comunicarte, 2008), pp. 163–66 (p. 164). In its online version, the article appears anonymously and is not attributed to any of the four journalists.
73. Acuña et al, '19 y 20 de diciembre de 2001'.
74. José Gobello, *Nuevo diccionario lunfardo* (Buenos Aires: Corregidor, 2014), p. 255.
75. Several contributors to Mu, including Rolnik and Benasayag have also collaborated with Colectivo Situaciones, a radical group of intellectuals and activists which emerged in Buenos Aires in 1999. For further details of the group and its activities see Colectivo Situaciones, *19 & 20: Notes for a New Social Protagonism* (Brooklyn, NY: Autonomedia, 2012).
76. Zibechi, *Territories in Resistance*, p. 8.
77. Sitrin, *Everyday Revolutions*, p. 91.
78. Cover matter, *Mu*, Issue 4, May 2007.
79. *Mu*, 'El fiolo que te parió: las mil y unas formas de proxenetismo', Issue 4, May 2007, p. 3.

80. *Mu*, 'El fiolo que te parió', p. 3.
81. *Mu*, cover matter, Issue 21, May 2007.
82. Sarah Churchwell, 'Roy Lichtenstein: From Heresy to Visionary', *The Guardian*, Saturday 23 February 2013 <https://www.theguardian.com/artanddesign/2013/feb/23/roy-lichtenstein-heresy-to-visionary> [accessed 10 August 2016].
83. Ibid. The verb *parir* can mean to give birth to a child and also to create something or come up with an idea. The phrase 'Que nos parió' is also a play on words, as variations on the colloquial expletive phrase 'la madre que te parió' are widely used to express offense, surprise or displeasure.
84. Feitlowitz, *Lexicon*, p. 6.
85. *Mu*, cover matter, Issue 29, October 2009.
86. Soledad Vallejos, 'Arruga, una causa que mantiene muchas dudas', *Página 12*, Saturday 18 October 2014, <https://www.pagina12.com.ar/diario/sociedad/3-257810-2014-10-18.html> [accessed 10 July 2016].
87. Ibid.
88. *Mu*, 'Una nueva generación de derechos humanos: la segunda desaparición de Julio López', Issue 1, December 2006, p. 6.
89. Draper, 'Question of Awakening', p. 89
90. Jameson, *Postmodernism*, p. 284.

CHAPTER 2

# A Spectre Calls: Hauntology as Historicity

El murmullo incesante de los muertos *es* la verdad de la historia.
[The incessant murmuring of the dead *is* the truth of history.]

IDELBER AVELAR

Some sixty-five years ago, the American novelist William Faulkner sagely observed that 'the past is never dead. It's not even past'.[1] As a statement of historicist potential, it is an epigraph that could well be applied to the 2004 novel *El cantor de tango* [The Tango Singer] by the Argentine author Tomás Eloy Martínez. Set in Buenos Aires in late 2001, as the economic storm clouds gathered in the months preceding the *Argentinazo*, the novel is a palimpsestic text, forged from the multiple strata of textual and material historicity upon which the modern urban imaginary of Buenos Aires has been constructed. In the novel, a North American graduate student, Bruno Cadogan, moves to Buenos Aires to research a postdoctoral project on Jorge Luis Borges and his writings on the tango. He hears of an enigmatic singer, Julio Martel, who gives impromptu musical recitals in apparently arbitrary locations around the city, in derelict buildings, in subway tunnels and on street corners. *El cantor de tango* chronicles Cadogan's quest to find the eponymous Martel and, moreover, his gradual comprehension of the spectral topographies which the singer invokes through his performances. In his renditions of archaic and long-forgotten tangos, Martel maps out the past utopias of Buenos Aires and the casual brutalities which destroyed these dreams of an alternative future.

This chapter will examine the many cities that Martel's tangos reveal beneath the skin of contemporary Buenos Aires, as his recitals divest the modern metropolis of its spectacular consumer trappings to reveal the layers of history which lie beneath. Within the novel, the edifices, streets and monuments of the *polis* constitute a series of crime scenes, where ordinary people have wrought acts of extraordinary cruelty upon one another. In charting the quotidian wickedness of the city's history, Martel seeks to highlight the hauntological traces of these occluded or forgotten pasts that linger on amidst the hustle and bustle of the urban *topos*. These ghosts, however, are far more complex entities than the stereotypical apparitions of Paco Cabezas's 2007 film *Aparecidos*. In his performances, the singer invokes the dead through the spectral revenants of place and time that punctuate the modern urban landscape, markers on a much larger map of the past where the injustices of the history underlie the inequities of the present. Where Martel is the cartographer, Cadogan assumes the role of detective, shadowing the singer's movements, recording the locations of his performances and attempting to decipher their meaning. As we shall see, the tangos which Martel sings are articulations of hauntological affect, in that they 'register the harm inflicted or the loss sustained by a social violence done in the past or present'.[2] Indeed, in the intermedial interplay between music and narrative, Martel's recitals highlight the more profound heteromediality of the novel, as it conjures up a genealogy of meaning between what Avery Gordon describes as 'materiality, sensorial aspects, time-space correlations, and a prototypical semiotic function'.[3] The elegiac laments of Martel's tangos encode a history of violence that informs all aspects of present lived experience and thus speaks of the dangers inherent within any wilful denial of historicity. However, as this chapter will also posit, *El cantor de tango* can also be interpreted as an admonitory text which warns of the perils of historicity as lamentation alone, devoid of the utopian impulse that precipitates notions of an alternative present and future.

But before we turn to the novel itself, it is pertinent to consider the particularities of the mode of historicist discourse which it encodes. Spatial historicity, particularly the way in which the signifiers of the past manifest themselves amongst the crowded vistas of the urban built environment, is one of the most prominent contemporary reminders of the inexorable passage of time. Furthermore, the architectural traces of history in our cities, if we allow ourselves to decipher them, provide an exigent reminder of the utopian designs for life of the past. In his 2003 monograph *Present Pasts: Urban Palimpsests and the Politics of Memory*, Andreas Huyssen asserts: 'one of the most interesting cultural phenomena of our day is the way in which memory and temporality have invaded spaces and media that seemed among the most stable and fixed: cities, monuments, architecture, and sculpture'.[4] He describes the contemporary spatial turn, and its problematization of the material traces of the past, as a divergence from the hegemonic historical discourse of the past two centuries, which guaranteed 'the relative stability of the past in its pastness'.[5] Tradition, albeit in itself a curated construction, affirmed spatial and monumental iterations of historiography as the material signifiers in a diachronic trajectory towards modernity, against which progress could be evaluated. Current departures from such discourse are, he explains, a symptom of 'a fundamental crisis in our imagination of alternative futures'[6] in an increasingly globalized world. The historical traces of the built environment no longer solely encode a single prescribed version of the past, having now become, in contrast, fluid spaces where a plurality of contested meaning awaits excavation, not only through the efforts of historians and memory scholars but also in the everyday interactions between the city's inhabitants and their surroundings. Huyssen's thesis finds parallels in the writings of Owen Hatherley, who, in the opening pages of his essay *Militant Modernism*, indignantly states:

> We have been cheated out of the future, yet the future's remains lie about us, hidden or ostentatiously rotting. So, what would it mean then, to look for the future's remnants? To uncover clues about those who wanted, as Walter Benjamin put it, to 'live without traces'? Can we, should we, try and excavate utopia?[7]

Hatherley's radical manifesto for a revivification of the utopian ideologies that underlay the material and cultural reconstruction of post-war Britain was written in 2008, in the twilight years of a New Labour government which, according to the author, had done all it could to exorcise the ghosts of its socialist origins in favour of a neoliberal agenda.[8] In a review of the text for the *New Statesman*, the critic Jonathan Meades enthused that *Militant Modernism* was the 'deflected Bildungsroman of a [...] velvet-gloved provocateur nostalgic for yesterday's tomorrow, for a world made before he was born, a distant, preposterously optimistic world which, even though it still exists in scattered fragments, has had its meaning erased, its possibilities defiled'.[9]

Primarily an architectural writer and theorist, the relics which Hatherley examines in *Militant Modernism* are those of the built environment, which he examines as a material articulation of the utopian spirit of those modernists who participated in what seems now an endeavour of near-Herculean proportions: replacing the slums and crumbling terraces of a decrepit post-war Britain with clean, well-lit and sanitary public housing, building 'an Eldorado for the working class'.[10] It is this spirit that Hatherley seeks to harness in *Militant Modernism* and indeed in his subsequent works, such as *A Guide to the New Ruins of Great Britain*. He finds it in the commonly vilified 'new brutalist' housing estate of Park Hill in Sheffield;[11] in Ernő Goldfinger's monolithic London skyscrapers Trellick and Balfron Towers, once denounced as 'Towers of Terror' yet now lauded by the National Trust as 'the welfare state in concrete';[12] and in the 1960s-built Scottish new town of Cumbernauld, the central protagonist of Bill Forsyth's tender comedy of teenage love and football, *Gregory's Girl*.

Hatherley's writings enunciate

> the conviction that the Left Modernisms of the 20th century continue to be useful: a potential index of ideas, successful or failed, tried, untried or broken on the wheel of the market or the state. Even in their ruinous condition, they can still offer a sense of possibility which decades of being told that 'There is no Alternative' has almost beaten out of us.[13]

Here, the utopian potential of futures past is to be found not in the civic monuments and show-pieces of historic urban architecture but in the everyday, the long-discarded, the commonplace and the ugly. Thus, it is by disinterring remnants of a much-maligned British modernism, that the possibility of an alternative future can be uncovered. This is a proposition which has clear origins in the work of the German Marxist thinker Walter Benjamin, whom the author refers to in the first page of *Militant Modernism* as the author of the modernist exhortation 'to live without traces'.[14] Whilst Hatherley explores the built environment and its utopian promise in his analysis of the contemporary cultural landscape, Mark Fisher explores the potential of the cultural discourse of 'popular modernism' of post-war Britain to liberate us from a future of what he terms 'capitalist realism'.[15] While Hatherley's writing is, in a positive sense, of an unrepentantly nostalgic bent, Fisher goes further, positing the legacy of such past utopianisms as spectral manifestations of futures lost and futures yet to come. In his 2014 work entitled *Ghosts of My*

*Life: Writings on Depression, Hauntology and Lost Futures*, Fisher explores notions of hauntology or spectrality, a school of academic thought which originated in Jacques Derrida's 1993 work *Specters of Marx*.[16] Before considering Fisher's interpretation of hauntology, and its relevance to *El cantor de tango*, it is useful to briefly examine the origins of the concept.

In the postmodern environs of the first decades of the twenty-first century, when technology and the functionalities of global connectivity have colonized everyday existence, the notion of ghosts is an incongruity, running contrary to the hegemonic codes of the Enlightenment, which privilege rationalism above all things. But, as Fredric Jameson asserts in his essay 'Marx's Purloined Letter', first published within *Ghostly Demarcations*, the 1999 symposium compiled in response to Derrida's text, 'spectrality does not involve the conviction that ghosts exist'.[17] A play on words in both English and the original French, Derrida's 'hauntology' merges the verb 'to haunt' with the noun 'ontology' and, in doing so, destabilizes the Manichean opposition which these two contradictory concepts denote. Jameson characterizes the metonymic ghosts summoned by Derrida as 'these moments in which the present — and above all our current present, the wealthy, sunny world of the postmodern and the end of history, of the new world system of late capitalism — unexpectedly betrays us'.[18] The spectral denotes the sensation that time and space are 'out of joint',[19] and provokes an uncanny sense of past events, feelings or ideologies revisiting us in the present and revealing an alternative to the hegemonic actuality. Thus, the spectral is neither past nor present nor future. Rather, it appears as an interstitial zone between chronologies.

Another important feature of hauntology is, as Jameson asserts, its refusal to relinquish 'the expression of a persistent yet generally subterranean Utopianism'.[20] For Hatherley, the architectural revenants of the British post-war consensus embody a felicitous yet short-lived effort to construct a society beneficial to all, where radical modernity was employed in the pursuit of such a goal. In Fisher's view, the 'cultural ecology'[21] of this aesthetic is embodied in a range of outlets as diverse as 'postpunk, brutalist architecture, Penguin paperbacks and the BBC Radiophonic Workshop'.[22] What unites this apparently disparate list of cultural relics is a utopian aspiration to live differently; to embrace and inhabit modernity despite the risks of failure. In reclaiming these cultural relics and the modernist impetus that spawned them, we defy what Jameson has termed 'the eternal present' of neoliberal capitalism and imagine an alternative future. Therefore, haunting is much more than a vague nostalgia; it is a positive recognition of the 'historical alternatives which haunt the established society as subversive tendencies and forces'.[23] By listening to the muttering of ghosts, we can recognise future possibilities outside the amnesiac discourse of neoliberalism.

For Fisher, Derrida's concept contains these two key notions; firstly, that 'which is (in actuality) *no longer*, but which remains effective as a virtuality'.[24] In other words, a spectre of what is absent but not erased. Secondly, hauntology embodies that which 'has *not yet* happened but which is *already* effective in the virtual (an attractor, an anticipation shaping current behaviour) [...] a virtuality whose present coming was already playing a part in undermining the present state of things'.[25]

Avery Gordon describes this second impetus more succinctly as 'utopian grace', where the spectral reveals glimpses of the past which incite a desire for change and betterment in the present and the future.[26] According to the interpretations of Fisher and Gordon, if hauntological narratives are to elicit a response other than lamentation, they must comprise a function beyond the disclosure of the occluded histories of our past. The spectral must also instigate a re-evaluation of the present that has the potential to ignite transformation of thought and action.

Moreover, the notions of nostalgia and spectrality used by Hatherley and Fisher have a resonance far beyond the specificities of post-war British cultural history. Whilst popular notions of ghosts have formed part of folk culture for centuries, Derrida's theory and its multiple subsequent interpretations are inextricably intertwined with modernity, in all its felicities and its traumas. Fisher quotes from the theorist Marshall Berman, who epitomizes the ambiguity at the heart of the modern in his statement that 'to be modern is to find ourselves in an environment that promises us adventure, power, joy, growth, transformation of ourselves and the world — and, at the same time that threatens to destroy everything we have, everything we know, everything we are'.[27] The urban *topos* epitomizes this temporal and epistemic conflict. As the cockpit of modernity, the city is a locus of perpetual change, where remnants of historical endeavours sit alongside the technological signifiers of a constant, headlong rush into the future. Simultaneously looking backwards towards the past and forward towards the future, the urban landscape is imbued with profound hauntological potential. As Julian Wolfreys asserts, the city is indeed 'a machine, albeit a spectral one'.[28] He goes on to cite Manfredo Tanfuri's concept of the *polis* as 'a sort of machine, emitting incessant messages'.[29] This is reflected in the numerous literary narratives of hauntology which take a metropolis, often London, as their setting. In novels such as Peter Ackroyd's *Hawksmoor* and Iain Sinclair's *White Chapell, Scarlet Tracings* London cannot truly be experienced as anything other than a paradigm of historicity. It is a city in flux, 'becoming constantly',[30] an epitome of modernity yet any true comprehension of its urban present can be achieved only through the excavation of 'the countless relationships of its subjects to its past, to its dead, to the traces of memory that maintain themselves and reiterate themselves'.[31]

With these tropes in mind, can *El cantor de tango* by Tomás Eloy Martínez be read as a novel of urban hauntology? It is a narrative which seeks to disinter, excavate and revisit the past utopias of Buenos Aires. But to what extent do its historicist excursions incite the potential for change in the present? By considering the dialogic interplay between the text and Fisher and Gordons's dual tenets of hauntology, we may evaluate the novel's hauntological potential. Like all cities, Buenos Aires is a palimpsest construct, where the new is built upon the ruins of the old, creating strata of time and space within the urban landscape. For the architectural historian Adrián Gorelik, the Argentine capital signifies 'tiempo grabado en las piedras, la marca presente de todas las pérdidas de la historia, de todas las heridas del hombre en el mundo, su presencia en bruto — en tiempo y espacio real' [time engraved upon the stones, the imprint of all the losses of history, of all the wounds of man in the world, this raw presence –– in real time and space].[32] As Cadogan takes his

FIG. 2.1. Calle Libertad, a typical central Buenos Aires streetscape. Image: Brigid Lynch

first stroll around Buenos Aires, on an evening excursion with El Tucumano, a new acquaintance from his boarding house, he remarks upon the aesthetic patchwork of the city streets, declaring:

> Apenas alzaba la vista, descubría palacios barrocos y cúpulas en forma de paraguas o melones, con miradores inútiles que servían de ornamento. Me sorprendió que Buenos Aires fue tan majestuosa a partir de las segundas y terceras plantas, y tan ruinosa a la altura del suelo, como si el esplendor del pasado hubiera quedado suspendido en lo alto y se negara a bajar o a desaparecer.[33]
>
> [Every time I looked up I discovered baroque palaces and cupolas in the shape of parasols or melons, with purely ornamental turrets. I was surprised that Buenos Aires was so majestic from the second or third story upwards and so dilapidated at street level, as if the splendor of the past had remained suspended in the heights and refused to descend or disappear].[34]

At street level, the urban landscape is nondescript, littered with the commercial paraphernalia of any modern city yet the beauty of the upper stories, crowded with architectural signifiers of other times and places, strike the narrator. The past literally hangs in the air; ghostlike, suspended and intangible, it haunts the streetscape (Fig. 2.1).

It was in an effort to capture something of the palimpsestic metropolis that, in October of the year 2000, the Bloomsbury publishing house commissioned

Martínez to write an essay on the Argentine capital, as part of a series entitled 'Writers and their Cities'.[35] He would be in illustrious company: Gunther Grass had been tasked with writing Berlin and Carlos Fuentes was to produce a chronicle of Mexico City. In his response to Bloomsbury's request, the author suggested he write a short piece based around a dream he had had of the city a few days previously, whilst he was visiting London. He described this dream in an interview in 2006, describing how 'en el sueño, yo trataba de oír a un cantor de tango insuperable, sin encontrarlo jamás en los lugares donde lo anunciaban' [in the dream, I tried to hear an incomparable tango singer, but I was never able to see him in the places where he was advertised to perform].[36] Struck by the strangeness of the dream, Martínez mentioned it to a colleague, Jean Franco, who told him about the existence of Luis Cardel, a tango singer whose performances were rumoured to be superior to the legendary Carlos Gardel.[37] However, Cardel suffered from haemophilia and had become seriously ill, having contracted the AIDS virus through a contaminated blood transfusion. 'A pesar de su persecución a este cantor por Buenos Aires' [Despite his pursuit of this singer all over Buenos Aires],[38] the author was never able to hear him perform, although he did befriend Cardel's widow following the singer's death. It was this dream and his subsequent pursuit of the enigmatic Cardel that provided the inspiration for *El cantor de tango*. Whilst his text quickly outgrew the word limit proscribed by Bloomsbury, they encouraged the author to continue writing and so the novel was born.

Thus, the novel was originally intended as an attempt to write the city of Buenos Aires, to represent the *polis* in text and to document both its historical and contemporary sensibilities. This was no small undertaking, given the wealth of illustrious authors who preceded Martínez in this task. For to write the city of Buenos Aires is also to write the nation of Argentina. With its paradigmatic relation to concepts of Argentine national identity, Buenos Aires has long been represented in literature as the seat of all progress within the nation, the engine of Argentine modernity, and as such, the 'locus of all civilizing projects'.[39] Conversely, in the works of authors such as Ezequiel Martínez Estrada, Roberto Arlt and Ricardo Piglia, it is often depicted as a dystopian *polis*, where alienation and inequality blight the lives of its inhabitants.[40] It is through the character of Cadogan that the author conveys the complex and conflictive textual historicity of Buenos Aires. As a North American academic researcher who has never before visited the Argentine capital, Cadogan's knowledge of the city is solely drawn from textual representations. For readers unfamiliar with Buenos Aires, his frequent reveries provide an educated commentary on the city, its history and above all, its literature. These elucidations are the fruit of years of academic research, during which he has explored the Argentine capital at length through its literary representations, from the confines of a university library. Indeed, in the opening lines of the novel, he admits to this predilection for textual, as opposed to material historicity, stating, in a distinctly Borgesian tone: 'Buenos Aires fue para mí solo una ciudad de la literatura hasta el templado mediodía de invierno del año 2000 en que escuché por primera vez el nombre de Julio Martel' [Buenos Aires was a city I knew only from literature until one mild winter's day in 2000 when I first heard the name Julio Martel].[41] Having never before visited the city, Cadogan considers himself, initially at least, unburdened by the weight of its material history. In fact, at first, he considers a visit to Buenos Aires unnecessary, so well-acquainted is he with the city through his study of its textual representations. He ruminates that 'podía imaginar la humedad, el Río de la Plata, la llovizna, los paseos vacilantes de Borges por las calles del sur con su bastón de ciego' [I could imagine the humidity, the Río de la Plata, the drizzle, Borges tottering along the southern streets with his white cane].[42] However, as the literary allusions of these admissions suggest, not only is his personal imaginary of Buenos Aires forged solely from textual representations of the city, so every aspect of his physical explorations of the metropolis will be informed by its literary subjectivities.

Paradoxically, Bruno's status as a foreigner, the quintessential stranger in a strange land, enhances his ability to perceive and experience the city in a more profound sense. As an outsider, he can avoid what Jason Wilson describes in his own guide to the city as the 'inevitability of over-familiarity'[43] that can encumber native *porteño* authors. In this assertion, that 'writers best perceive place from outside their own cultures',[44] Wilson cites Borges, one of the city's most famous literary sons. Although a native *porteño*, Borges left the city for Europe with his family in his mid-teens, returning permanently over a decade later.[45] Alluding to his rediscovery of Buenos Aires following his return, he famously asserted that: 'I was able to see Buenos Aires keenly and eagerly because I had been away from it for a long time. Had I never gone abroad, I wonder whether I would ever have seen it with the particular shock and glow it now gave me.[46] For Borges, and subsequently for Wilson, it is this distance and the attendant clarity of perspective that it facilitates which is fundamental to capturing a sense of the city in textual form. Attuned to the unfamiliar and the unusual, visitors are often better able to perceive the city than its inhabitants, who have become inured to their surroundings and are no longer affected by the layers of visual, cultural and historical meaning that permeate their native urban landscape. As the old saying goes, familiarity breeds contempt. In *Memories of Buenos Aires*, the American academic Max Page describes his experience of visiting the city for the first time:

> In our eagerness to learn the ways of the city and connect it to past travels and our home, we are alive to every detail, even as we are oblivious to the many levels of experience that the inhabitant knows deep within herself, which operates almost like instinct. As I explored Buenos Aires, all my senses were in peak form, absorbing and filtering the uniqueness of the city.[47]

Therefore, by employing a North American as his narrator, Martínez can view the city with fresh eyes and an affective distance unavailable to a native protagonist. The author's personal history may have also influenced this narrative modality. Born in Tucumán, in Northwest Argentina, he lived and worked as a journalist in Buenos Aires during the turbulent period of the 1960s and 70s before fleeing into political exile in Venezuela in 1975. Following the transition to democracy in 1983, he returned to the Argentine capital but his subsequent career as a writer and academic was punctuated by long periods of residence in the United States. Setting to one side issues of intentional fallacy, it is not unreasonable to assume that such absences and the insights gleaned upon subsequent returns to the city may have influenced the author's decision to encode narratorial authority within the novel in the character of a visitor.

It is worth exploring our narrator's intertextual conceptualizations of Buenos Aires further, since in the impressions he draws from literary representations of the city, Cadogan replicates the ubiquitous foundational discourse of the Argentine nation — the binary opposition of civilization and barbarism. First conceptualized by the nineteenth-century statesman Domingo F. Sarmiento in his 1845 work *Civilización y barbarie: vida de Juan Facundo Quiroga* [Civilization and Barbarism: The Life of Juan Facundo Quiroga], this ideologeme views the nation's entire history as a metonymic struggle between these two forces. A Unitarian, who frequently sought political exile in Chile during the Federalist regime of the *caudillo* Juan Manuel de Rosas from 1829 to 1852, Sarmiento was convinced of the modernizing impetus of Buenos Aires in contrast to the savagery and feudalism of the interior.[48] Laura Podalsky provides a concise summary of this complex antinomy, defining it succinctly as: 'Buenos Aires-civilization-European influences versus interior provinces-barbarism-autochthonous tradition'.[49] Within the oppositional discourse of civilization and barbarism, Buenos Aires epitomises a civilized modernity entirely absent from the infinite and perilous horizons of the Pampas and the gauchos who populate these desolate plains. Within Cadogan's textual historicity, barbarism is encoded within the short story 'El matadero' [The Slaughterhouse] by Esteban Antonio Echeverría, which he describes as 'el primer cuento argentino' [the first Argentine work of literature].[50] Written in 1841, the narrative unfolds in 'the Convalescencia, or Alto Slaughterhouse [...] located in the southern part of Buenos Aires, on a huge lot, rectangular in shape, at the intersection of two streets, one of which ends there while the other continues eastward'.[51] It depicts the squalor, brutality and inhumanity of the slaughterhouse, and the torture and murder of a young Unitarian by the Federalist soldiers of Rosas. The cattle that are brought to the site for slaughter are emblematic of 'the Unitarians who suffer through Rosas's repressive and violent reign',[52] and their slaughter foreshadows the savage killing of the young man in the final pages of the story. The violence and cruelty of 'El matadero' are an allegorical representation of the alleged barbarity that the *caudillo* Juan Manuel de Rosas has wrought upon the city, and in turn the nation. Thus, when Cadogan hears that Martel is to perform on the site of the old slaughterhouse, in the peripheral district of Liniers, it is his literary knowledge that informs his deductions as to the singer's motivations. He theorizes that Martel has chosen the slaughterhouse since, within Echeverría's fictional narrative, 'la crueldad con el ganado es la réplica de la bárbara crueldad que en el país se ejerce con los hombres' [the cruelty to the cattle is a metaphor for the barbarous cruelty inflicted on men in the country].[53] Yet, as we shall see shortly, Martel is motivated by an alternative sense of the past, beyond Cadogan's purely textual notion of historicity.

For our narrator, just as the literary historicity of Echeverría's 'El matadero' encodes the barbarism embedded within the Argentine national imaginary, so the oppositional discourse of civilization is also to be found in fiction, in the short story 'El aleph' [The Aleph] by Borges. The story's protagonist, a fictionalized version of Borges himself, happens upon a mythical sphere known as the aleph in the basement of a house on the Calle Garay. The essence of all knowledge, the aleph contains all points of space and time within the universe, bestowing all those who gaze upon it with immeasurable wisdom. It is the fictional aleph, along with certain other recurrent Borgesian metaphors, such as the labyrinth, the maze and the library, which Cadogan employs as his primary spatio-temporal reference points when he first arrives in Buenos Aires. In one example, he takes a room at a dilapidated boarding house solely because he believes it to be the house described within the short story. Moreover, convinced that through his recitals, Martel is tracing out a secret map which will lead to the immutable truth of the city's existence, Cadogan employs his literary knowledge to decipher the problem. As he explains:

> compré algunos mapas de Buenos Aires y fui trazando en ellos líneas de colores que unían los lugares donde Martel había cantado, con la esperanza de encontrar algún dibujo que descifrara sus intenciones, algo parecido al rombo con el que Borges resuelve el problema de 'La muerte y la brújula'.[54]
>
> [I bought some maps of Buenos Aires and drew coloured lines on them joining the places where Martel had sung, in the hope of finding some picture that might decipher his intentions, something like the rhombus with which Borges solves the riddle in 'Death and the Compass'.][55]

The singer's recitals and the truth which underlies these excursions become, for Cadogan, a new incarnation of the aleph: in order to truly understand Buenos Aires, he must find Martel and discover the secret. Thus, Bruno's perceptions of the city are irrevocably informed by his knowledge of its textual historicity. His Buenos Aires is populated by spectres, in the ghosts of the texts he has studied and their authors. He is not yet able to view Buenos Aires as anything other than an intertextual entity, ensnared as he is within a web of literary references that cannot represent the totality of its lived existence. For, as Podalsky suggests, 'cultural analysis must be wed to material history'[56] in order for some truth of the *polis* to emerge, and indeed, for hauntology to move beyond mere lament. It is only in his encounter with Martel, towards the end of the novel, that he is able to comprehend Buenos Aires as a nexus of lived experience, beyond the page.

Just as Cadogan's literary histories constitute one form of hauntology within the novel, so the material historicity which informs Julio Martel's perception of Buenos Aires is representative of another spectral discourse. In the novel's epigraph, taken from Benjamin's unfinished magnum opus *The Arcades Project*, we glimpse the interrelation between these two spectralities. It reads: 'el conocimiento llega solo en golpes de relámpago. El texto es la sucesión larga de truenos que sigue' [Knowledge comes only in lightning flashes. The text is the long roll of thunder that follows].[57] In this separation of knowledge, acquired through lived experience and its subsequent textual representations, Benjamin's epigraph addresses the historicist dichotomy at the heart of *El cantor de tango*. Whilst Cadogan espouses a purely literary historicity, Martel is consumed by the material past in the lives of those dead he evokes through his performances. As a chronicler of hauntological affect, Benjamin was fascinated by urban landscapes and, in many of his essays and monographs, he attempts to trace the spectral pathways beneath the physical geography of the city, in his native Berlin, and in Naples and Paris. It is in one of these chronicles, *Berlin Childhood Around 1900*, that we find an autobiographical vignette which could equally be applied to Martel's hauntological endeavours. As Benjamin recalls:

> Accidents and crimes [...] Each day the city promised me them afresh and when evening came it was still in my debt [...] a looted display window, the house from which a dead person had been removed, the place on a carriageway where a horse had collapsed –– I would plant myself in front of them to feed on the evanescent breath left behind by the event.[58]

These recollections of Berlin constitute a vision of a haunted place, a collection of micro-histories, the 'evanescent breath' of thousands of interactions, events and accidents that interpellate the quotidian reality of urban existence. For Martel, the affective topography of Buenos Aires is punctuated by the innumerable accidents and crimes of the past, in both the individual casual cruelties of its citizens and the collective violence of the state. In his performances at the sites of these past injustices, he feels the 'evanescent breath' of this material historicity upon him. It is these micro-histories that form the narrative motor of the novel and in their placement throughout the text that the significance of Benjamin's epigraph is evident. Although Martel's performances coalesce around three central historical vignettes, there are numerous other historiographies contained within *El cantor de tango*, stories which ebb and fade, subsumed within the broader narrative, only to reappear later in the text. Such diegetic fragmentation and the subsequent sporadic elucidation of these micro-histories delivers the truth of the past 'en golpes de relámpago', a series of minor narrative epiphanies as opposed to a neat linearity. Moreover, this resistance of a diachronic narrative mirrors both the often-disorientating material reality of the *polis*, and more broadly the fragmentary nature of history itself, particularly in a post-dictatorship society like Argentina.

Before we consider some of the specific historiographies around which Martel's hauntological incursions revolve, it is useful to examine one of the earliest of the singer's performances that Cadogan hears of, a recital in the subway beneath the Obelisk on the Avenida 9 de Julio. For it is in this short episode, little over one page in length, that the full weight of the past upon the tango singer becomes evident. Built in 1936 and designed by Alberto Prebisch, the monument reaffirmed the 'founding gesture' of the establishment of the city and, as Adrián Gorelik and Graciela Silvestri suggest, it symbolized 'a very typical way of being modern; its form conjures up the frenzied time of modernity itself'.[59] An architect and prominent figure in the celebrations of 1936, Prebisch became known as the 'leader of the classical-modern avant-garde'[60], modernizer in chief and one of the leading lights of the quarticentennial celebrations of the founding of Buenos Aires. The design and construction of the Obelisk was much more than the erection of a commemorative civic monument; it formed part of a wider ideological impetus to relocate the cultural nucleus of the city from the Borgesian *arrabales* of the periphery to the heart of the downtown grid.

Therefore, the celebrations of 1936 represented the endeavour 'to turn Buenos Aires into the ideological embodiment of four hundred years of predestined utopia'.[61] As the only public monument constructed for these celebrations, the Obelisk was an architectural statement of intent and stood in sharp opposition to the 'fin de siècle eclecticism, outcome of the ostentatious whims of the parvenu immigrant'[62] embodied in the *cocoliche* structures of the Avenida de Mayo, such as the Palacio Barolo.[63] For Prebisch, the simplicity and purity of the Obelisk constituted a timely riposte to the decadent ornamentation of such buildings, and their melange of architectural styles that have been described as 'a literal "Tower of Babel" of stylistic languages'.[64] Here, we see the conflictive discourse of civilization and barbarism once again make its presence felt, now re-sited from the interior to the urban, in the baroque extravagancies of the Eurocentric architecture of the city centre.

In the contemporary reality of the novel, the state of the subterranean networks beneath the Obelisk is a far cry from the modernist idealism of Prebisch. The tunnels are dirty, ill-lit and home to a variety of cottage industries. Shoe-shiners, magazine sellers and numerous other businesses crowd the tunnels. Bruno describes the scene as a chaotic melee, saying:

> dos de los desvíos conducen a kioscos y baratillos de ropa militar, diarios y revistas usados, plantillas y cordones de zapatos, perfumes de fabricación casera, estampillas, bolsos y billeteras, reproducciones industriales del *Guernica* y de la *Paloma* de Picasso, paraguas, medias.[65]

> [Two of the branches lead to kiosks and shops selling army surplus, second-hand magazines and papers, shoelaces and insoles, homemade perfumes, stamps, handbags and wallets, industrial reproductions of Picasso's *Guernica* and *Paloma*, umbrellas and socks.][66]

The disorganized commerce of this unregulated subterranean market is a world away from the purity and order of the 'white city' that Prebisch envisioned in the construction of the Obelisk.[67] It is another world entirely, a mercantile dystopia beneath the gleaming angles of the monument. This underworld of ersatz commerce is, in its depredation and decay, the antithesis of the formal mercantile structures of the neoliberal city. It is an Arltian vision of a parallel economy, far from the glittering window displays of the exclusive boutiques that populate the city's upmarket shopping streets.

Yet, paradoxically, it mimics the ethos of free-market buying and selling embodied by such establishments. Here too, is a place of commerce but the customers are those who could never gain admittance to the hallowed halls of the upmarket shopping mall. In this way, with the makeshift clutter of its stalls and the homemade ephemera on sale, the market underneath the Obelisk embodies some small utopian sensibility, an attempt to reclaim the quotidian necessities of buying and selling from the grand neoliberal temples to consumption. In this, it is reminiscent of a Sheffield market that Hatherley visits in his work *A Guide to The New Ruins of Great Britain*. Castle Market, he tells us, has been condemned by

Sheffield City Council as a 'rotting, abandoned time capsule'.[68] Yet for Hatherley, this 1960s-built indoor market exemplifies the utopian spirit of 'modernism as montage, messiness, and the drama of multiple levels and scales'.[69] It is 'a modernist design which specifically tries to engineer bustle and individuality, so that you notice both the ingenious design of the labyrinthine structure and the competing design ambitions of the many stalls and built-in shops'.[70] Whilst the teeming informal economy of the labyrinthine subways beneath the Obelisk is far from Prebisch's idealised urban classicism, the existence of this parallel agora is both an indictment of and a triumph over the homogenizing forces of neoliberal capital.

Martel does not sing here, since his voice would not be heard above the din of traders touting their wares. Instead he moves towards 'una de las oquedades sin salida, donde algunas familias sin techo habían montado su campamento de nómades'. [in one of the dead-end hollows where some homeless families had set up camp.][71] Amongst the dispossessed and down on their luck, he sings the tango *Caminito* and his voice reverberates throughout the tunnels, carrying his elegiac lament to an unexpectant audience. But it is only much later in the novel that we learn the reason for Martel's performance here. Obsessively attempting to decipher the tango singer's secret map, Cadogan searches through the newspaper archives of the national library. He finally locates a report of a violent incident at the Obelisk in an edition of the British publication *The Economist* from mid-1976, 'donde el corresponsal en Buenos Aires escribía que un domingo de junio de 1976 — el 18, creo — un grupo de hombres con cascos de acero llegó poco antes del amanecer a la Plaza de la República en un automóvil sin placas de identificación'[where the Buenos Aires correspondent wrote that one Sunday in June 1976 — the 18th, I think — a group of men in steel helmets arrived at the Plaza de la República slightly before dawn in an unmarked car].[72] The men drag a young person from the vehicle and, having forced their captive up against the monument, they unleash a barrage of machine gun fire towards the victim and the glistening white stone of the Obelisk. Like so many of the micro-histories within Martínez's work, this incident has its origins in a real historical event. In a series of brutal reprisals that followed several left-wing guerrilla bombings in June and July of 1976, including that of the police headquarters building at Coordinación Federal in Buenos Aires, 'a teenager was taken by police from his cell at the first light of dawn. Put up against the gleaming white Obelisk, towering over downtown Buenos Aires, he was executed'.[73] Martínez does not name the victim, nor the murderers. These factual omissions go beyond literary device. Rather, they reflect a broader pattern of omission and occlusion in the historical record of the last dictatorship. This anonymity imbues the death of this murdered youth with a paradigmatic status. Here Martel sings not only to commemorate the death of one young man but of the senseless massacre of a generation of Argentines, perpetrated by a military government determined to eradicate the threat of perceived subversion. His song fractures the oppressive silence of impunity that still pervades the Argentine society of the novel.

Moreover, in this particular location, his music is a repudiation of the message that adorned the Obelisk in late 1975, in the months immediately prior to the military coup — that 'Silencio es Salud' [Silence is Health] (Figs 2.2 and 2.3).[74]

Fig. 2.2. The Obelisk, Avenida 9 de Julio, Buenos Aires, late 1975. A municipal government campaign against excessive traffic noise advises motorists that 'silencio es salud'. Image: Archivo DiFilm.

Fig. 2.3. A wider view of the 'silencio es salud' placard that adorned the Obelisk. Image: Archivo DiFilm.

Ostensibly erected to discourage motorists from the liberal use of their car horns, in the febrile socio-political climate of early 1976, the slogan resonated with a far more sinister meaning: that acquiescence would be enforced by any means necessary. In breaking this silence and evoking the ghost of the anonymous victim of state violence, Martel's song memorializes the damage done to the Argentine body politic during the punitive years of *el Proceso*. Yet, as we shall observe, to move beyond a state of haunting, commemoration alone is insufficient, since in order to enact change, the activity of listing and cataloguing the atrocities of the past must be conjoined with the praxis of hope.

From this one minor incident in the novel, the weight and complexity of the past which the tango singer articulates is fully illustrated. A heavy burden to bear, the 'imposibilidad material de convivir con todo el pasado' haunts Martel, exacerbating his ill health and physical frailty.[75] In a further examination of the hauntological potential that Martel reveals through his performances, we will now consider the three central vignettes around which the text is structured. The first of these Benjaminian micro-histories centres around the Waterworks Palace, a huge baroque edifice embellished with ornate stonework in the *cocoliche* style so popular in Buenos Aires in the period immediately preceding the first centenary of liberation from Spanish rule in 1910. As Cadogan informs us, the intricacy of the building's exterior decoration belies the ugly functionality of its interior, a maze of pipes and ironwork which filter the silt-laden water of the Río de la Plata and transform it to potable water for the bathrooms and kitchens of the city. He describes the Palace as a riot of 'mosaicos calcáreos, cariátides de hierro fundido, placas de mármol, coronas de terracota, puertas y ventanas labradas con tantos pliegues y esmaltes' [limestone mosaics, cast iron caryatids, marble plaques, terracotta tiled roofs, doors and Windows with so many carved folds and glazes] (Fig. 2.4).[76]

In all its neo-colonial splendour, this water purification depot is emblematic of the architectural discourse of the 1910 Centenary celebrations, which 'looked to the neo-colonial style in an attempt to develop a didactic language that would strengthen the pedagogical construction of a common origin'.[77] Designed by Belgian, Norwegian and British architects in the baroque French style, the building exudes a distinctly European beauty, transplanted to the shores of the River Plate. Its aesthetic speaks of the discourse of civilization and of the utopian aspirations of the city modernizers who sought to transform Buenos Aires from a colonial port to the most modern and advanced city of the Americas. It is of a similar ilk to the buildings of the city centre which prompted Meades to remark, on a visit to Buenos Aires in 2004:

> This is a city which is, then, founded on nostalgia in its purest, most literal sense — in an aching yearning for a forsaken place across the sea, a yearning which expresses itself so variously, so ubiquitously, that it defies the reason and the desire that this city should still be here [...] It is in a state of perpetual anticipation, about to travel hopefully'.[78]

The utopian origins of the Waterworks Palace are bespoiled by a crime which takes place in the year 1899: the murder and subsequent discovery of the body of

Fig. 2.4. Palacio de las aguas corrientes, Buenos Aires. Image: www.info.bae.com.

teenager Felicitas Alcántara. Her abduction and murder take place on the cusp of the new century, on New Year's Eve, and are considered 'un crimen tan atroz que aun se hablaba de el en Buenos Aires, donde abundan los crimenes sin castigo' [a crime so atrocious [...] that it was still spoken of in Buenos Aires, where unpunished crimes abound].[79] She disappears while bathing in the river, a short distance from her home, and despite the considerable efforts of the police, no trace of her can be found. Witnesses who saw her bathing on the day of her disappearance mention the presence of a tall, dark moustachioed man watching the beach from a rowing boat, with the aid of a spyglass. Yet this information is not acted upon, as this description bears significant similarities to the physical appearance of Colonel Ramón L. Falcón, the investigating officer in the case. It is not until over a year later, in April 1901, that the body of the young girl is discovered in a room in the south west wing of the Waterworks Palace by a caretaker (Fig. 2.5).

Once again, there are few clues that can be gleaned from the crime scene, save for a handkerchief embroidered with the initials RLF, initials which also correspond to the initials of the investigating officer. The culprit is never found and the Alcántara family move away, fleeing Argentina to begin a new life in France.

In the possible involvement of Colonel Falcón in the death of Felicitas Alcántara, there is an allusion to the venality and incompetence of Argentine officialdom and to the impunity that would flourish throughout the twentieth century for those

Fig. 2.5. Interior of the Palacio de las aguas corrientes, Buenos Aires.
Image: Brigid Lynch

committing such crimes on behalf of the state. But there is another significant element to the crime. As Cadogan informs us, years after the murder, in 1915, 'el presidente de la República en persona ordenó que las habitaciones malditas eran clausuradas, lacradas y borradas de los inventarios municipales' [the President of the Republic personally ordered the wretched rooms to be closed, sealed and removed from the public records.][80] By official decree, the past was erased from the record. The room where the victim of such a barbarous and inconvenient crime was found simply ceased to exist, thus removing the stain of an inglorious death from a building with such utopian origins. It is through his performance there that Martel reclaims the existence of Felicitas Alcántara from bureaucratic oblivion, refuting the national custom 'de suprimir de la historia todos los hechos que contradicen las ideas oficiales sobre la grandeza del país' [suppressing from history all the facts that contradict the official ideas of the grandeur of the country.][81] Once again, he memorializes past accidents and crimes. But he undertakes his commemorative practices alone, or latterly with only his companion Alcira, and so must bear the weight of these traumatic histories himself. Martel's precarious health is failing, and, with each performance, he grows weaker and more fragile, as if absorbing the pain and suffering of these ghosts of history.

The second vignette takes place in another location intimately linked with the history of the city and with the industry upon which much of the nation's wealth was built: the buying and selling of cattle. The location is Liniers, on the western periphery of Buenos Aires, and whilst Cadogan theorizes that Martel's performance here is a reference to the bloody violence of Echeverría's short story 'El Matadero', the truth, when revealed, is more complex. In 1977, in a house close to the old slaughterhouse, ex-prostitute Violeta Miller informs on her nurse Catalina Godel, whose real name is Margarita Langman. We are told that Miller was brought to Buenos Aires in the 1920s from Eastern Europe under the false pretence of a happy marriage and a new life in the new world by a member of the Zwi Migdal, a Jewish mafia that specialized in the trafficking of young women from the old countries of Eastern Europe to staff the brothels of the Argentine capital. As the narrator explains:

> A comienzos del siglo XX, casi todos los burdeles de Buenos Aires dependían de esa mafia de cafishios judíos. Los enviados de la Migdal viajaban por las aldeas míseras de Polonia, Galitzia, Besarabia y Ucrania, en busca de muchachas también judías a las que iban seduciendo con falsas promesas de matrimonio.[82]
>
> [At the beginning of the twentieth century, almost all the brothels of Buenos Aires were run by that mafia of Jewish pimps. The Migdal's envoys travelled through the poorest villages of Poland, Galicia, Besarabia and Ukraine, in search of Jewish girls they would seduce with false promises of matrimony.][83]

A victim of white slavery, Miller was the illiterate third child of a tailor from suburban Lodz, Poland who, in 1914, fell prey to just one such outwardly respectable businessman whom she met at her local synagogue. After a swift but respectable courtship, he proposes to her and after their marriage the couple emigrates to Argentina, only for Miller to discover during the journey that she is one of eight 'wives' who are to be auctioned upon arrival. This trade in human beings mirrors the trade in cattle for which the area is renowned and, fittingly, the tangos that Martel sings here are from the brothels and bordellos of 1920s Buenos Aires.

It is of no little significance that both Miller and Godel are Jewish. Following the mass immigration of the late-nineteenth and early-twentieth centuries, Buenos Aires become home to the world's largest Jewish community outside New York and Jewish citizens suffered particular persecution during el *Proceso*.[84] The tragedy of this vignette is Miller's inhumanity in reporting Godel to the authorities, and her negation of a common bond of solidarity which could have united the two women. As a former militant in the Montoneros guerrilla organization, who has escaped from a clandestine detention centre, Godel is a fugitive.[85] She has disguised her identity, applying for the role of Miller's nurse in order to evade capture and certain death at the hands of a military task force. For this performance, Martel is too unwell to leave the car and sing for Godel, so he asks a friend to lay the flowers he has brought in tribute to the murdered woman. In truth, he mourns not only her death but, moreover, her betrayal by Miller, a woman whose past traumas have damaged her irrevocably. In reporting her nurse to the authorities, she demonstrates that she is no longer capable of trust, nor of love for another human being. Finally, Martel goes to the ruins of Miller's house on the Avenida de los Corrales, where he

Fig. 2.6. The former clandestine detention centre Club Atlético, Buenos Aires. Image: *La Nación*.

finds Godel's old and mildewed copy of Julio Cortázar's *Rayuela* and is overcome with grief. Yet he persists, determined to sing for the lost lives of both women and through his song, it is almost as if Catalina Godel returns. '*Hoy te evoco, emocionando*, cantaba, y la Margarita del tango regresaba al caserón como si el tiempo no hubiera pasado, con el cuerpo de veinticuatro años atrás' [*Today, overcome, I invoke you*, he sang, and the Margarita of the tango returned to the big house, as if time had not passed, with her body of twenty-four years earlier] .[86]

As we have seen, Cadogan's perception of the historicist forces which Martel summons at Liniers are dominated by his perception of the city and its past as a textual entity, as opposed to the material site of countless accidents and crimes. It is only in the final section of the novel, as he talks with Martel's partner Alcira, that Cadogan realises the true motivation behind this particular performance, in that the subject of Martel's commemoration was not the brutal slaughterhouses described in Echeverría's short story but rather other more recent murderous events. In this realization, he recognizes the existence of a city beyond the text, where it is the spectral revenants of deeds, not words, which linger on. But it is only after Martel's death that Cadogan comes to understand the enormity of the singer's historicist project. With Alcira's help, he begins to piece together the puzzle that Martel had inscribed upon the urban landscape and learns of the locations of other performances: under a motorway flyover, alongside the ruins of Club Atlético, the clandestine prison where thousands of so-called 'subversives' were held captive and tortured during *el Proceso*; opposite the Jewish community centre on the Calle Pasteur, where in 1994 a truck bomb killed eighty-six people; and at the gates of the former Vasena metalworks, where during the workers' uprising of the 'semana trágica' [tragic week] of 1919, police fired on the crowd, killing thirty workers (Fig. 2.6).

At each of these sites, Martel performs his tangos to demarcate a time and space that are 'out of joint', a fractured spatio-temporality which is no longer fully extant in the present but remains as 'an anticipation, shaping current behaviour'.[87] As Cadogan remarks:

> El mapa, entonces, era más simple de lo que imaginé. No dibujaba una figura química ni ocultaba el nombre de Dios o repetía las cifras de la Cábala, sino que seguía, al azar, el itinerario de los crímenes impunes que se habían cometido en la ciudad de Buenos Aires. Era una lista que contenía un infinito número de nombres y eso era lo que más había atraído a Martel, porque le servía como un conjuro contra la crueldad y la injusticia, que también son infinitas.[88]

> [The map, then, was simpler than I'd imagined. It didn't draw any alchemic figure or hide the name of God or repeat phrases from the Kabbalah, but followed, by chance, the itinerary of crimes committed with impunity in the city of Buenos Aires. It was a list that contained an infinite number of names and that was what had most attracted Martel, because it served as an incantation against cruelty and injustice, which were also infinite.][89]

Thus, the spectral discourse of material historicity is revealed to Cadogan in the minutiae of the forgotten accidents and crimes that Martel evokes in his performances. As he grasps the true purpose of Martel's peregrinations, our narrator finally realizes just how erroneous his literary theorizing has been and his disappointment is palpable. Here, Cadogan epitomizes Ricardo Piglia's assessment of the literary critic as 'un aventurero que se mueve entre los textos buscando un secreto que a veces no existe, [...] un personaje fascinante: el descifrador de oráculos, el lector de la tribu' [an adventurer who moves between texts searching for a secret that sometimes does not exist, [...] a fascinating character: the decipherer of oracles, the reader of the tribe.][90] But he also highlights the danger inherent within the scholarly vocation, citing the fate of the detective Lönnrot in 'La muerte y la brújula', a character who, he asserts, 'va hacia la muerte porque cree que toda la ciudad es un texto' [meets his death because he believes the whole city is a text.][91] Piglia's Borgesian allusion is particularly relevant to Cadogan, who undergoes something of an intellectual and emotional crisis towards the end of the novel, as his personal imaginary of Buenos Aires is fractured by his encounters with the material reality of the city. In the final chapter, entitled 'Diciembre 2001', even before he discovers the truth behind the singers' performances, Cadogan's literary fetishizations of the city are undone by the violence and social unrest of the *Argentinazo*, in particular the spontaneous mass demonstrations which followed the declaration of a state of siege on the evening of 19 December 2001. At this point in the narrative, Martel has been hospitalized due to the worsening of his haemophilia, and Cadogan finds himself with little to do except sit and wait for news of the singer's condition. Even in his genuine concern for Martel, the narrator cannot conceptualize his friend's predicament through anything other than a literary reference, likening himself to Truman Capote, 'esperando que ahorcaran a Perry y Dick, los asesinos de *A sangre fría*, para poner punto final a su novela' [waiting for Perry and Dick, the murderers of *In Cold Blood*, to be hanged, so he could finish his book.][92] Leaving the hospital briefly, he joins the crowds moving towards the Plaza de Mayo. But it is not a desire for social justice that provokes his participation. Rather, it is the glimpse of his ex-lover, El Tucumano, at the head of the protest that acts as catalyst for his involvement. He follows the crowd to the city centre, increasingly shocked at the violence and barbarity of both the multitude itself and the response of the authorities. He describes how 'la gente corría agitada por las calles. La mayoría estaba casi desnuda' [people were running through the streets in a state of agitation. Most of them were practically naked].[93] In the midst of the crowd, 'las mareas humanas' [human tides] that throng the streets of the city, Cadogan feels little solidarity with the protestors. Rather, he feels 'solo como un perro' [as alone as a dog], alienated from the collective impetus by his own private fixations: his failed romance with El Tucumano and the possibility that Martel may die in hospital before revealing his secret map. He sees the helicopter of outgoing president de la Rúa rise up from the roof of the Casa Rosada and cries out: 'no nos dejés, [...] aguantá y no nos dejés, pero yo sabía que no era a él quien se lo decía. Se lo decía al Tucumano, a Buenos Aires, y también me lo decía a mí mismo, una vez más' [Don't leave us, I shouted at him, hang on, don't leave us, but I knew that it wasn't him I was saying it to. I was saying it to El Tucumano, to Buenos Aires, and to myself, once more.][94]

Cadogan's outburst reveals that what he fears most is the desecration of his own personal conceptions of Buenos Aires, visions of the city which he has carefully constructed from his readings of its literary representations. As he witnesses his cherished abstractions of the textual city disintegrate around him, he is bereft, cast adrift upon a material reality that his own curated subjectivities have previously occluded. In this mode, he views the resignations of several presidents that followed the popular uprising of December 2001 not as a move towards positive change, but rather as an apocalyptic series of events. From his perspective, the *Argentinazo* of December 2001 signifies the end of history, and he expresses his personal desolation, berating himself for his inability to stop what he considers to be the desecration of his urban text. As Janice Radway asserts, spectropolitics, or the praxis of hauntology, can be defined as the opportunity to 'revivify our collective capacity to imagine a future radically other to the one ideologically charted out already by the militarized patriarchal capitalism that has thrived heretofore on the practice of social erasure'.[95] Yet the historicity that consumes Cadogan is disconnected from material reality. He can see the ghosts of the past, but only those that populate his textual urban imaginary. He luxuriates in the presence of these spectres, since they offer him a stable and fixed version of the city's history. Thus, when this sense of the past is imperilled by change in the present, Cadogan struggles to comprehend his surroundings. This intransigence in the face of change is emblematic of the narrator's reluctance to accommodate an alternative version of history, and, moreover the radical vision of the present and the future that such a version may encode.

As the *El cantor de tango* ends, Martel is dead and Cadogan leaves for New York in a state of confusion and despair. How, then, given the apparent negativity of the novel's conclusion, can we utilize the theoretical tenets of Fisher and Gordon to extricate any hauntological meaning from the text? Throughout the narrative, Cadogan and Martel suffer from an excess of historicity, with both characters seeking to uncover a past that Fisher describes as '(in actuality) *no longer*, but which remains effective as a virtuality'.[96] But whither the 'utopian grace' that Gordon describes as central to the purpose of any truly hauntological endeavour? At first reading, the historicist projects of both characters appear devoid of the potential to effect change in the present. Although Martel's tributes to the dead are a form of mourning work, they seem to speak only of the destruction of past utopianisms. Moreover, the burden of his lone commemoration of these violent micro-histories ultimately proves insufferable and hastens the deterioration of the singer's health. In the case of Cadogan, his disillusionment with the material reality of his textual city also appears to negate any utopian aspirations. He cannot, or will not, link his cherished city of words to the material and spatial realities of Buenos Aires and its past.

However, there is a redemptive capacity at work within the novel which does not reveal itself diachronically, but, rather, as the Benjaminian epigram suggests, in 'golpes de relámpago'. In the final pages of the text, as Cadogan boards his evening flight to New York and surveys the dark immensity of Buenos Aires from above, he muses upon his experiences there and a truth which had previously eluded him reveals itself. The nocturnal vista of the city by night provokes the realization that 'el verdadero laberinto no estaba marcado por las luces, donde sólo había caminos que llevaban a ninguna parte, sino por las líneas de oscuridad, que señalaban los espacios donde vivía la gente' [the true labyrinth was not marked out by the lights, where there were only paths that led nowhere, but by the lines of darkness, which indicated where the people lived].[97] The truth, Cadogan understands, is to be found in the places where light is absent, for it is just this occlusion that denotes the presence of the city's inhabitants. Considered alone, Cadogan's newly-acquired knowledge appears to verify a reading of the novel as lacking in spectral potential, as it reinforces the absence of utopian sensibilities. It is not until the final sentence that the novel articulates the full extent of its hauntological potential. Having heard from a colleague about another tango singer in Buenos Aires, he is unable to sleep. At dawn, he tells the reader, 'me senté ante la computadora y escribí las primeras páginas de este libro' [I sat down at the computer and wrote the first few pages of this book].[98] As Gordon suggests, 'the ghost registers *and* it incites'.[99] It is, therefore, paradoxically, in the act of writing that Cadogan renders the novel a truly hauntological text. Previously paralyzed by the words of others, he is finally able to convert his lived experience of Buenos Aires into text and so reconcile the literary imaginary of the Argentine capital with its material reality. In the act of writing, Cadogan is no longer immobilized by the prospect of recognizing alternative past histories, nor immune to the practice of hope that such genuine hauntological endeavour engenders. Moreover, in his textual representations of Martel's historicist excursions, the narrator aligns himself with the tango singer's attempts to fracture the silence that has surrounded the quotidian accidents and crimes of the city for so long. In doing so, he amplifies Martel's efforts, transforming what was a series of lonely and apparently futile commemorative acts into a collective project that unites the singer, the writer and the reader. The lives and deaths of Felicitas Alcántara, Catalina Godel and the countless other dead to whom Martel dedicated his performances form the foundations for a new history of Buenos Aires, upon which a radically different version of the present can be shaped.

Therefore, *El cantor de tango* is a truly hauntological novel, a palimpsest text which warns of the dangers of the spectral as lamentation alone. As this consideration of the text has demonstrated, if historicity is to be harnessed in the pursuit of anything other than elegiac lament, it must be married with a defiant utopianism and a vision of a future brighter than the past. *Horizontalidad* is largely absent from the novel, although it is implicit in the exigencies of Martel's autonomous crusade for an active form of remembrance of the past accidents and crimes of Buenos Aires. In the following chapter, we will further explore the dynamic relations between historicity and *horizontalidad*, with reference to the documentary *La multitud* and the feature film *Elefante blanco*. Both films historicize the inequality and injustice of contemporary existence, linking the failures of the present to the depredations of the past. In contrast to Cadogan's conclusion that the truth of the city is to be found in the lives of its inhabitants, the texts analysed in Chapter Two foreground the spatial in their examinations of the urban *topos*. But as we shall see, beyond their common focus upon the liminal topographies of greater Buenos Aires, each of these two cinematic texts encodes an entirely different vision of the city in the post-Crisis era.

## Notes to Chapter 2

1. William Faulkner, *Requiem for a Nun* (New York: Vintage, 1996), p. 32.
2. Avery Gordon, *Ghostly Matters: Ghosts and the Sociological Imagination* (Minneapolis: University of Minnesota Press, 2008), p. xvi.
3. Jorgen Bruhn, 'Seeing Without Understanding: Mediality, Aspects of Literature and Memory in Vladimir Nabokov's "Spring in Fialta"', *Orbis Litterarum*, 70:5 (2015), 380–404, (p. 387).
4. Andreas Huyssen, *Present Pasts: Urban Palimpsests and the Politics of Memory* (Stanford, CA: Stanford University Press, 2003), p. 7.
5. Ibid., p. 1.
6. Ibid., p. 2.
7. Owen Hatherley, *Militant Modernism* (Ropley: Zero Books, 2008), p. 3.
8. For a summary of Hatherley's argument, see ibid., pp. 3–14.
9. Jonathan Meades, 'Yesterday's tomorrow — Militant Modernism by Owen Hatherley', *New Statesman*, 30 April 2009 < https://www.newstatesman.com/books/2009/05/militant-modernism-hatherley> [accessed 18 April 2018]
10. Hatherley, *Militant Modernism*, p. 9.
11. New Brutalism is the term coined by the critic Reyner Banham to describe a particularly British interpretation of the modernist architectural style pioneered by Le Corbusier in buildings such as the Unité d'Habitation. Amongst its most prominent practitioners in Britain were the architects Alison and Peter Smithson. For a full discussion of the history of the New Brutalist movement, see Alexander Clement, *Brutalism: Post-War British Architecture* (London: Crowood Press, 2011).
12. Oliver Wainwright, 'Wayne Hemingway's "Pop-up plan" Sounds the Death Knell for Legendary Balfron Tower', *The Guardian*, 26 September 2014 <http://www.theguardian.com/artanddesign/architecture-design-blog/2014/sep/26/wayne-hemingways-pop-up-plan-sounds-the-death-knell-for-the-legendary-balfron-tower>[accessed 7 November 2014].
13. Hatherley, *Militant Modernism*, p. 13.
14. Hatherley, *Militant Modernism*, p. 3.

15. Mark Fisher, *Ghosts of My Life: Writings on Depression, Hauntology and Lost Futures* (Zero Books: London, 2013), p. 47.
16. Jacques Derrida, *Specters of Marx: The State of the Debt, the Work of Mourning and the New International* (Abingdon: Routledge, 1994).
17. Fredric Jameson, 'Marx's Purloined Letter', in *Ghostly Demarcations: A Symposium on Jacques Derrida's Specters of Marx*, ed. by Michael Springer (London and New York: Verso, 1999), pp. 26–67, (p. 39).
18. Jameson, 'Marx's Purloined Letter', p. 39.
19. Derrida, *Specters*, p. 27.
20. Ibid., p. 33.
21. Fisher, *Ghosts*, p. 22.
22. Ibid., p. 22.
23. Gordon, *Ghostly Matters*, p. xvii
24. Fisher, *Ghosts*, p. 19.
25. Ibid., p. 19.
26. Gordon, *Ghostly Matters*, p. 57.
27. Marshall Berman, cited in Fisher, p. 51.
28. Julian Wolfreys, *Writing London, Vol.2: Materiality, Memory, Spectrality* (Basingstoke: Palgrave Macmillan, 2004), p. 7.
29. Cited in ibid., p. 7.
30. Ibid., p. 21.
31. Ibid.
32. Adrián Gorelik, *Miradas sobre Buenos Aires: historia cultural y crítica urbana* (Buenos Aires: Siglo Veintiuno, 2004), p. 148.
33. Tomás Eloy Martínez, *El cantor de tango* (Buenos Aires: Planeta, 2004), p. 22.
34. Tomás Eloy Martínez, *The Tango Singer*, p. 12. All English translations are taken from Anne McLean's original translation of the novel: Tomás Eloy Martínez, *The Tango Singer*, trans. by Anne McLean (London: Bloomsbury, 2006).
35. Susana Rosano, 'En definitiva, en Argentina todos caemos en el barroco fúnebre: reportaje a Tomas Eloy Martínez', *Revista Iberoamericana*, LXXII (2006), 657–62, (p. 662).
36. Rosano, 'En definitiva', p. 662.
37. Aída Nadi Gambetta Chuk, 'Soma y sema: *El cantor de tango* (2004) de Tomás Eloy Martínez', *Graffylia*, 40 (2007), 40–45 (pp. 40–41).
38. Ibid., p. 40.
39. Laura Podalsky, *Specular City: Transforming Culture, Consumption, and Space in Buenos Aires, 1955–1973* (Philadelphia, PA: Temple University Press, 2004), p. 32.
40. For example, see Ezequiel Martínez Estrada, *La cabeza del Goliat: microscopía de Buenos Aires*, Roberto Arlt, *Los siete locos*, and Ricardo Piglia, *Respiración artificial*.
41. Eloy Martínez, *El cantor de tango*, p. 13. Eloy Martínez, *The Tango Singer*, p. 3.
42. Eloy Martínez, *El cantor de tango*, pp. 13–14. Eloy Martínez, *The Tango Singer*, p. 3.
43. Jason Wilson, *Buenos Aires: A Cultural and Literary Companion* (Oxford: Signal, 1999), p. xi.
44. Ibid.
45. Alfred Mac Adam, 'Introduction', in *Jorge Luis Borges, On Argentina* (London: Penguin Classics, 2010), pp. ix–xvi (p. xi).
46. Jorge Luis Borges, 'Autobiographical Essay', in *The Aleph and Other Stories 1933–1969*, ed. and trans. by Norman di Giovanni (London: Lowe and Brydone, 1971), pp. 203–60, (p. 223–24).
47. Page, 'Introduction', in *Memories*, pp. xii.
48. David Rock, *Argentina 1561–1982: From Spanish Colonization to the Falklands War* (London: Tauris, 1985), p. 114.
49. Podalsky, *Specular City*, p. 33.
50. Eloy Martínez, *El cantor*, p. 105. Eloy Martínez, *The Tango Singer*, p. 95.
51. Esteban Antonio Echeverría, 'El Matadero', in *The Argentina Reader* ed. by Gabriela Nouzeilles and Graciela Montaldo (Durham, NC: Duke University Press, 2002), pp. 107–14 (p. 107).
52. Ibid.

53. Eloy Martínez, *El cantor*, p. 105. Eloy Martínez, *The Tango Singer*, p. 95.
54. Eloy Martínez, *El cantor*, p. 207.
55. Eloy Martínez, *The Tango Singer*, p. 197.
56. Podalsky, *Specular City*, p. xii.
57. Eloy Martínez, *El cantor*, p. 9. An English translation of this epigram can be found in Walter Benjamin, *The Arcades Project*, trans. by Howard Eiland and Kevin McLaughlin (Cambridge, MA: Harvard University Press, 1999), p. 456.
58. Walter Benjamin, *Berlin Childhood Around 1900* (Cambridge, MA: Harvard University Press, 206), p. 89.
59. Adrian Gorelik and Graciela Silvestri, 'The Past as Future: A Reactive Utopia in Buenos Aires', in *The Latin American Cultural Studies Reader*, ed. by Ana del Sarto, Alicia Rios and Abril Trigo (Durham, NC: Duke University Press, 2004), pp. 427–40 (p. 437).
60. Adrian Gorelik, 'A Metropolis in the Pampas: Buenos Aires 1890–1940' in *Cruelty and Utopia: Cities and Landscapes of Latin America*, ed. by Jean-François Lejeune (New Jersey: Princeton University Press, 2003), pp. 146–59 (p. 158).
61. Gorelik and Silvestri, 'The Past as Future', p. 428.
62. Ibid., p. 434.
63. In an architectural sense, the term cocoliche refers to the hybrid baroque style visible in the ornate palaces of areas such as the Avenida de Mayo in central Buenos Aires. According to Ana Cara-Walker, the notion of a hybrid Argentine-Italian subjectivity first emerged in the second half of the nineteenth century, in response to the wave of immigration from southern Europe. Walker cites the first formal cultural expression of the concept as appearing in a dramatic adaptation of the Juan Gutierrez novel *Juan Moreira* (1879), in the form of the character of the Italian immigrant labourer Antonio Cocoliche. As she summarizes, 'cocoliche in all its forms expressed and mediated socio-cultural negotiations that tempered a new Argentine way of life'. See Ana Cara-Walker, 'Cocoliche: The Art of Assimilation and Dissimulation among Italians and Argentines', Latin American Research Review, 22: 3 (1987), pp. 37–67 (p. 40).
64. Gorelik, *Cruelty and Utopia*, p. 157.
65. Eloy Martínez, *El cantor*, p. 44.
66. Eloy Martínez, *The Tango Singer*, p. 35.
67. Gorelik, *Cruelty and Utopia*, p. 157.
68. Owen Hatherley, *A Guide to The New Ruins of Great Britain* (London: Verso, 2011), p. 86.
69. Ibid., p. 82.
70. Ibid., p. 83.
71. Eloy Martínez, *El cantor*, p. 44. Eloy Martínez, *The Tango Singer*, p. 35.
72. Eloy Martínez, *El cantor*, p. 208. Eloy Martínez, *The Tango Singer*, p. 208.
73. Martin Edwin Andersen, *Dossier Secreto: Argentina's Desaparecidos and the Myth of the 'Dirty War'* (Oxford: Westview Press, 1993), p. 231.
74. Feitlowitz, *Lexicon*, p. 39.
75. Gorelik, *Miradas*, p. 148.
76. Eloy Martínez, *El cantor*, p. 70. Eloy Martínez, *The Tango Singer*, p. 60.
77. Gorelik and Silvestri, 'The Past as Future', p. 434.
78. Jonathan Meades, *Museums Without Walls* (London: Unbound, 2013), pp. 84–85.
79. Eloy Martínez, *El cantor*, p. 74. Eloy Martínez, *The Tango Singer*, p. 65.
80. Eloy Martínez, *El cantor*, p. 83. Eloy Martínez, *The Tango Singer*, p. 73.
81. Eloy Martínez, *El cantor*, p. 83. Eloy Martínez, *The Tango Singer*, p. 73.
82. Eloy Martínez, *El cantor*, p. 113.
83. Eloy Martínez, *The Tango Singer*, p. 103.
84. See Feitlowitz, *Lexicon*, p. 113.
85. The Montoneros were a leftist Peronist guerrilla group, active during the 1970s, that supported armed struggle as the means to achieve their political objectives. Chapter Five explores the history and legacy of the Montoneros in detail.
86. Eloy Martínez, *El cantor*, p. 138. Eloy Martínez, *The Tango Singer*, p. 128.
87. Fisher, *Ghosts*, p. 19.

88. Eloy Martínez, *El cantor*, pp. 248–49.
89. Eloy Martínez, *The Tango Singer*, p. 239.
90. Ricardo Piglia, *Crítica y ficción* (Buenos Aires: Penguin Random House, 2014), p. 15.
91. Ibid.
92. Eloy Martínez, *El cantor*, p. 226. Eloy Martínez, *The Tango Singer*, p. 216.
93. Eloy Martínez, *El cantor*, p. 214. Eloy Martínez, *The Tango Singer*, p. 204.
94. Eloy Martínez, *El cantor*, pp. 219–20. Eloy Martínez, *The Tango Singer*, p. 210.
95. Janice Radway, 'Foreword', in Gordon, *Ghostly Matters*, pp. vii-xiii (p. xiii).
96. Fisher, *Ghosts*, p. 19.
97. Eloy Martínez, *El cantor*, p. 251. Eloy Martínez, *The Tango Singer*, p. 241.
98. Eloy Martínez, *El cantor*, p. 253. Eloy Martínez, *The Tango Singer*, p. 243.
99. Gordon, *Ghostly Matters*, p. 207.

CHAPTER 3

# The Map and the Territory: Space and Place in Post-Crisis Buenos Aires

> Architecture is the real battleground of the spirit. Architecture wrote the
> history of the epochs and gave them their names.
> MIES VAN DER ROHE

Chapter 3 considers how the discursive forces of historicity and horizontalism are inscribed upon the urban cartographies of Buenos Aires in two cinematic texts from 2012: Martín Oesterheld's documentary, *La multitud* [The Crowd], and Pablo Trapero's feature film *Elefante blanco* [White Elephant]. Using the notion of cognitive mapping, the chapter investigates the spatio-temporal subjectivities of both films in their explorations of the liminal spaces of Villa Lugano, a district situated on the border between the capital and the deindustrialized suburbs of greater Buenos Aires. Both films explicitly historicize these peripheral landscapes, assembling reticulations of meaning between the material remnants of the past and the spatial dimensions of the present. In doing so, they reflect the topographical specificities of the now established structure of feeling that emerged in the wake of the *Argentinazo*. Furthermore, both films interrogate the tensions between official cartographies of the suburban, popular conceptions of these liminal territories and the existing reality of life there. In a similar approach, this chapter seeks to historicize the topographical iterations of both texts, exploring each film's visual subjectivities through the prism of the past.

*La multitud* foregrounds the ruined theme park Interama, casting its dilapidated attractions and the surrounding landscape as a metonymic signifier of the social damage wrought by the ideologies of *el Proceso*. The film presents the theme park, along with the neighbouring districts featured in *La multitud*, as spatial traces of the modernizing impetus of the last dictatorship and the neoliberal economic model it imposed upon society. In *Elefante blanco*, Trapero, an alumnus of the new Argentine cinema movement of the 1990s, explores that most marginalized of urban spaces, the *villa miseria*, a *topos* which looms large in the popular imaginary as a locus of crime, poverty and social unrest. This chapter investigates the film with reference to the innovative focus of this alternative form of national cinema upon liminal spaces, and to the wider history of representations of the *villa miseria* in Argentine cinema. In contrast to these largely negative portrayals, Trapero's film enunciates a more complex historiography of the shanty town, and its influence upon the development of the liberation theology movement of the 1960s. In connecting this history of activism to the struggles of the present, the film uncovers the spatial potential of the villa as a site of resistance and utopian aspiration.

In the prologue to his 2005 work, *El último lector* [The Last Reader], Ricardo Piglia recounts the strange, fable-like tale of a man who has devoted years of his life to the planning and construction of a scale model of the city of Buenos Aires in his workshop in the district of Flores. The story's narrator has heard rumours of this miniature city and of its obsessive creator, a photographer named Russell, who believes his model to be the repository of the real Buenos Aires and the city surrounding his workshop a mere simulacrum. Piglia's text is rich in a quintessentially Argentine ludic intertextuality, employing a playful re-interpretation of the short story by Jorge Luis Borges, 'Del rigor en la ciencia', in which an ancient civilization seeks to perfect the cartographic art through the creation of a life-size map of its territories. The unwieldy chart is eventually discarded and left to rot, although its scale is such that vagabonds, beggars and wild animals continue to shelter amongst its ruins.[1] In adapting this Borgesian leitmotif to the contemporary urban milieu of Buenos Aires, Piglia seeks to interrogate the strategies we deploy in order to extract meaning from the physical topography of urban space. His narrator arrives at the conclusion that:

> la ciudad trata entonces sobre réplicas y representaciones, sobre la lectura y la percepción solitaria, sobre la presencia de lo que se ha perdido. En definitiva, trata sobre el modo de hacer visible lo invisible y fijar las imágenes nítidas que ya no vemos pero que insisten todavía como fantasmas y viven entre nosotros.[2]
>
> [The city, then, is about replicas and representation, about reading and lonely perception, about the presence of what has been lost. Ultimately, the city addresses a way of making visible the invisible and of fixing clear images of that we no longer see but which persist like ghosts and still live amongst us.]

Essentially then, the practices of model-making and cartography facilitate the construction of these 'replicas and representations' that we create to impose order upon the chaos of the physical world. Beyond their geographical function, in such maps and maquettes we see idealized expositions of a curated spatial imaginary; that is, they depict a particular version of the *topos*, frozen in space and time, which privileges and excludes certain features, landmarks and edifices in its depiction of a specific topographical imaginary. In a similar fashion, as city dwellers we each construct our own abstract maps of the landscape, a gathering of 'discourses, symbols, metaphors and fantasies through which we ascribe meaning to the modern experience of urban living'.[3] In doing so, we imbricate personal experience with the historicity of the *polis*, weaving links of cognition and affect between individual histories and our urban environs. In contrast to the material permanence of the map and the model, these psychic cartographies are fluid, porous, and able to accommodate the recalibrations of cognition and affect wrought by our lived experience of the urban. Moreover, such individual 'cognitive maps'[4] are informed

Fig. 3.1. Promotional poster for *La multitud*. Image: DA Films

and shaped by the urban cartographies of popular culture. Building on the work of both Kevin Lynch and Fredric Jameson, David Harvey describes the resultant admixture of subjectivities as exemplars of a broader 'spatio-temporal imaginary, [...] the senses of space and time that course through consciousness and which present themselves in works of art, poetry, novels, films and multimedia forms'.[5]

Whilst these forms of urban cultural discourse can enhance our conception of the city, they can also engender dislocations between individual cognitive maps and the territory we inhabit. In the urban spatio-temporalities of the neoliberal era, with their emphasis on money, the affective landmarks of the past often become relics, the alien signifiers of a more primitive era before our cities were transformed into mere 'production sites and marketplaces for global capital'.[6] Seduced by the 'effervescent montage of continuous images'[7] that characterizes the postmodern urban imaginary, we often disregard the everyday ruins of the past. Moreover, as our perceptions of the city are colonized by the hegemonic discourse of capital, the peripheries of these cognitive maps shrink ever further, excluding those urban communities that exist outside the networks of power and capital. In short, the ubiquity of the neoliberal urban imaginary can inhibit our ability to view the city as manifold and heterogeneous, as all our imaginary cities are inevitably coloured by the hues of the global consumerist marketplace. In examining the documentary *La multitud* and the feature film *Elefante blanco*, this chapter will analyse if, and how, the urban hinterland and its historicist relics enable the formulation an alternative spatio-temporality of post-Crisis Buenos Aires. By mapping the derelict sites and

Fig. 3.2. The diorama of the Interama theme park in *La multitud*. Image: DA Films

the shantytowns of the city's periphery, both films challenge the hegemonic spatio-temporality of the Argentine capital post-*Argentinazo*. Yet, as this chapter will demonstrate, it is only within *Elefante blanco* that these uncovered tensions between map and territory elicit new conceptions of urban citizenship.

As María Arenillas suggests, the most prominent narrative modality of Martín Oesterheld's *La multitud* is the 'materiality of places and their afterlives' (Fig. 3.1).[8] Classifying the work as representative of a recent 'non-discursive turn' in Argentine documentary, Arenillas aligns the film alongside recent works by Jonathan Perel, such as *Tabula Rasa* (2013) and *Toponimia* (2015). In calling these films 'non-discursive', she refers to the absence therein of established narrative conventions, such as plot, characters and dialogue. Instead, these productions focus upon what Arenillas, citing John Cage, terms 'quiet sounds', and the gaze of the camera.[9] In privileging the historicist potential of landscapes over depictions of human interaction, and excluding all non-diegetic sounds, both Perel and Oesterheld construct a gaze that is predominantly spatial in its focus. Here, it is through the built environment that the past impinges upon the present, consistently challenging us to decipher these ruined topographies. Two thirds of the way through *La multitud*, in one of the few interior sequences in the film, we briefly glimpse a miniature city reminiscent of that crafted by Piglia's photographer Russell. Ensconced on a tilted dais and encased in glass, the diorama is a small-scale representation of the Parque de la Ciudad, originally known as Interama, a large amusement park constructed in the early 1980s in the Villa Lugano district of Buenos Aires (Fig. 3.2).

Resembling an architect's maquette, it is decorated with doll's house versions of the myriad attractions scattered throughout the 105-hectare park; glued to a verdant felt carpet, a selection of around fifty tiny rollercoasters, Ferris wheels and water rides demarcates the vast and ambitious size and scale of Interama. In the centre of the model, the camera lingers on the architectural centrepiece of the park, the vertiginous Torre Espacial, or Space Tower.[10]

At the time of its opening in 1985, the tower was, at a height of 176 metres, the tallest structure in the Argentine capital, with thousands of visitors flocking daily

FIG. 3.3. . The ruined landscapes of the Interama theme park in *La multitud*.
Image: DA Films

FIG. 3.4. The derelict remains of themepark rides under a motorway flyover in
*La multitud*. Image: DA Films

to its panoramic viewing platforms for a bird's-eye view of the city.[11] Almost thirty years on, it has fallen into disuse, transformed into a dilapidated relic of a bygone era (Fig. 3.3).

The surrounding amusement park is similarly neglected; the miniature trains that ferried thrill-seekers around the five zones of the park now lie rusting under a motorway flyover (Fig. 3.4). Vertigorama, the gigantic rollercoaster that was once the park's premier attraction, is partially hidden under a canopy of trees and burnt out and abandoned cars litter the site. This is one of the ruined landscapes

THE MAP AND THE TERRITORY   71

FIG. 3.5. A photograph of the Ciudad Deportiva, during its construction in the mid-1970s. Image: DA Films

FIG. 3.6. An image of Interama, shortly after its official opening in 1982. Image: DA Films

of contemporary Buenos Aires which Oesterheld's documentary explores. The derelict vistas of the Parque de la Ciudad are mirrored in the similarly neglected Ciudad Deportiva de La Boca, a pharaonic development project launched by the Boca Juniors football club in 1964. On the Costanera Sur, on land reclaimed from the River Plate, construction began on a series of seven interconnected islets that would house sports facilities, cinemas, swimming pools and a new stadium for the club. Designs for this 'futuristic suburban Venice'[12] were highly lauded, yet, as with Interama, the project languished in financial difficulty and was never completed (Fig. 3.5, 3.6).

Alongside the hubristic futurism of these abandoned landscapes of leisure, the film uncovers further hidden spaces in the housing developments that border both parks. Moreover, it also charts the industrious terrain of neoliberal capital in the ever-expanding business district of Puerto Madero and in the gigantic nearby power plant, the Central Térmica Costanera Sur.[13] Featuring scant human interaction and entirely diegetic audio, Oesterheld's documentary demarcates the alienating spatio-temporalities of the neoliberal city. In the frequency of its vertiginous panoramic shots, which disorientate the viewer and inhibit spatial and affective connections, the landscape is miniaturized, and the human forms below rendered tiny and insignificant. Indeed, in a striking visual metonym, the camera momentarily lingers upon a weathered giant model of the fictional character of Gulliver, which sits amidst the ruins of the Parque de la Ciudad. Just as Swift's explorer found himself a giant in the land of the diminutive Lilliputians, from the viewing platforms of the Torre Espacial the camera's gaze deforms our perception of the landscape, engendering a sense of material distance and estrangement. Here, the spatial disorientation of the declivitous vista foments alienation, as the territory below becomes abstract in its map-like qualities. Unlike Martel's hauntological dérives in *El cantor de tango*, which immerse the reader in the urban streetscape, the spatial gaze of *La multitud* incites distance and detachment. As James Scorer asserts, 'the panoramic and panning shots of abandoned spaces highlight how the city is failing the multitudes that inhabit it'.[14]

Florian Freitag describes the concept of the theme park as 'a bounded commercial leisure space that offers a variety of rides, restaurants, shops, and shows that are all themed around one or several past, exotic, or fictional cultures'.[15] It is, he asserts, a cultural medium which imposes its own distinct narrative and spatial boundaries upon the landscape, through the use of 'painting, architecture, sculpture, landscaping, music, theatre and film'.[16] This intermedial *mise en scène* is employed to create a discrete universe, where visitors experience a series of distinct and thrilling environments in safety and security. Linking this controlled sequence of narratives and the 'spatial logic of the theme park'[17] to the experience of watching a film, Freitag highlights the heteromediality of these leisure environments. In its depiction of Interama and Ciudad Deportiva, *La multitud* compounds such medial transference, adding another layer of meaning to these ruined sites through the creation of a cinematic *mise en abyme*. The camera's gaze permits a vicarious experience of the 'film' that is the theme park, distorting its spatial boundaries

Fig. 3.7. The construction site in Puerto Madero. Image: DA Films

through frequent panoramas which mimic the dramatic movement of one of the park's long-closed rides. Here, this heteromediality enhances the sense of ruination and degradation the viewer sees amongst the former attractions. It is as if the film stock of the 'movie' that would have constituted a visitor's original experience of Interama has, over time, become warped and out of shape.

This sense of spatial alienation is present throughout Oesterheld's documentary. Beyond the ruined landscapes of the derelict parks of Interama and Ciudad Deportiva, it is also palpable in the spaces of neoliberal capital which the film depicts. In Puerto Madero, the hordes of construction workers are dwarfed by the vast size and scale of the skyscrapers that they labour within. Forests of iron rods obscure our view, forming the skeletal outlines of new offices and apartment blocks, whilst in the glass facades of surrounding buildings we see reflected the purposeful machinations of cranes, ropes and pulleys. In the deep canyon between two skyscrapers, the camera rests upon the surreal image of a half-completed avenue, a road to nowhere from whose edges a web of steel cables teeter over the abyss (Fig. 3.7).

Formerly docklands, the largely derelict Buenos Aires district of Puerto Madero was subject to a campaign of redevelopment and modernization from 1989 onwards, with the construction of high rise office blocks, expensive restaurants and luxury accommodation.[18] As with similar developments, such as London's Docklands, it is an exclusive and exclusionary space, a topos of capitalist speculation and consumption. For Adrián Gorelik, the redevelopment of Puerto Madero is one local symptom of the broader global paradigm shift in notions of the urban in the neoliberal age, 'una concepción política del estado y de la sociedad urbana que se traduce en una formula económica: *la ciudad de los negocios*' [a political conception of the state and of urban society which is translated into an economic formula: *the city of business.*][19] This city of neoliberal commerce is present in the material reality of the concrete and steel of Puerto Madero, but it also exists beyond the confines of the remodelled business district. It has become a hegemonic spatio-temporality that colonizes our urban subjectivities, altering personal notions of citizenship in the post-Fordist era, 'un modelo de la ciudad que ha convertido su espacio público y sus infraestructuras públicas en objeto de negocio' [a model of the city which has converted its public space and infrastructure into something to be bought and sold, the stuff of business.][20]

Iterations of this neoliberal chronotope are also visible in the brief human interactions *of La multitud*. In the shantytown of Villa 20, we encounter Ukrainian immigrant Lyudmila, whose basic living space sits alongside a vast informal wrecker's yard of abandoned vehicles. A shot of her makeshift heater, a Heath Robinson contraption comprised of a pile of bricks and an electric element, is a visual leitmotif which links her surroundings with the earlier images of construction work in neighbouring Puerto Madero. Presumably scavenged from a building site, the heated bricks are the sole source of warmth in Lyudmila's flimsy shack of wood and corrugated iron. Her friend and compatriot Yuri lives in slightly better conditions, in the public housing complex of Lugano 1 and 2, close to the Interama park. But his existence is equally precarious, as his rent has increased twice in one month and his earnings as a coffee vendor are meagre. Economically vulnerable to the waning demand for his products during the hot summer months, Yuri may have to seek alternative accommodation and move to an informal housing settlement like Lyudmila's. The émigrés are not the only residents we encounter; two other unnamed men walk amidst the ruins of Interama and the Ciudad Deportiva. All exist on the margins of the city of commerce, estranged from its workings and stranded in a landscape they struggle to negotiate. For example, we watch one resident as he makes his way home from the Parque de la Ciudad. Attempting to cross the busy highway that lies between the park and the high-rise blocks of Villa Lugano, he is forced to weave his way between the lanes of speeding cars in a hazardous attempt to reach the other side. Such is the dislocation here amidst this urban hinterland and those who are forced to navigate its terrain that even basic movement is difficult and fraught with risk.

Thus, within Oesterheld's urban spatio-temporality, the peripheral spaces which exist outside the boundaries of the '*ciudad de los negocios*' are an alienated and alienating terrain. Whether from the heights of the Torre Espacial or from the landscape below, constructing a cognitive map of this landscape is a near-impossible endeavour. The inhabitants here, economically disenfranchised by the post-Fordist marketplace and largely forgotten by civic institutions, live in a state of continued precarity with little or no possibility of improvement in their circumstances. They eke out a basic existence in the corners of the map, struggling to make ends meet in a largely hostile environment. The ruined playgrounds of curated pleasure in Interama and Ciudad Deportiva, the bustling construction sites of free market leviathan Puerto Madero, and the shantytowns and dilapidated public housing of Rodrigo Bueno and Villa Lugano form the metonymic landmarks of Oesterheld's map. Looming above them all, the Torre Espacial dominates the territory, sentinel-like, surveying the ruins and the wreckage that surround it (Fig. 3.8).

Fig. 3.8. The Torre Espacial by day. Image: DA Films.

In the film's closing shot, the screen is filled with the image of the tower by night, illuminated in the *celeste y blanco* of the Argentine flag. Bedecked in this patriotic decoration, the rapier-like structure is a beacon of the ruinous urban spatio-temporality that permeates *La multitud*: a ruined landmark for a ruined cartography.

As we have seen, in tracing the topographical antinomies of state and market amidst these landscapes of past, present and future, Oesterheld's documentary refutes any possibility of spatial and affective recuperation in the neoliberal present. It excoriates the failures of the neoliberal city and the urban imaginary it engenders, yet ultimately the film withholds the potential for change. However, as Harvey asserts, 'any search for an alternative to neoliberal globalization must search for a different kind of spatio-temporality'.[21] Accordingly, in the feature film *Elefante blanco*, Trapero moves beyond a remapping of the urban limens towards the construction of an alternative spatio-temporality, where the ruins of the past inform the contemporary struggle for a reinvigorated urban citizenship.

Like *La multitud*, *Elefante blanco* also unfolds within the environs of the Villa Lugano neighbourhood of Buenos Aires. Its primary setting is the shanty town of Ciudad Oculta, a settlement of approximately 30,000 inhabitants on the southern outskirts of the federal capital. The absence of civic infrastructure and investment, unsanitary living conditions and crippling poverty blight the existence of those who inhabit the *villas miseria* of Buenos Aires, a population alternately ignored or demonized in the popular media. At odds with the hegemonic discourse of the city as civilizing project, the *villa miseria* has long been considered a no man's land within the popular urban imaginary, 'an outside space that has somehow found its unwarranted way into the city'.[22] This liminality is starkly underscored by the comment of central character Padre Julián (Ricardo Darín) early in Trapero's film. Explaining that no official records exist for the population of Ciudad Oculta, he adds: 'Además, esto no figura en el mapa' [What's more, this doesn't appear on the map]. Thus, within *Elefante blanco* Trapero seeks to recuperate this absence of representation by tracing the spatial subjectivities of the *villa* upon the popular cognitive map. The film is a fictional representation of the daily reality of life in a Buenos Aires *villa miseria* and the struggles of the parish priests who minister to the marginalized communities within them. Conflicts arise when the construction of a new public housing project falters and, consequently, the residents begin to organize themselves autonomously. *Elefante blanco* offers a performance of existence in the *villa*, of the alienation and cruelty that neoliberal economic policies have precipitated, and of the strategies that the *villeros* devise to cope with this reality. Whilst the work was filmed mainly within Ciudad Oculta itself and in the ruined hospital building from which it takes its title, as Clara Garavelli theorizes, 'many scenes were filmed in other informal settlements, such as Villa 31 and Villa Rodrigo Bueno, as if to state, through a fictionally constructed space, that this is a common reality of all slums'.[23]

Despite a lukewarm reception in Argentina upon its release, Trapero's film merits closer analysis for its aesthetic hybridity, populist dramatic discourse and most significantly, its cognitive mapping of the *villa*. It delineates the physical and affective geography of the settlement, depicting its historicist landmarks alongside the inchoate space of horizontalism that offers to reinvigorate this hidden city. In a break from the well-established *modus operandi* of the movement known as 'New Argentine Cinema', with a stellar cast and international funding and distribution, *Elefante blanco* offers the first big budget depiction of the shanty town in Argentine film history; a cultural product tailored to the demands of the mass-market. Moreover, the participation of Ricardo Darín, one of the country's most popular and bankable actors, is illustrative of the cultural reach of this production. Whilst it has been said that Trapero is the one director that is 'least likely to accept political readings of his films',[24] as this chapter argues, his fusion of space and history in *Elefante blanco* is indeed a political statement. In its depiction of the landmarks of Ciudad Oculta, it proffers an alternative spatial territory, tracing out a new cognitive map of this no man's land of the hegemonic urban imaginary. Between the crumbling ruin of a modernist public hospital and the precarious reality of the private dwelling places of the *villa*, the film encodes a third space, a *topos* that Chantal Mouffe describes as a 'space of agonism'.[25] It is upon this terrain that historicist sensibilities and horizontalist praxis come together to reconfigure notions of urban citizenship and in doing so, initiate an alternative spatio-temporality.

Written, produced and directed by Trapero, *Elefante blanco* received a mixed reception upon its release. The film garnered some favourable reviews in both the national and European press and was selected for the 'Un Certain Regard' prize at the 2012 Cannes film festival. Yet it failed to attract much serious critical interest in either academic circles or in specialized film journals. Gonzalo Aguilar dismissed the production, lamenting that 'stereotypes are everywhere [...]. Once more we see the *villa* as a dead-end labyrinth, a shantytown priest as a morally-impeccable character, and drugged zombie-like kids who will never go to school'.[26] Indeed, the film does feature its fair share of familiar stock characters, such the young priest

Padre Nicolás (Jeremy Renier), who struggles with the challenges of his vocation and the temptations of the flesh. His vows of chastity are tested by the beautiful social worker Luciana (Martina Gusmán), whose youthful idealism is waning in the face of the everyday cruelties and violence of the *villa*. Another cliché is to be found in the characterization of Monito (Federico Barga), a bright adolescent whose future is jeopardized by his involvement with drugs and crime. The plot is also somewhat confused, as elements of human drama vie for prominence with action sequences in which the ever-present threat of violence from local drug dealers erupts into indiscriminate killing. However, as a non-documentary production, *Elefante blanco* is cinematically *sui generis*: it is the only mainstream Argentine feature film produced between 2001 and 2012 in which a *villa miseria* is the primary setting. While, as Aguilar affirms, 'the crisis of 2001 propelled a series of new representations of the *villa*', such portrayals were largely limited to the field of documentary.[27] Given the segregation of cinema-going in the country, where national productions are usually screened in smaller, independent venues and imported Hollywood productions shown in newer multiplexes, Argentine audiences often sought succour in the latter, with cinema as a form of escapism. The appetite for entertainment vehicles with a shanty town setting was arguably marginal.

More generally, unlike contemporaneous Brazilian films, which capitalize on the urban prominence, vitality and the frequently fetishized criminality of Rio's *favelas*, the depiction of shanty towns in Argentine cinema is conspicuous by its absence. In an essay examining representations of the shanty town throughout national cinema history, Aguilar theorises that the reason for this omission is twofold: firstly, the *villas* of Buenos Aires lack the 'visual presence of Rio's *favelas*, but more significantly, 'the existence of the *villas* creates disharmony with the image of modernity that Buenos Aires has always projected as the "most European" of Latin American cities'.[28] Gorelik goes further, emphasizing the disquiet that the emergence of the *villa* engendered within the popular urban consciousness, signifying as it did 'the appearance of the radical other in the very core of the city'.[29] Furthermore, in Rio, the physical topography of the city, where the *favelas* line the hills overlooking Guanabara Bay, repudiates a lack of representation. In contrast, in the flat lowlands of Buenos Aires, the *villas miseria* are less prominent, and consequently, easier to ignore. As Scorer opines, 'despite its physical proximity to the rest of the city [...] the *villa* is surprisingly distant, always lying beyond –– beyond the railway tracks, beyond the avenue, beyond the river, even beyond the bus route'.[30] As we observed in *La multitud*, the shanty town of Villa Rodrigo Bueno abuts prosperous Puerto Madero yet few connections, either spatial or affective, exist between the two districts.

Interestingly, one of the earliest Argentine films in which a representation of the *villa miseria* appears is a light-hearted musical comedy. In *Puerto Nuevo* (1936), directed by Mario Soffici and Luis César Amadori, the eponymous *villa* is a settlement spawned by the commerce of the bustling port, providing a temporary home for immigrants and dock workers. The narrative reflects the historical reality; in 1931, the Argentine government housed a group of Polish immigrants in a temporary encampment, or *villa de emergencia*, in several vacant lots in Puerto

Fig. 3.9. 'Wall Street', as depicted in the 1936 film *Puerto Nuevo*. Image: Youtube.

Nuevo. The settlement was originally dubbed 'Villa Desocupación' but later renamed as the more aspirational 'Villa Esperanza'.[31] In this film, amongst the *villeros* lives our leading man, a handsome troubadour. He is discovered by 'a rich girl who has him make his debut in a theatre. After a series of adventures, including comic moments, the singer and the girl fall in love'.[32] Or, to paraphrase the old cliché, girl meets boy, girl makes boy famous, girl and boy live happily ever after. However, despite its somewhat formulaic plot, *Puerto Nuevo* is significant in its depiction of the *villa* itself. Here, as a bespoke studio set, the *villa* is a safe and sanitized space, resonant of the bounded security of a theme park. Although poor and ramshackle, the settlement is depicted as a lively and productive community. Makeshift shops and kiosks line the main street, with hand-painted signs advertising their wares. A barber and a tailor can be seen attending to their clients, whilst a tobacco vendor chats to a customer, perhaps regarding the quality of the 'puchos de habanos legítimos' that his kiosk advertises. On 'Wall Street', a group of would-be investors sits outside the 'negocios de bolza' [*sic*] and our hero stands on the corner of 'Calle Florida', playing the bandoneon and extolling the virtues of Puerto Nuevo in song (Fig. 3.9).

As in the maps and models of Borges and Piglia, here we are presented with a particular urban imaginary, a benign spatio-temporality in which the shanty town has not yet acquired the threatening connotations it will later accrue. In its replication of the civic and commercial signifiers of Buenos Aires and New York, the shanty town of *Puerto Nuevo* is rendered a non-threatening space, whose inhabitants are merely hard-working folk seeking to emulate the civilizing values of the great urban centres. This reflects the concurrent popular conception of the shanty town as a *villa de emergencia*, an impermanent community which is a mere staging post on the immigrant's path to economic improvement. Aspiration and self-betterment are the dominant sensibilities here; once the inhabitants of this temporary settlement find gainful employment and greater financial stability, they will move on and the makeshift shacks of Puerto Nuevo will become redundant.

However, in its largely positive representation of life in a *villa miseria*, *Puerto Nuevo* is an anomaly in the history of Argentine feature film. As these informal settlements grew, further swelled by internal migrants from the interior, popular notions of the shanty town as a locus of exception within the urban landscape waned. In *Detrás de un largo muro* (1958), a melodrama directed by Lucas Demare, a father and daughter who leave their rural existence for a better life in Buenos Aires are confronted by the cruel and brutal reality of daily life in the *villa*. Having been promised employment and modern housing, they are taken to 'Villa Jardín' by their new employer, with the assurance that once construction is completed in the new housing development nearby, they will be able to move in. Visiting dignitaries arrive with similar promises but leave swiftly after the obligatory photo opportunity. Here, the film articulates a growing fear of the permanence of the *villa* within the public consciousness. In contrast to the rustic and congenial community of *Puerto Nuevo*, here the shanty town is vast and sprawling. There is little order and organization; feral children roam the terrain in gangs; idle and lascivious young men ogle our heroine and water must be fetched from a communal tap. The sense of menace, a threatening subjectivity that exists beyond the narrative arc, is palpable.

Thus, from the late 1950s onwards, the *villa miseria* largely disappeared from the popular cinema screen, relegated to the documentary form in works such as David José Kohon's 1958 short *Buenos Aires* and Fernando Solanas' seminal 1968 film *La hora de los hornos*. Accordingly, it is not without significance that the shanty town in which Trapero's film is set is popularly known as Ciudad Oculta, the 'hidden city' of Villa 15. The name reflects the physical boundaries installed around the settlement in early 1978, as the military dictatorship sought to beautify the capital in preparation for the football World Cup of that year. According to the Buenos Aires daily newspaper *Clarín*, 'fue durante la última dictadura y a meses del Mundial 78 que el Gobierno de facto decidió construir dos muros que ocultaran la villa. Desde ese día casi nadie llama al barrio por su verdadero nombre; todos le dicen Ciudad Oculta' [It was during the last dictatorship, a few months before the 1978 football World Cup that the de facto government decided to build two walls that would hide the *villa*. From that day forward, almost nobody referred to the area using its actual name: everyone called it Ciudad Oculta.][33] The name reflects the broader liminality of the shanty town in the popular urban imaginary, a marginality that has undoubtedly contributed to its lack of representation, other than in the field of documentary. Yet, this is not to suggest that, both pre-and-post-*Argentinazo*, national cinema shied away from the task of reflecting the impact of the neoliberal economic policies of *Menemismo* upon the urban landscape. In fact, the resurgence in cinematic output which followed the 1994 'Ley de Cine', widely heralded as the 'New Argentine Cinema' movement, is notable for its focus on such issues.[34] As Joanna Page affirms, 'from this point onward films began to testify in earnest to the impact of growing unemployment, rising crime, and the expansion of the informal economy'.³⁵ Moreover, the straightened economic circumstances of the mid 1990s informed not only the subject matter but also the aesthetic modalities of works by such young directors such as Israel Adrián Caetano, Bruno Stagnaro, Martín Rejtmann and Pablo Trapero. With money short and the costs of imported film materials and equipment high, they had little option but to seek out cheaper alternatives to advance their film-making, thus 'turning that scarcity of means into an aesthetic choice of formal austerity'.³⁶ Their use of cheaper equipment and film stock, such as '16-mm, black-and-white, Beta, or (increasingly) digital video cameras',³⁷ lends a gritty, sordid air to films such as Caetano and Stagnaro's 1998 *film Pizza, Birra, Faso* and Trapero's *Mundo Grúa* (1999); an aesthetic entirely in keeping with the alienating sub-urban landscapes which these works depict.

In fact, one of the foremost visual tropes of this alternative form of national cinema is the primacy of (sub)urban spaces within these films, and in particular the eschewal of the iconic spaces of the capital in favour of the more homogenous, *lumpen* landscapes of Greater Buenos Aires. As with Oesterheld's later work *La multitud*, in many of these films, conspicuous in their absence are the paradigmatic geographical signifiers of the capital, the baroque European elegance of the Plaza de Mayo, the modernist magnificence of the Obelisk monument or the rustic cobbled streets of the *barrios* of La Boca and San Telmo. When such locations do appear, as in the opening minutes of *Pizza, Birra, Faso*, they are often portrayed as the degraded revenants of a past era. After forcing their way inside the Obelisk, the protagonists are confronted with 'the remnants of half-visible political graffiti, pornographic magazines and tetra-pack wine', the detritus of a post-political consumerist society, which renders the landmark 'devoid of its monumental powers'.³⁸ Indeed, a direct parallel can be drawn between this depiction of the Obelisk and Oesterheld's framing of the derelict interiors of the Torre Espacial in *La multitud*, wherein outdated office furniture and deafening silence speak of a long-neglected monument (Fig. 27).

For the main part, the films of the 'new Argentine cinema' are concerned with the landscapes of the peripheral territory of Greater Buenos Aires, outside the civic borders of the federal capital. This is an area which Aguilar describes as 'una especie de alfombra debajo de la cual la ciudad capital escondió todo aquello que no quiso ver' [a kind of rug under which the capital city hid all those things that it did not want to see.]³⁹ Here, the specificities of quotidian urban existence is foremost; the legitimate and illegitimate commercial spaces of the neoliberal economy; offices, petrol stations, banks, local shops and markets, budget restaurants and takeaway food outlets. It is, as Beatriz Urraca suggests, a sordid spatial reality, 'a virtual, composite city', [...] 'where people do not live together, and which is never situated in the centre of anything'.⁴⁰ Two of Trapero's later works, *El Bonaerense* (2002) and *Carancho* (2010) epitomize this liminal *topos* of the suburban in a distinctly modern Latin American context. Here, the suburbs bear no relation to the idealized Anglo-Saxon notion of leafy, prosperous neighbourhoods with close-knit communities. Rather, these areas are 'the expendable locations of the global consumerist marketplace',[41] non-descript streets and avenues that line the arterial roads linking the deindustrialized outer city to the prosperous inner metropolis. It is indeed the 'alienated city' that finds voice in Trapero's films, an urban subjectivity which is absent from the tourist brochures or promotional material of civic heritage. Here, cognitive maps have ceased to function, overridden by the daily struggle for survival in a post-Fordist urban environment. This sense of alienation is also prominent in *La multitud*, where, as previously observed, one resident of Villa Lugano struggles to cross a busy motorway on his way home. Therefore, urban spatial subjectivities are prominent in the output of the group of directors at the centre of the 'new Argentine cinema' and particularly in Trapero's body of work. *Elefante blanco* is no exception. Moreover, as a shanty town within Villa Lugano, on the border between the federal capital and Greater Buenos Aires, Ciudad Oculta is a doubly liminal space.

Therefore, the film presented many middle-class Argentines with their first glimpse of the spatial reality of a *villa,* outside the formulaically menacing images disseminated through the popular news media. As film scholar Steven Shaviro explains, 'cinema is at once a form of perception and a material perceived, a new way of encountering reality and a part of reality perceived for the first time'.[42] In his film Trapero is not only attempting to remap this 'alienated city' for his characters but also for the cinema-going public at large. In an interview, he explained the workings of his film:

> El cine nos permite ver y descubrir realidades de una manera muy especial y muy íntima. Uno pudo haber visto muchas entrevistas a curas de la villa o a las familias que viven en cualquiera de estos barrios, pero la manera en que el público se va a relacionar con esta película es diferente a la manera de la gente que leyó la crónica en el diario o que escuchó una noticia en la radio.[43]
>
> [Cinema allows us to see and discover realities in very special and intimate way. One might have seen many interview with priests from the *villa* or with families who live in whichever one of these districts, but the way that the public is going to relate to this film is different to the way that people read newspaper reports or listen to a radio news bulletin about these places.]

Therefore, within Trapero's film, two distinct yet contiguous cartographies are drawn. Within the narrative arc, there is a retracing of the cognitive map of the *villa* by its inhabitants, as they challenge the validity of existing spatial boundaries. More broadly, as a cultural product which makes visible that which was unseen, *Elefante blanco* seeks to disseminate an alternative spatio-temporality and to recuperate the *villa* as a legitimate space within the popular cognitive map.

To begin any examination of the film, it is worth considering in detail the title sequence and the two scenes which frame it, since these eight minutes of film introduce the viewer to two of the three distinct *topoi* which form the metonymic core of Trapero's cartography. After returning from Amazonas, Padres Julián and Nicolás are driven to Ciudad Oculta by Liliana. The ambient noise of the traffic and wailing police sirens signal their entry into the urban landscape. They arrive after dark, during a torrential rainstorm. The little we see of the *villa* at this point acts as a warning, a precursor of things to come. In the darkness and the rain, we catch glimpses of the sordid spatial reality of the shanty-town; stacks of broken and discarded wooden pallets, muddy, unpaved roads and low-hanging electricity cables. But the darkness and inclement weather occlude the full squalid totality of the *villa* and inhibit our ability to clearly perceive the surroundings. However, in the following shots, we do see the interior of the parochial apartment, the new home of Padre Nicolás. The storm has knocked out the electrical supply, so the only light comes from candles. It is not until the next morning, when the priests awake to the sound of gunfire and profanities, that the reality of life in the *villa* begins to reveal itself. A raucous rock soundtrack heralds the title shot; a wide-angled image of the hospital overlaid with the words 'ELEFANTE BLANCO' in a giant white typeface. The grey-white typography mimics the concrete exterior of the building and its enormous proportions. After no more than two seconds, the camera switches to a panoramic shot of the *villa* in daylight, slowly panning diagonally across the rooftops of the huge cluster of dwellings that surround the old hospital. Here, finally, we can clearly see the physical reality of the shanty town. A series of rapidly cut compilation shots follows, micro vignettes of life in the *villa*. We see rickety housing units, protected from the elements by flimsy metal sheets and blocks of red brick precariously balanced one upon the other. These are the haphazard dwellings constructed by the inhabitants of Ciudad Oculta, 'makeshift homes built with found materials (wood, bricks, stones, corrugated tin)'.[44] This landscape is, in both aesthetic and theoretical terms, considered the antithesis of the modernist civic impetus, an architectural *mêlée* which 'upset[s] the conceptualization of the city as civilizing unit'.[45] Yet here, amidst the precarity of this marginalized settlement and the abject poverty that besets it, there is also community and industriousness. We see children playing, neighbours passing the time of day with one another and men sifting through the mounds of rubbish that litter the streets.

Immediately after these compilation shots, the camera embarks on a single long-take tracking shot within which lies one of the key tropes of *Elefante blanco*: that of historicity and the failure of past utopias. The scene is approximately four minutes in duration, with no visible cuts, lending a documentary realism to the narrative. As it begins, the raucous rock soundtrack that accompanied the film's opening shots segues into the background; it becomes a tinny, incidental noise emanating from an old radio in the parochial flat, thus providing a diegetic link between the camera's panoramic gaze and the viewpoint of the priests. They stand on the balcony of their apartment, surveying the sheer vastness of the settlement. It is here that Padre Julián informs his newly-arrived colleague Nicolás that despite its vastness, Ciudad Oculta is absent from any official maps of the city. He elaborates, explaining that, according to baptismal records the diocese has accumulated, the population is estimated to be around 15,000. However, this is the number of families who live there; therefore, the true figure is likely to be closer to 30,000 inhabitants. The prosaic tone of the priest's explanation belies the shocking significance of these two facts. That a community of over 30,000 people can exist, living and working on the fringes of Buenos Aires and yet be omitted from official maps is a stark paradigm

Fig. 3.10. The ruined hospital in Ciudad Oculta, Buenos Aires. Image: Página12.

of the social inequality that permeates modern urban existence in Latin America.

This neglect is most visible in the building where the priests have made their home, the titular white elephant that was once envisioned as the largest public hospital in all Latin America. It lies in ruins, the shell of the building now home to the priests of the parish. (Fig. 3.10)

The hospital's utopian origins only serve to underline its sordid contemporary state, a proverbial white elephant, an entity which the *Oxford English Dictionary* defines as 'a possession that is useless or troublesome, especially one that is expensive to maintain or difficult to dispose of'. As Padre Julián continues his tour, he provides Nicolás with a potted history of the building that has languished in incompletion for over thirty years. The two priests leave the apartment, descending ill-lit staircases with walls emblazoned with graffiti. Padre Julián continues his narration, explaining that construction of the building first began in 1937 and was the brainchild of Alfredo Palacios. Elected as the first Argentine socialist deputy in 1904 for the district of La Boca, Palacios was a committed social reformer who spearheaded several campaigns to combat poverty.[46] The priest's historiographical narration is sketchy, and his timeline of the building's construction littered with chronological gaps. But this is symptomatic of the lack of information on the building within the historical record. Just as Ciudad Oculta has been erased from official cartographies, so the details of its most prominent building are largely absent from the written histories of Buenos Aires. What is clear is that, as a major civic project, the hospital's construction was subject to the caprices of the political zeitgeist and construction was halted soon after it began. Work on the hospital was restarted under the populist administration of Juan Perón but abandoned yet again following the 1955 coup that ousted the Justicialist Party leader and led to the military government of the so-called Revolución Libertadora [Liberating Revolution]. As one critic asserted, the building has become a 'símbolo viviente de las idas y vueltas de la a veces kafkiana historia argentina, tanto como el oscilante compromiso de la comunidad con los desposeídos' [a living symbol of the ebbs and flows of the often Kafkaesque tides of Argentine history, and of society's fluctuating commitment to the dispossessed.][47] As the priests descend to the ground floor, Julián concludes this tour with the remarks: 'Iba a ser el hospital más grande de Latinoamérica. Y ahora le dicen "el elefante blanco"' [It was going to be the largest hospital in Latin America. And now they call it the 'white elephant'.]. In short, the hospital is a ruin of modernity, a relic that, in the words of Michel de Certeau 'designates what is no more: "Look: here there was" but can no longer be seen'.[48]

All lived experience in the *villa* is presided over by this eponymous white elephant, as its castellated towers dwarf the two-storey shacks that surround it. It lies unfinished and open to the elements, yet its vast scale and structural obduracy imbue the hospital with a solidity and a permanency that is otherwise absent from the spatial landscape of the *villa*. In its current ruined state, the building speaks of its long-forgotten origins as modernizing civic project, and the unfulfilled socialist vision of Palacios. Within the ruined leviathan of the *elefante blanco*, we see the decayed promise of a long-forgotten civic utopia, an insistent reminder of a 'future preterite'.[49] Yet, with the passage of time the building has accrued myriad new meanings. In its current state, home to three hundred families, it signifies the social disenfranchisement of the *villeros*, disowned by civic authorities and condemned as unworthy of the attentions of the neoliberal marketplace. As the hospital sits perched above the shanty town, we are reminded of the now-neglected Torre Espacial in the Interama park. An austere and unforgiving sentinel presiding over the precarious lived existence of the *villeros*, the building speaks of the economic inequality and subjugation of those deemed unfit for citizenship. It is the first landmark upon Trapero's cognitive map of Ciudad Oculta.[50] But what distinguishes the hospital from the neglected landscapes of *La multitud* is the cinematic gaze through which its meaning is conveyed. Although *Elefante blanco* opens with a series of panoramic shots that recall Oesterheld's approach, the viewer is relocated almost immediately to street level and the interactions between inhabitants. During Padre Julián's tour, we descend once again, this time from the overview of the villa seen from the priest's balcony to the bowels of the building and then out into the bustling main street. Through this combination of camera shots, a change in subjectivity manifests itself, dispelling the distance and alienation of the title sequence.

The second landmark presented to the viewer during Padre Julián's tour is another space of historicity, one which could be considered the second white elephant within the film. It is the *villa*'s chapel, a rudimentary single-storey building located a few hundred yards from the old hospital. As Padre Julián, Padre Nicolás and a third priest, Lisandro, arrive, volunteers busy themselves clearing out the flooded ground floor, after the torrential rain of the previous evening. The exterior walls of the chapel are adorned with murals which depict the popular Marian icon, the Virgin of Luján, and the murdered priest Carlos Mugica. Mugica was one of the first *curas villeros*, priests who live within the *villas miseria* and minister to the spiritual needs of the inhabitants. In 1968, he was amongst the founding members of *el Movimiento de Sacerdotes para el Tercer Mundo* [Movement of Priests for the Third World], a group of 'worker priests' inspired by the Second Vatican Council and 'Pope Paul VI's proclamation of *Populorum progressio*, the most important synthesis of the ideas of Vatican II'.[51] The interpretation of these papal edicts in a specifically Latin American context led to the emergence of Liberation Theology, a movement within the Roman Catholic Church that re-framed the teachings of the gospels as a manifesto for socio-economic change in an increasingly unequal society. As Ivan Petrella asserts, 'Latin American liberation theology was born at the crossroads of a changing Catholic Church and the revolutionary political-economic ferment of the late 1960s and early 1970s'.[52] Mugica typified this fusion of spiritual devotion and political commitment. Like Padre Julián, the Jesuit priest was from an affluent porteño family but forsook his personal wealth in order to live and work among the poor and the disenfranchised. As Eduardo Blaustein writes:

> El cura Mugica encabezaba protestas y movilizaciones, reclamaba la entrega de los restos del Che Guevara, había andado en Paris en pleno mayo del '68 y en Cuba, jugaba al fútbol con los villeros de YPF y Saldia. Eso fue días después de que Juan Perón, en su retorno al país, se apareciera en la villa para saludar a los vecinos y entrevistarse con el padre Mugica.[53]
>
> [The priest Mugica headed protests and demonstrations, demanded the return of the remains of Che Guevara, he had visited Paris in May of '68 and in Cuba, and he used to play football with the *villeros* of YPF and Saldia. This last incident was just days after Juan Perón, having returned to Argentina, appeared in the villa to greet the inhabitants and to talk with Father Mugica.]

A charismatic and well-known figure, Mugica acted as mentor to several young Peronist activists who would go on to become leading figures within the Montoneros guerrilla group. Perhaps due to his close links with this left-wing Peronist faction, the priest was assassinated on 11 May 1974.[54] Reflecting the reality of Mugica's stature within the shanty towns of Buenos Aires, particularly Villa 31, where he was based, Trapero portrays the martyred cleric as an icon within *Elefante blanco*. As Hugo Vezzeti observes, 'la figura de Mugica en el espacio y en la comunidad de la villa es un emblema incorporado a cierto estado de la vida social, de la conciencia y la auto representación de la comunidad villera' [the figure of Mugica in the space and community of the *villa* is an emblem which embodies a certain form of social life, conscience and self-representation of villa community.][55] In the mural that adorns the exterior of the chapel, he is pictured alongside some of his most famous words, 'Señor, sueño con morir por ellos' [Lord, I dream of dying for them.] His devotion and the strength of his vocation is an article of faith for Padre Julián in particular, who, in a later scene, counsels a distraught Nicolás with the example of Mugica.

Fig. 3.11. The chapel in *Elefante blanco*. Image: Youtube.

Yet, like the hospital, the chapel is a neglected, semi-ruined space (Fig. 3.11). The roof leaks and the stray dogs of the *villa* frequently use it as a toilet. We see mass celebrated there, but it is a basic venue ill-equipped to accommodate its congregation. A new chapel is under construction as part of the larger building project in the *villa*, an endeavour that Padre Julián repeatedly refers to as 'the project'. This term also holds a deeper significance within the lexicon of liberation theology. As the theologian José Miguez Bonino explains:

> The historical project is an expression frequently used in our discussions as a midway term between an utopia, a vision which makes no attempt to connect itself historically to the present, and a program, a technically developed model for the organization of society. A historical project is defined enough to force options in terms of the basic structures of society. It points in a given direction. But frequently its contents are expressed in symbolical and elusive forms rather than in terms of precise technical language [...] It is in this general sense that we speak of a Latin American socialist project of liberation.[56]

Therefore, Padre Julián's recurrent references to 'el proyecto' speak not only of the ongoing programme of social housing and community facilities that the Church, in conjunction with the civic authorities is developing; it is a synecdochal allusion to the wider aim of the Liberation Theology movement, the creation of 'a Christian utopia that orients its work within history'.[57] This broader spiritual project, of which Mugica is the totemic representation within the *villa*, is continued through the work of the three priests in *Elefante blanco*. Just as shots of the old hospital and its attendant utopian discourse are interspersed with longer scenes in the film, so brief shots of the chapel and of the priests praying appear throughout. One particular montage begins with a wide shot of the priests praying a decade of the rosary in the parochial apartment. The camera cuts to a close-up of Padre Julián's face as he recites the first part of the Hail Mary, then moves to another close-up, of his hands as he clutches the rosary beads while Nicolás and Lisandro complete the prayer. The sound of their praying continues as we see a series of brief shots depicting the abject poverty of the *villa*. It is a moving sequence, not least in that it demonstrates the enormity of the challenge facing the priests. Gunshots and the barking of stray dogs are the responses that their prayers elicit. As the sequence suggests, their faith in the redemptory potential of 'the project' may prove inadequate in the face of the increasing violence and alienation that pervades in the shanty town. Their incantations cannot ward off the crisis that is fomenting there. Just as the chapel is no longer fit for purpose, so, this montage seems to suggest, the priests' faith and their spiritual commitment to alleviating the poverty and degradation of the *villa* may not be sufficient in overcoming the social and economic desolation that surrounds them.

There is a third space on the cognitive map of the *villa* that Trapero draws. Between the historicist landmarks of hospital and chapel lies the contested territory of the *villa* itself. The unpaved streets are lined with piles of rubbish, stray dogs meander around and abandoned rusting vehicles dot the landscape. That this is a dystopian space is highlighted even more by the fact that it sits in the shadow of the high-modernist aspirations of the ruined hospital. It is a *topos* that reflects the failures of neoliberalism, the radical economic discourse which, in Argentina, emerged in the 1970s as the favoured policy of the military junta. In their discussion of global cinema and the neoliberal economic doctrine, Jyotsna Kapur and Keith Wagner define this particular brand of free-market capitalism as 'the radical restructuring of relations between labour and capital in favour of the latter; the dismantling of social welfare; the conversion of one nation-state after another to advancing the free-market; and a rampant culture of commodification, abstraction, and dehumanization'.[58] However, the state is not completely absent from the *villa*; we see it represented by the social worker Luciana and her efforts to register local residents for the new social housing project. But her makeshift office in a cramped portacabin is redolent of a tokenism that characterizes the attitudes of civic institutions towards the residents of Ciudad Oculta. In the eyes of the state and the market, the *villeros* are what Zygmunt Bauman has described as 'flawed consumers' or 'vagabonds'.[59] Lacking in social and economic capital, Bauman characterizes vagabonds as those at the sharp end of decades of neoliberal economic praxis, whose inability to adapt to the demands of the new consumer society renders them useless as modern citizens. As he asserts, for this marginalized demographic, 'their potential for consumption is as limited as their resources. This fault makes their position in society precarious. They breach the norm and sap the order. They spoil the fun simply by being around.'[60] As vagabonds, the residents of the *villa* are viewed with prejudice and suspicion each time they leave the confines of the shanty town and venture out into the wider world. Marginalized by the disdainful glances of their more affluent neighbours and frequently harassed by the police, such treatment serves only to further alienate the community, fostering a wariness of outsiders which is not easily overcome.

This atmosphere of distrust is evident in an early scene, where Padres Lisandro and Nicolás descend the external staircase of the hospital and enter the *villa* proper, with the former explaining how to negotiate this space. Advising Padre Nicolás to wear his dog-collar at all times, so that residents will recognize him as a priest, his colleague explains the potential consequences of any deviation from this established rule. Two weeks previously, a volunteer tutor was threatened at gunpoint by local youths who did not recognize him and were suspicious that he may have been an undercover police officer. He escaped shaken but unharmed. In this perilous landscape the dog-collar is a signifier of identity and acts as a pass of safe conduct. It underlines the historical commitment of the *curas villeros* and the recognition of their vocation by the local community. As is evident from the interaction between the priests and the residents who greet them during their walk to the chapel, there is community here. That violence and poverty dominate everyday life in the *villa* is irrefutable. But there is also human warmth and interaction. Yet Trapero is at pains to avoid any romanticization of these affective bonds between clergy and residents of the shanty town. Daily life here is frequently punctuated by acts of violence, many of which are linked to the illegal manufacture and trade of narcotics. One evening, when out visiting a local resident, Padre Nicolás and Luciana are caught up in a gunfight between feuding criminal gangs. The violence erupts without warning and there is no place to hide as youths on mopeds fire indiscriminately at one another. In an instant, the public spaces of the *villa* become a battlefield, where market supremacy is attained through the physical elimination of business rivals. This is indeed 'capitalism at its most pitilessly predatory'.[61] The shootings are part of a wider conflict, a turf war between two rival drugs producers, Sandoval and Carmelita, which threatens to consume the *villa* as their foot soldiers roam the streets, killing and maiming with impunity. All lived existence in the shantytown is subject to the vagaries of this illicit industry. Furthermore, just as the *villa* itself does not figure on any maps, so within it there are proscribed places which lie out of bonds to all those save the criminal gangs that control this territory. Both within the film and in reality, violence and criminality are an everyday part of life within Ciudad Oculta and venturing into such forbidden spaces can have lethal consequences. As the director explained in an interview with the Spanish newspaper *El País*, 'la relación con la gente de Ciudad Oculta no nació de una visita de turista, sino de la cotidianeidad de nuestras estancias. Por supuesto, en algunos sitios no pudimos entrar: los mismos vecinos nos avisaban si no era seguro' [the relationship with the people of Ciudad Oculta didn't come about through tourist visits but rather through the regularity of our stays there. Naturally, there were places that we could not enter: the neighbours themselves advised us if somewhere wasn't safe.][62]

In *Elefante blanco*, one such place is Carmelita's 'lab', a highly-fortified, labyrinthine dwelling place where *paco*, a type of cocaine paste, is manufactured and prepared for sale, and stolen goods are collated and distributed. This site of commerce may be, in legal terms, an illegitimate one but its success lies in its application of the tenets of free-market capitalism to the production and distribution of hard drugs. The link between late capitalism and criminality in Argentine film of the 1990s and 2000s is a relation explored at length by Page in her monograph *Crisis and Capitalism*. As she suggests, the apparently endemic corruption and malfeasance of the political elite and their commercial cronies during this period informs the national cinematic output of the time, where the juxtaposition of so-called 'white-collar' financial crime with the more traditional malfeasance of those on society's margins in genre films such as *Nueve reinas* [Nine Queens] and *Un oso rojo* [Red Bear] begets an interrogation of concepts of criminality.[63] In the febrile economic environment of December 2001, a crime of previously inconceivable magnitude was perpetrated against the Argentine body politic in the guise of capital flight, as investors moved millions upon millions of dollars from national banks to a place of greater safety, resulting in what became known as el *corralito*.[64] Literally overnight the banks, devoid of collateral, withdrew customers' rights of access to savings and current accounts in what, legally, did not constitute a crime. Put simply, money disappeared, vanishing into the ether. Such events and their reflection in contemporary cinema destabilized traditional notions of the legitimacy of both state and market.

It is through the prism of the *Argentinazo* that Trapero asks us to view the narcotics dealers of *Elefante blanco*. For what are the business enterprises of Carmelita and Sandoval if not the ultimate incarnation of the *laissez-faire* doctrine of neoliberal economics? Like all good entrepreneurs, they have identified a niche in the market — namely the demand for cocaine and its by-products — and so constructed a cottage industry around the production and distribution of the drug. The cheaper *paco* is the drug of choice within the *villa*, whilst the purer powder version will be bought and consumed by the more affluent citizens of the city proper. In the absence of legitimate opportunities, Carmelita and Sandoval are merely applying the tenets of free-market capitalism to their pursuit of criminal enterprise. Such efforts resonate with intertextual echoes of another criminal hideout from the annals of Argentine culture; that of the Astrologer's Temperley base of operations in Roberto Arlt's seminal 1929 novel *Los siete locos*.[65] In this text, it was Arlt who first fully called into question the relations between capitalism and urban civil society. From his lair in the suburban hinterland of the city, Arlt's criminal mastermind the Astrologer concocts his plans of global domination through the creation of a new world order, to be financed by mass-enslavement and a transnational network of brothels. Like the Astrologer, the drug dealers who control the villa do not seek their fortune through the subversion of the hegemonic practices of free-market capitalism but rather through the adoption and refinement of such processes. The product that they offer to the 'flawed consumers' of the *villa* facilitates a temporary, pharmaceutically-induced respite from the poverty of the shanty town; the opportunity to escape the misery of their surroundings through the consumption of narcotics.

Like the locals, the priests are subject to the invisible borders that govern this neo-liberal *topos*. There is an unwritten agreement that as long as they desist from interfering in the affairs of the criminal fraternities, they will be allowed to conduct their ministry in safety. However, in a crucial scene forty minutes into the film, the new 'padre gringo' deviates from the established rules of conduct and ventures into this forbidden and uncharted territory. This dangerous excursion arises following the street shooting in which Mario, a nephew of the narcotics king-pin Sandoval, is murdered. Implored by his distraught grandmother to recover Mario's body, Padre Nicolás ignores the advice of Luciana and Lisandro and sets out, along with the caretaker Cruz, to retrieve the teenager's corpse from Carmelita. Cruz guides Nicolás to Carmelita's lab but refuses to accompany him beyond the door, ominously declaring 'yo llego hasta acá' [This is as far as I go.] What follows is a foray into previously unexplored territory and in undertaking such a quest, Nicolás assumes the role of Dantean explorer, proceeding beyond an invisible sign that reads 'all hope abandon ye who enter here'.

In another lengthy uncut sequence, similar to the introductory tour given to him by Padre Julián, and again around four minutes in duration, Padre Nicolás negotiates the network of corridors, doorways and cluttered rooms that comprise Carmelita's headquarters. At times alone, urged on by the directions of unseen voices, at times hooded and guided through the maze-like building by armed henchmen, he navigates his way through the hazardous terrain. Along the way, he passes teenagers in fugue states of narcotic intoxication, guards equipped with walkie-talkies and sawn-off shotguns, and employees stripping stolen electrical goods for parts. He emerges into a makeshift field hospital, where an injured teenager is undergoing basic treatment for gun wounds, before returning once again to the darkness of a half-lit passage-way, illuminated only by the candles of a devotional shrine. Finally, he finds himself in the operational heart of this territory, the drug lab itself, where he encounters Carmelita and asks her to give him Mario's corpse (Fig. 3.12.).

She accepts, indicating the corridor where the boy's body has been unceremoniously dumped, and provides the priest with a wheelbarrow to ferry Mario's remains back to his loved ones. This is indeed a hellish topography, where the violence and brutality enacted upon the body politic by a rapacious neoliberal business model is duplicated and re-enacted upon the bodies of unfortunates like Mario. It is a neoliberal space par excellence, where human life is another commodity to be bought and traded away in the struggle for survival that the market perpetuates. Yet, by entering this *topos* and leaving it unharmed, Nicolás converts the unmapped territory into a known space, another marker on Trapero's cognitive map of the *villa*. Consequently, he is castigated by Padre Julián for undertaking such a dangerous mission. The senior priest berates him saying, 'nunca fuimos allí. No es nuestro lugar' [We have never gone there. It's not our place.] But by violating the established spatial codes and entering Carmelita's laboratory, Nicolás has breached the boundaries of a previously inviolable space and emerged intact. The unknowable space is now known and can be recognized. It can now be mapped.

Having established these three landmarks on a physical and conceptual map of Ciudad Oculta, it is important to consider the fourth and final space which Trapero

FIG. 3.12. Padre Nicolás enter's Carmelita's narcotics lab in *Elefante blanco*. Image: Youtube

delineates within *Elefante blanco* –– the space of agonism. Chantal Mouffe outlined this theoretical topos in an interview with Markus Miessen in 2012. For Mouffe, the development of such a space is critical in order to enact a democratic renaissance in what she terms the 'post-political society', where hegemonic political discourse insists that 'the partisan model of politics has been overcome, there is no Left and Right and the consensus at the centre doesn't really allow for an alternative'.[66] This is a state of existence akin to Fisher's notion of capitalist realism, where the capitalist cycle of production, consumption and obsolescence 'seamlessly occupies the horizons of the thinkable'.[67] Just as the advent of neoliberalism brought about the subjugation of sovereign governmental institutions to the economic flows of the transnational marketplace, so traditional political parties coalesce around a safe yet meaningless centre-ground, a discursive space where radical political convictions are discarded, since 'there is no alternative'[68] to contemporary capitalist society. Mouffe believes that an alternative does exist, quoting the slogan of the anti-globalization movement, 'another world is possible'.[69] She continues: 'the present state of globalization, far from being "natural", is the result of a neo-liberal hegemony, and it is structured through specific relations of power. This means that it can be challenged and transformed, and that alternatives are indeed available'.[70] It is in *Elefante blanco* that one such alternative is articulated, in the horizontalist endeavours of the community, a praxis which fractures the boundaries of the possible within the villa.

Indeed, a fracturing of consensus lies at the heart of Mouffe's theory. Whilst her body of work is often popularly aligned with the work of theorists such as Michel Hardt and Antonio Negri, an exploration of Mouffe's notion of consensus reveals a clear and distinct divergence from the horizontalist orthodoxy. As a movement that began in the struggles of the Zapatista uprising in Mexico in the mid-1990s, *horizontalidad* came to global prominence following the 2001 Argentine economic crisis. Its most prolific chronicler, Marina Sitrin, defines horizontalism as a movement of 'non-hierarchical and anti-authoritarian creation, rather than reaction. It is a break with vertical ways of organizing and relating'.[71] As such, it repudiates interaction with established institutions and their representatives, instead seeking consensus within the movement itself through neighbourhood assemblies, workers' collectives in occupied factories and *piquetero* groups. In contrast, Mouffe views this withdrawal from hegemonic structures as counter-productive and defeatist. Arguing that true consensus is unattainable, since political change is not a finite objective but rather an ongoing process, she highlights the need for activists to confront the 'post-political' hegemony of neoliberalism by developing a space outside their own political networks, where 'productive engagement to disturb the consensus' can flourish.[72] Such territory is, for Mouffe, embodied by the space of agonism, in which non-agreement and a vibrant lack of consensus can revitalize a stagnant body politic.

In *Elefante blanco*, this metonymic space is present in the building site that sits adjacent to the old hospital. As Padre Julián explains to Padre Nicolás, this is where the local community has come together to build housing, a canteen, a health clinic and a new chapel. But there is discord, as we see initially in a scene where the workmen, themselves local residents, complain to the clergyman about delayed wage payments. The building project is a joint venture between the municipal authorities and the construction company, which, it later transpires, is actually managed by the Church. Despite great efforts on the part of the *curas villeros* and Luciana, the project eventually falters, becoming ensnared in a seemingly insoluble bureaucratic dispute between the two institutions. But the catalyst for the cessation of all construction work is the murder of Cruz, a caretaker and community worker in the *villa* who is posthumously revealed to have been an undercover police officer. After this crime, funding is withdrawn, and the project is mothballed. In a wide-shot resonant with meaning, we see the bulldozers leave the site, trundling slowly away out of the shadow of the derelict hospital. History, it seems, is doomed to repeat itself, as once again the *villeros* have been failed by the institutions of church and state.

The next day, however, the residents return and occupy the now vacant site, bringing building materials scavenged from around the settlement. Despite the official closure of the project, they are determined to continue building and realize their ambitions of a safe and stable new home for themselves and their families. It is a venture which is ultimately thwarted by the forces of law and order, when riot police attack the residents and evict them from the construction site. But for a brief period of time, this place resembles Mouffe's space of agonism. Repudiating the validity of the officially sanctioned decision, the residents come together to build, discuss and progress their vision of a new community (Fig. 3.13).

Furthermore, against the wishes of Padre Julián, Nicolás, along with Luciana, joins the gathering. This is significant as it signals a rupture in the established codes of behaviour that the old guard of priests in the *villa*, represented by Padre Julián, have always observed. Once again, as with his visit to the forbidden zone of Carmelita's drug laboratory, Nicolás breaks with administrative orthodoxies,

Fig. 3.13. Nicolás and Luciana discuss the lack of progress on 'el proyecto' with workers on the building site in *Elefante blanco*. Image: Youtube

motivated by his sense of solidarity with the *villeros*. By this point in the film, he has also embarked upon a physical relationship with Luciana, discarding his vows of celibacy. Therefore, through his dissenting actions, the 'padre gringo' has come to embody an alternative to the status quo, calling into question the validity of the 'post-political' discourse which has prevailed for so long and galvanizing the residents into action.

In *The Space of Agonism*, Mouffe asserts that, often, it is 'an outsider to the consensus' within a given community who acts as the catalyst for the creation of such an agonistic space.[73] However, she is at pains to emphasize that her notion is not simply a return to the Marxist cliché of the intellectual revolutionary who leads the *lumpen* masses to political victory. Rather, it is more frequently a voice from *within* the community, someone previously unable to articulate a discourse of resistance, since adherence to 'the whole culture of consensus simply does not allow for people to envisage that things could be different'. Here Mouffe argues that, by viewing issues in a different way, raising their voice against the prevailing view and articulating a discourse of opposition, this actor is able to 'subvert the consensus that exists in so many areas, and to re-establish a dynamic of conflictuality'.[74]

Padre Julián is unable to assume this role, as his health is fragile, and, over time, he has become somewhat inured to the everyday injustices of life in the *villa*. We see his tacit acceptance of the situation in his remark to the bishop, when he complains 'hace más de diez años que estoy ocupando ilegalmente una obra que ningún Gobierno terminó' [for more than ten years I've been illegally occupying a public building that no government ever finished.] In the context of *Elefante blanco*, it is Padre Nicolás who assumes the role of outsider, impelled to act by what he considers his failure to prevent the brutality visited upon his previous rural parish and the senseless violence of the criminal feuds within the *villa*. Whilst the other priests visit the offices of the bishopric in central Buenos Aires in a last-ditch attempt to save the ailing project, deferring to hegemonic codes of space and authority, we see him moving amongst the protesting residents out in the building site. Unlike

Padres Julián and Lisandro, he realizes that 'the political dimension cannot be localized in a privileged space'.[75] Rather, dissent must be articulated within all spatial realms beginning with the primary space of the *villa*. Despite the ultimate failure of the protest, and the violence inflicted upon the residents by the tear gas and rubber bullets of the police, the insurrection has demarcated this territory as a space of agonism, a site of potential, where authority can be contested. Indeed, in the response of the forces of law and order, and the defiance of the protestors, the conflict is itself resonant of the scenes filmed around the Plaza de Mayo during the *Argentinazo*. It is another landmark on Trapero's cognitive map of the *villa*, a place of the possibilities of the present, in contrast to the historicist utopian spaces of the hospital and the chapel. Whilst those landmarks speak of a utopia firmly located within the hierarchical structures of the civic government and the Catholic church, the nascent utopia of the building site is a site of horizontalism, where change is devised by the community itself, rather than imposed by external institutions. Yet, the old utopian landmarks of church and hospital are not obsolete ruins. The historical significance of both structures and the failures which their histories encode will continue to inform and influence this space of agonism.

In fact, in the closing scenes of the film, in the depiction of Padre Julián's funeral procession, we see this discursive syncretism of historicity and horizontalism in action. As the mourners file past the white elephant of the old hospital, they brandish images of the two martyred priests, Padres Julián and Padre Carlos Mugica. The placards speak of the historicist legacy of the *curas villeros*. But it is the assembled multitude, here mourning the deaths of their priests, who have created a space of agonism, a locus that encodes the potential for greater equality and a new subjectivity of urban citizenship. In commandeering the building project and organizing themselves autonomously, the *villeros* have mapped out a site of *horizontalidad*, a space of embryonic renewal and *autogestión* where the future can be built upon the ruins of utopias past, amidst the ghosts and the wreckage. In Oesterheld's *La multitud*, this sense of community and collective endeavour is entirely absent, as is the potential for change that it can enact.

In conclusion, through the cinematic gaze of both films, new meanings are generated by the decaying and demolished structures of the past. In contrast to the human spectres of *El cantor de Tango*, the ghosts here are spatial. The abandoned 'future[s] preterite'[76] of the urban landscape are re-signified in the present through their cinematic exploration and the historicity which the camera invokes. In *La multitud*, this process is truncated: we see the faded technicolour splendour of Ciudad Deportiva and the Interama theme park in the stills from the time of their construction and in their current state of neglect. But the panoramic distance imposed by the camera negates the possibility of renewal. Whilst Oesterheld's documentary invests these derelict landscapes with historicist significance, the spatial and affective estrangement it engenders denies the potential for transformation. As *El cantor de tango* infers, historicity alone is not enough. In contrast, in Pablo Trapero's *Elefante blanco*, the ruins of the hospital that tower above the *villa* inform the struggles of the present, fostering a horizontalist impetus that transforms the building site below into a nascent space of agonism. Moreover, in the most marginalized of spaces in post-Crisis Buenos Aires, the film posits an alternative to the hegemonic spatio-temporalities of the neoliberal metropolis, tracing new lines of meaning upon the cognitive map of the capital city. By so doing, it reflects the evolving subjectivities of the new structure of feeling that emerged following the *Argentinazo* of 2001.

Chapter 4, 'Back in Time for Dinner', moves from the spatial referents of horizontalism and historicity in the built environment to a consideration of the significance of material objects within the home in the 2010 television mini-series *Lo que el tiempo nos dejó*. In its historicist narratives, the series retells historically significant events from a quotidian perspective, placing the *mise en scène* of the home and the workplace at the centre of these personal histories. As we shall see, in a similar mode to *Elefante blanco*, the series blends the discourses of historicity and horizontalism to create a revitalized vision of the past which encodes an emboldened demand for change in the present.

## Notes to Chapter 3

1. Jorge Luis Borges, 'Del rigor en la ciencia', in *Obras completas* (Buenos Aires: Emecé, 1974), p. 847.
2. Ricardo Piglia, *El último lector* (Barcelona: Anagrama, 2005), p. 13.
3. James Donald, 'Metropolis: The City as Text', in *The Social and Cultural Forms of Modernity*, ed. by Robert Bocock and Kenneth Thompson (London: Polity Press/Open University, 1992), pp. 417–70 (p. 417).
4. I refer here to Kevin Lynch's concept of 'cognitive maps' in his monograph *The Image of the City* (Cambridge: MIT Press, 1960); and to Fredric Jameson's exploration of the notion in *Postmodernism*.
5. David Harvey, *Spaces of Capital* (Edinburgh: Edinburgh University Press, 2001), p. 224.
6. Saskia Sassen, 'Rebuilding the Global City', in *Re-presenting the City: Ethnicity, Capital and Culture in the 21$^{st}$ Century Metropolis*, ed. by Anthony D. King (Basingstoke: Macmillan Press, 1996), pp. 23–42 (p. 31).
7. Néstor García Canclini, *Consumers and Citizens: Globalization and Multicultural Conflicts* (Minneapolis: University of Minnesota Press, 2001), p. 84.
8. Maria Guadalupe Arenillas, 'Towards a Nondiscursive Turn in Argentine Documentary Film', in *Latin American Documentary Film in the New Millennium*, ed. by Maria Guadalupe Arenillas and Michael J. Lazzarra (New York: Palgrave Macmillan), pp. 275–90 (p. 276).
9. Arenillas, 'Towards a Nondiscursive Turn', p. 287.
10. This structure's name derives from the its location within the 'Future' zone of the park. In its original design, the Parque de la Ciudad was composed of five discrete zones; Latino, carnival, future, fantasy and international. For further information, see Mauricio Giambartolomei, 'El Parque de la Ciudad, olvidado y arruinado como una fantasma', *La Nación*, 31 May 2013 <http://www.lanacion.com.ar/1587106-el-parque-de-la-ciudad-olvidado-y-arruinado-como-una-feria-fantasma> [accessed 30 January 2018].
11. Daniel Gutman, 'Un símbolo porteño', *Clarín*, 17 May 2011 <https://www.clarin.com/ciudades/Buenos-Aires-vista-mirador-elevado_0_BJDWe8faw7g.html> [accessed 30 January 2018] The tower remains the tallest structure in Buenos Aires.
12. Arenillas, 'Towards a Nondiscursive Turn', p. 283.
13. For more information on the geographical specificities of the various landscapes that appear in *La multitud*, see Niall H. D. Geraghty, and Adriana Laura Massidda, 'The Spatiality of Desire in Martín Oesterheld's *La multitud* and Luis Ortega's *Dromómanos* (2012)', in *Creative Spaces and Urban Marginality in Latin America*, ed. by Niall H. D. Geraghty and Adriana Laura Massidda, (London: University of London Press, 2019), pp. 201–40.

14. Scorer, *City in Common*, p. 187.
15. Florian Freitag, '"Like Walking into a Movie": Intermedial Relations between Theme Parks and Movies', *The Journal of Popular Culture*, 50:4 (2017), 704–22 (p. 705).
16. Ibid., p. 706.
17. Ibid., p. 715.
18. For a brief history of Puerto Madero, and details of its redevelopment in the late 1980s, see Wilson, *Buenos Aires*, pp. 20–23.
19. Gorelik, *Miradas*, p. 192.
20. Ibid., p. 193.
21. Harvey, *Spaces of Capital*, p. 224.
22. Scorer, *City in Common*, p. 172.
23. Clara Garavelli, 'White Elephant/Elefante blanco', in *World Film Locations: Buenos Aires*, ed. by Santiago Oyarzabal and Michael Pigott (Bristol: Intellect Books, 2014), pp. 120–21 (p. 120).
24. Gonzalo Aguilar, *Other Worlds: New Argentine Film*: Basingstoke: Palgrave Macmillan, 2008), p. 123.
25. Markus Miessen and Chantal Mouffe, *The Space of Agonism* (Berlin: Sternberg Press, 2012).
26. Gonzalo Aguilar, 'Shantytowns: Buenos Aires, the Shattered City', in *World Film Locations: Buenos Aires*, ed. by Santiago Oyarzabal and Michael Pigott (Bristol: Intellect Books, 2014), pp. 48–49 (p. 49).
27. Aguilar, 'Shantytowns', p. 48. Prominent examples of documentaries which do address the reality of life within a *villa miseria* include *Memoria del saqueo* (2004), directed by Fernando 'Pino' Solanas and *Estrellas* (2007), directed by Federico León and Marcos Martínez.
28. Aguilar, 'Shantytowns', p. 48
29. Adrián Gorelik, 'Buenos Aires is (Latin) America Too', in *City/Art: The Urban Scene in Latin America*, ed. by Rebecca E. Biron (Durham, NC: Duke University Press, 2009), pp. 61–84 (p. 61).
30. Scorer, *City in Common*, p. 171.
31. Eduardo Blaustein, *Prohibido vivir aquí* (Buenos Aires: Punto de encuentro, 2006), p. 22.
32. Jorge Finkielman, *The Film Industry in Argentina: An Illustrated Cultural History* (Jefferson, NC: McFarland & Company, 2004), p. 206.
33. Nahuel Galotta, 'Ciudad Oculta por dentro, la villa que se revela en el cine' *Clarin.com*, 27 May 2012 http://www.clarin.com/capital_federal/Ciudad-Oculta-dentro-villa-revela_0_707929263.html [accessed 23 January 2016].
34. For further info on 'New Argentine Cinema' see, Page, *Crisis*, and Jens Andermann, *New Argentine Cinema* (London: Tauris, 2012)
35. Page, *Crisis*, p. 3
36. Andermann, *New Argentine Cinema*, p. xi.
37. Page, *Crisis*, p. 2.
38. Fernando Sdrigotti, 'Pizza, Beer and Cigarettes/Pizza, birra, faso' in *World Film Locations*, pp. 71–72 (p. 72).
39. Aguilar, *Miradas*, p. 211
40. Beatriz Urraca, 'Transactional Fiction: (Sub)urban Realism in the Films of Trapero and Caetano' in *New Trends in Argentine and Brazilian Cinema*, ed. by Cacilda Rego and Carolina Rocha (Bristol: Intellect, 2011), pp. 147–61 (p. 152).
41. Ibid., p. 152
42. Steven Shaviro, *The Cinematic Body* (Minneapolis: University of Minnesota Press, 1993), p. 41.
43. Horacio Bernades, 'Elefante blanco, social y masivo', *Pagina12*, 17 May 2012, <http://www.pagina12.com.ar/diario/suplementos/espectaculos/subnotas/25232-6708-2012-05-17.html> [accessed 23 January 2016]
44. Podalsky, *Specular City*, p. 100.
45. Ibid., p. 107.
46. Wilson, *Buenos Aires*, p. 189
47. Bernardes, 'Elefante blanco'.
48. Michel De Certeau, 'Practices of Space', in *On Signs*, ed. by Marshal Blonsky (Baltimore, MD: John Hopkins University Press, 1985), pp. 122–45 (p. 143).

49. Andermann, *New Argentine Cinema*, p. 74.
50. In 2018, the hospital was demolished and construction began on a complex of government buildings to replace the structure, including a new site for the Ministerio de Desarrollo Humano y Habitat [Ministry of Human Development and Habitat]. See Mauricio Giambartolomei, 'Ciudad Oculta: Un nuevo ministerio en el predio que ocupaba el Elefante Blanco', *La Nación*, 23 June 2019 https://www.lanacion.com.ar/buenos-aires/ciudad-oculta-nuevo-ministerio-predio-ocupaba-elefante-nid2260576 [accessed 3 July 2019]
51. Richard Gillespie, *Soldiers of Perón: Argentina's Montoneros* (Oxford: Clarendon, 1982), p. 53.
52. Ivan Petrella, *The Future of Liberation Theology: An Argument and Manifesto* (London: SCM Press, 2006), p. 1.
53. Blaustein, *Prohibido*, p. 44
54. Gillespie, *Soldiers*, p. 154.
55. Hugo Vezzeti, *Sobre la violencia revolucionaria: memorias y olvidos* (Buenos Aires: Siglo Veintiuno, 2013), p. 183.
56. Petrella, *Future of Liberation Theology*, pp. 11–12.
57. Ibid., p. 4.
58. Jyotsna Kapur and Keith B. Wagner, 'Introduction: Neoliberalism and Global Cinema', in *Neoliberalism and Global Cinema: Capital, Culture and Marxist Critique*, ed. by Jyotsna Kapur and Keith B. Wagner (New York: Routledge, 2011), pp. 1–18 (p. 2).
59. Zygmunt Bauman, *Globalization: The Human Consequences* (Cambridge: Polity Press, 1998), p. 96
60. Bauman, *Globalization*, p. 96
61. Naomi Klein, *The Shock Doctrine* (London: Penguin, 2007), p. 12.
62. Gregorio Belinchón, 'Pablo Trapero contra la hipocresía', *El País*, 27 June 2012 <http://cultura.elpais.com/cultura/2012/06/27/actualidad/1340812132_977262.html> [accessed 24 May 2016]
63. See Page, *Crisis*, pp. 81–109.
64. The *corralito* was, literally, a run on the banks which led to the restriction of withdrawals from bank current accounts. It occurred in early December 2001.
65. Roberto Arlt, *Los siete locos* (Madrid: Cátedra, 2011).
66. Markus Miessen and Chantal Mouffe, *A Space of Agonism* (Berlin: Sternberg Press, 2012) p. 22.
67. Fisher, *Capitalist Realism*, p .8.
68. Ibid.
69. Miessen and Mouffe, *Space of Agonism*, p. 22.
70. Chantal Mouffe, *Agonistics: Thinking the World Politically* (London: Verso, 2013), pp. 131–32.
71. Sitrin, *Horizontalism*, p. 3.
72. Miessen and Mouffe, *Agonism*, p. 22.
73. Miessen and Mouffe, *Agonism*, p. 22.
74. Miessen and Mouffe, *Agonism*, pp. 21–22.
75. Miessen and Mouffe, *Agonism*, p. 22.
76. Andermann, *New Argentine Cinema*, p. 74.

CHAPTER 4

❖

# Back in Time for Dinner: Living History on the Small Screen

The past is a foreign country: they do things differently there.
— L. P. Hartley

This chapter examines the 2010 television mini-series *Lo que el tiempo nos dejó* [What the Past Has Left Us] as an articulation of what cultural historian Raphael Samuel describes as 'living history', a form of historiographic discourse which privileges verisimilitude and affect over orthodox historical objectivity. Produced during the 2010 Bicentenary year, in collaboration with the popular historian Felipe Pigna, the series adopts the sensibilities of living history, along with the genre markers of both historical docudrama and the *telenovela*, to create a distinctive historicist fictionscape of alternative national histories (Fig. 4.1).

In its depictions of the role played by ordinary citizens in several significant events of the Argentine twentieth century, *Lo que el tiempo nos dejó* foregrounds the

FIG. 4.1. Promotional poster for the 2010 mini-series, *Lo que el tiempo nos dejó*.
Image: Telefe Argentina.

Fig. 4.2. Photograph from the 1999 installation 'El pañol', by Marcelo Brodsky. Image: Marcelo Brodsky.

specificities of the everyday, in the *mise-en-scène* of home, school and workplace. By recreating the sights and sounds of the past through outmoded consumer artefacts, popular music and archive media footage, the series interpellates an emotive and controversial historicist fictionscape. This chapter begins with an examination of the significance of the material traces of the past in post-dictatorship Argentina, with reference to a 1999 visual installation created by the artist Marcelo Brodsky. Situating the artwork within Samuel's tradition of 'living history', the case study continues by evaluating the historicist potential of audio-visual media, with a specific focus on the narrative modalities of both the docudrama and the *telenovela* and their use by the Madres and Abuelas of the Plaza de Mayo. We then consider the narrative specificities of *Lo que el tiempo nos dejó*, examining what the histories it depicts reveal of the past and of the contemporary present during the latter years of the Kirchner era.[1]

Brodsky's installation, entitled 'El pañol', was exhibited at the Centro Cultural Recoleta in Buenos Aires in 1999 as part of a colloquium entitled 'La desaparición — Arte y Política' (Fig. 4.2).[2] Although the artwork itself was subsequently dismantled, Brodsky's photographs of the installation were later included in his 2001 collection of photo-essays, *Nexo* [*Nexus*]. The exhibit itself was housed in an unremarkable room of whitewashed walls and comprised an amalgamation of sounds, objects and odours. In the photographs, the detritus of obsolete technology is prominent, with manual typewriters, tape recorders, rotary dial telephones and polaroid cameras visible, in varying states of disrepair. Three refrigerators and a washing machine are lined up, heaped with more random items. An open briefcase reveals a jumble of old photographs, the yellowing images of people and places competing for attention. At the rear of the room, a child's stuffed toy glares accusingly through its one remaining eye from the bottom shelf of a ramshackle bookcase. The incongruity of an empty pram, parked haphazardly alongside an antiquated sewing machine, arrests the gaze. Still more objects compete for attention; stamp collections, a balding doll and a framed black and white photograph of two laughing toddlers. However, what the photographs cannot show is that amidst this bric-à-brac, this jumble of affective keepsakes and remnants of outmoded consumer culture, the ubiquitous institutional smell of disinfectant pervades. Overhead, the rhythmic thrum of a helicopter taking off pulses, its rotors slicing through the air. Another, more subtle noise is also discernible; the grating of metal chains over concrete, like an insistent ghost. In this work of 'mnemonic art',[3] constructed with the aid of testimonial accounts from survivors, Brodsky recreates the spatial reality of a storeroom within the Escuela Mecánica de la Armada (ESMA): the largest and most notorious of the clandestine detention centres which operated during the so-called 'Process of National Reorganization'. The objects displayed are not lost property, but rather the looted possessions of the people imprisoned in the ESMA during *el Proceso*, and who were subsequently disappeared.

According to the testimony of those who were illegally held within the complex and survived, the ESMA 'held around 5000 prisoners between 1976 and 1983, around 90 per cent of whom were assassinated'.[4] The mechanics of the repression were first publicly documented in the 1984 report by Argentina's National Commission on

Disappeared People (CONADEP), a volume which catalogued the practices of abduction, torture and summary execution favoured by the military regime in their mission to rid the country of 'subversive elements'. Amongst the findings of the CONADEP report, it was noted that 62 per cent of abductions took place in or around victims' homes.[5] In addition to the extra-judicial detention of suspects, task forces such as the ESMA's Grupo de Tareas 3.3.2 would also systematically loot the possessions of the victims and their families.[6] From washing machines to televisions, jewellery to soft toys and keepsakes, any object coveted by the officers involved was appropriated, kept or removed for storage within the camps. As one witness testified, 'While they kept me detained and held my mother hostage, I saw them looting all our goods and belongings and piling them on to trucks. The house was left without any trace that people had lived there'.[7] In the perverse argot of *el Proceso*, these stolen objects were referred to as 'botín de guerra' [war booty], a material perk of the fight against subversion. Whilst task force members often retained the most valuable items, the remaining loot was transported to camps such as the ESMA, where it was deposited in a storeroom adjacent to the prisoners' quarters. In an essay accompanying Brodsky's photographs, survivor Lila Pastoriza describes the surreal moment when, hooded and shackled and waiting to use the bathroom, she glimpsed from behind her blindfold the outline of a pile of miscellaneous objects. She recalls: 'A la derecha, como en la bruma, atisbo las pilas espectrales de cosas, y, arriba de todo, alucinantes, un par de esquíes. Olor a sótanos viejos, vahos de cloro. Es el pañol' [On the right, as if in a mist, I glimpse spectral piles of objects, and, on the top, absurdly, a pair of skis. The smell of old basements, a whiff of chlorine. This is the storeroom.][8]

'To dwell means to leave traces', Walter Benjamin once wrote.[9] Yet no trace now remains of the contents of the ESMA storeroom, material signifiers of the personal and professional lives of their owners. Following the decommissioning of the depository in early 1978, its contents were dispersed, likely resold or otherwise disposed of.[10] In the absence of physical remnants, Brodsky's installation enacts a metonymic reconstruction of the lived existence of the thousands of *desaparecidos* who passed through the ESMA, amongst them the artist's younger brother Fernando. Using survivors' accounts of the room, his collation of miscellaneous objects is exacting in its verisimilitude, with the original installation including not only the visual stimuli of the prison storeroom but also its distinctive sounds and odours. In fact, the apparent authenticity of the artwork was such that, following the exhibition's opening, Brodsky was compelled to assure a concerned public that the contents of his installation were not the original stolen objects from the ESMA. However, he stressed: 'No hay gran diferencia entre este pañol y el que estaba en la ESMA. Los mismos objetos, el mismo olor a desinfectante, el mismo sonido de cadenas arrastradas por el suelo y de helicópteros levantando vuelo' [There is no great difference between this storeroom and the one from the ESMA. The same objects, the same smell of disinfectant, the same sound of chains being dragged along the floor and of helicopters taking off.][11] Whilst Brodsky's installation is a facsimile of the actual storeroom that functioned within the ESMA, its rich materiality evokes in the viewer a genuine emotional response.

For those who care to look beyond the initially bewildering disorder of 'El pañol', its contents articulate a profoundly historicist narrative of loss and recuperation. The technological artefacts featured denote the relative youth and social affluence of their former owners; as the CONADEP report confirmed, in approximately 71 per cent of reported cases, those abducted were aged between 21 and 35.[12] The children's toys present allude to the disappearance of entire families as do the white goods and other kitchen appliances, signifiers of a ruptured familial domesticity. The jumble of photographs contained within the leather briefcase speaks of former lives now inscribed with the temporal before and after of disappearance. And in the inclusion of that most benign of objects, an infant's pram, there is an expression of perhaps the most notorious of all the regime's crimes: the appropriation and illegal adoption of an estimated five hundred infants during the dictatorship, many of whom were born within the ESMA.[13]

Thus, 'El pañol' is an inherently historicist artwork that employs material artefacts to enunciate the panoply of trauma inflicted upon Argentine society by the military dictatorship. The alterity of the individual items, their essential incongruity in this institutional *mise-en-scène* arises from the absence of their former owners. Here is the unutterable horror of disappearance that José Pablo Feinmann has described as 'the obscenity of death without bodies'.[14] Furthermore, in depriving family members of the affective souvenirs of their abducted loved ones, such as the photographs, books and assorted keepsakes, all of negligible commercial value, the regime compounded the primary trauma of disappearance. For in these stolen objects lie the traces of existence, the everyday remainders of individual lives. In the erasure of these traces, the operatives of *el Proceso* publicly exercised their absolute power over the population. As Pastoriza indicates, 'que personas y cosas se desvanecieran sin dejar rastros era la señal, la amenaza inequívoca' [that people and things should disappear without a trace was the signal, the unequivocal threat].[15] In its reanimation of the past through material artefacts, Brodsky's installation seeks to breach the vacuum of disappearance and silence that had enveloped Argentine society and to recuperate an alternative historical truth.

In 2000, a Canadian television company approached Brodsky with a request to use his film and photographs of 'El pañol' in a documentary exploring the dictatorship, entitled 'Argentina's Dirty War'. In the absence of any contemporaneous photographic evidence of the storeroom, Brodsky's images were employed within the documentary as a visual recreation of a past that had been presumed unsalvageable. And so, through this process of transmediality, 'El pañol' acquired new and diverse layers of meaning. The historicist immanence of the objects within the storeroom, the traces of the past which they embody are amplified by their transferral to the televisual medium: for the television viewer, Brodsky's images move beyond mimetic recreation to visually become the past. Summarizing the complex series of entanglements that this collaboration engendered, the artist asserts that 'arte y documento, memoria e historia, recreación, creación y transmisión manifiestan su ambigüedad en este programa de la televisión canadiense' [art and archive, memory and history, recreation, creation and transmission all demonstrate their ambiguity in

Fig. 4.3. Photographs from the installation 'El pañol', in Marcelo Brodsky. Image: Marcelo Brodsky.

this Canadian television programme].[16] Yet, the extraordinary potential of material artefacts such as these in historical television, be it documentary or drama, can, in part, be ascribed to their inherent ordinariness. As relics of everyday lives from the past, such objects provoke an affective response. Joe Moran theorizes that outdated everyday miscellanea, such as the objects featured in Brodsky's installation, afford us the opportunity to grasp at the past and 'render it visible, disrupting the illusion of the timeless routine and connecting it again with historical processes'.[17] In our recognition of objects from our own lived experience, *as seen on TV*, we are able to relocate our everyday lives within specific moments of a broader national past. Indeed, as Idelber Avelar posits, such discarded commodities are particularly important in post-dictatorship societies, since 'they offer anchors through which a connection with the past can be re-established'.[18] It is just such a connection that the television mini-series *Lo que el tiempo nos dejó* seeks to forge in its foregrounding of the material minutiae of the past. In its televisual histories, the series endows these artefacts with a haptic primacy which encodes a deeper narrative significance than that of mere temporal signposts. In the discursive *mise-en-abyme* of the series, old shoes and coats, outdated consumer gadgets, cosmetics and even the television set itself are synecdochal representations of an alternative national past.

The series, a collection of six one-hour individual dramas, was the fruit of a collaboration amongst the production companies Underground Contenidos, Endemol Argentina and Telefe Contenidos. The first episode, entitled 'Mi mensaje' [My Message], was broadcast on 1 September 2010 on the Telefe national television channel in the peak-time slot of 10:30pm. The scheduling of the series is illustrative of its target audience, given that, in Argentina, this is the time of the traditional *sobremesa*, when families remain at the dinner table after their meal to chat and watch television. 'Mi mensaje' achieved a substantial 19.4 points in ratings, having attracted the second-largest audience of all programmes transmitted on that date.[19] Advertised with the promotional tagline 'Historias del Bicentenario, en un ciclo de unitarios imperdible' [Histories of the Bicentenary, in a collection of unmissable episodes] the series presents history as mediated through its everyday remnants: the objects, sights and sounds that populate the domestic topography of the past. In the home, the workplace, and the classrooms of the school and the university, the characters enact their workaday routines as they become embroiled in important historical events. Against a backdrop of clothes, media and consumer artefacts which embody 'la iconicidad de una cultura material ligada a un determinado tiempo histórico' [the iconicity of a material cultural bound to a particular historical period], these histories unfold .[20].

Where the novel *El cantor de tango* and the films *La multitud* and *Elefante blanco* assert the material proximity of history through their depictions of space and the built environment, *Lo que el tiempo nos dejó* enunciates its alternative vision of the past by exploiting the historiographic immanence of objects. The centrality of historical artefacts in *Lo que el tiempo nos dejó* merits detailed analysis since it is emblematic of a broader materialist turn in post-Crisis Argentine historicist discourse. A constituent element of the revitalized sense of the past which began to emerge in the late 1990s, this trend in historicist representation is visible in an inchoate form before the Crisis of 2001, in cultural texts such as Brodsky's 'El pañol'. But it is only in the years after the *Argentinazo* that we may observe the materiality of history become more pervasive, as the historicist structure of feeling of which it is part evolves into a 'particular community of experience hardly needing expression'.[21] Thus, by 2010, this particular historicist modality has become an established form of cultural communication, finding voice in the primetime historical narratives of *Lo que el tiempo nos dejó*. In this material turn, there are parallels with the form of historiographical representation that Samuels terms 'living history': a form of historical knowledge that favours 'the poetics of the ordinary' over the diachronic orthodoxies of academic history. Living history, he writes,

> eschews epic and grand narrative in favour of personal observation and local knowledge. It invites us to play games with the past and to pretend that we are at home in it, ignoring the limitations of time and space by reincarnating it in the here-and-now. It pins it faith in surface appearances, visible artefacts, 'evidence...which can be seen, touched and photographed', rather than aggregates and abstractions. [...] Instead of being an alp on the brain of the living, the past dissolves into a thousand different views.[22]

As Samuel's description affirms, this type of popular history is grounded in the material, in objects and artefacts that reanimate the past in the environs of the present, rendering the spectator 'an eavesdropper on the past, an eyewitness to everyday transactions and events'.[23] It is also a form of historical knowledge with a distinctly horizontalist bent, since it focuses upon the everyday lives of ordinary individuals who become involved in or witness formative historic events, rather than on the experiences of the politicians and statespeople at the centre of power.

The notion of living history is key to the historical narratives of *Lo que el tiempo nos dejó*, since, as James Young writes, 'historical artefacts are used not only to gesture toward the past, to move us toward its examination, but also to naturalize particular versions of the past'.[24] By privileging the materiality of living history, the series articulates a specific vision of the past. This narrative and epistemic framework is what Milly Buonanno terms a 'fictionscape': a specific selection and use of events, relationships, objects and spaces through which meaning, and affect are encoded. She defines the fictionscape as 'un territorio (paisaje) imaginario determinado y desplegado por el conjunto de las historias de ficción ofrecidas y disponibles en un determinado periodo de tiempo' [an imaginary territory (landscape) determined and deployed by the ensemble of fictional histories on offer and available in a particular period of time.][25] One other element crucial to the fictionscape of *Lo que el tiempo nos dejó* can be found in its medial self-reflexivity, namely, its fusion of the narrative modalities of historical television programming and the *telenovela*.

As a mini-series specifically produced to coincide with the national Bicentenary celebrations of 2010, *Lo que el tiempo nos dejó* can be categorized as a work of 'historical event television', audio-visual texts that commemorate historical figures or events but which are 'shaped by the ideological and cultural conditions of the present'.[26] These texts are usually produced and broadcast on or around national celebrations, significant historical anniversaries or other important events that connect the past with the present in the national imaginary. For Tobias Ebbrecht, who coined the term, one of the most potent forms of historical event television is the docudrama, a hybrid narrative that combines the narrative re-presentation of drama with the archive footage and historical artefacts of the factual documentary. As such, the docudrama encodes 'a sensual and subjective historical space which is not bound to facts but reinvents historic development by reorganizing and recreating images of the past as subjective images of remembrance'.[27]

Furthermore, as a Latin American and specifically Argentine televisual text, the mini-series exhibits certain narrative traits common to that most enduringly popular of Latin American televisual genres, the *telenovela*. In its continued success as the 'género popular por excelencia de la ficción televisiva latinoamericana' [popular genre par excellence of Latin American televisual fiction],[28] the *telenovela* has, since its origins in the 1960s, become a staple of television schedules across Latin America. Whilst bearing certain thematic similarities to the soap opera, its British cultural counterpart, the *telenovela* is unique in its inherent versatility. As Mar Chicharro notes, it is a televisual product that, whilst retaining certain basic characteristics, can be tailored to the demands and expectations of audiences across Latin America and even further afield, as the success of recent Spanish television productions have demonstrated.[29] This is arguably due to the universality of its subject matter, which is always centred around inter-personal relationships, their caprices and cruelties. Feelings, emotions and the machinations of affect are foremost within the *telenovela*, as the characters are propelled through often labyrinthine and outlandish story arcs, provoking sympathy or disdain from audiences. Viewers are further guided by the Manichean morality that is another narrative constant of the *telenovela*; in this televisual universe, the central protagonists are demonstrably virtuous and the villains extravagantly villainous.

One further textual conceit of the *telenovela*, particularly relevant to post-dictatorship societies, is its focus on that which is hidden or occluded, particularly in terms of identity and past behaviours. Jenny Amaya describes this as 'el reconocimiento como esencia de la trama; el modo melodramático de representación es siempre "el drama de la virtud" menospreciada, "hecha visible y reconocida"' [recognition as the essence of the plot; the melodramatic mode of representation is always "the drama of the virtue of truth" underappreciated, "made visible and recognized".][30] In the Southern Cone, where the transition from dictatorship to democracy has been dominated by a search for the truth of the crimes committed by the state against its citizens, the narrative motor of *anagnorisis* inherent within the *telenovela* genre has made it the perfect vehicle for dramatic explorations of the recent past. Within Greek tragedy, *anagnorisis* occurs when a character uncovers their truth of their identity or circumstances, thus moving from a state of ignorance to one of knowledge and self-awareness. The 1992 Brazilian telenovela *Años Rebeldes* [Rebel Years], produced by the Globo television network, was 'the first serial drama ever to portray the political violence and repression that took place under the military regime'.[31] Despite critical reviews in the press and the controversy over alleged censorship, the series attracted over thirty million viewers. In Argentina, it was over a decade later that the first *telenovela* to deal with the legacy of *el Proceso* appeared. In 2006, the human rights organization Asociación Abuelas de Plaza de Mayo collaborated extensively with Telefe in the production of the serial *Montecristo: Un Amor, Una Venganza* [Montecristo: Love and Revenge], a *telenovela* whose protagonist Laura comes to realise that she is the child of *desaparecidos*, appropriated and illegally adopted by a family with connections to the Argentine military. The producers of the series collaborated closely with the Abuelas on *Montecristo*, even filming within the Asociación's headquarters in Buenos Aires.[32] As a result, the *telenovela* depicted the challenges faced by illegally appropriated adult children with great detail and accuracy, showing the legal and scientific processes involved in the recuperation of identity, along with the psychological trauma that many such young people face. Consequently, the broadcast of *Montecristo* was accompanied by a huge increase in the number of enquiries received by the Grandmother's association from young adults concerned that they too might be the child of *desaparecidos*.[33]

For the Abuelas, this demonstrated the huge latent potential of television drama to circulate the purpose of their organization, the recuperation of over five hundred children born to disappeared parents in clandestine prisons such as the ESMA and illegally appropriated by military personnel. In 2007, the organization would again collaborate with Telefe in the production of *Televisión por la Identidad*, a serial which dramatized the cases of three young adults who recovered their identities and were reconciled with their biological families through the efforts of the Abuelas. The first episode depicted the case of Tatiana Ruarte Britos, the first child found by the grandmothers. The second instalment narrated the case of Juan Cabandié, who was born in the ESMA and recovered his identity at the age of twenty-six, whilst the third part was a fictionalized amalgam of various cases.[34] This mini-series, whilst technically not a telenovela, replicated the form, thematic motifs and melodramatic style of such productions in its depictions of the restitution of identity. It garnered a raft of plaudits from critics and audiences alike and went on to win an Emmy award in 2008 for best foreign television film or mini-series.[35] Therefore, in emplotting the stylistic motifs of the telenovela upon the personal histories of *el Proceso*, series such as *Montecristo* and *Televisión por la Identidad* constructed and disseminated innovative narratives of living history, where affect and the truth of personal experience is privileged over chronological accuracy and historical objectivity. As Amaya suggests, 'lo que está en juego en este tipo de discursos no es la verdad, sino la verisimilitud en la representación del pasado' [what is in play in this type of discourse is not the truth, but rather the verisimilitude of the representation of the past.][36]

Therefore, in combining the narrative and aesthetic traits of docudrama and the *telenovela*, *Lo que el tiempo nos dejó* clearly demarcates the boundaries of its historicist representation. Its subjective reorganization of historical events is resonant of the docudrama genre, along with its eschewal of objective historiography. Like the *telenovela*, it favours verisimilitude over historical accuracy, formulating a broader sense of historicity through its use of period *mise-en-scène*, specifically the consumer artefacts of the past and the sights and sounds, in music and television of the period. What is crucial here is not minute historical accuracy but rather 'la construcción de representaciones del pasado, desde otros principios, con otros recursos y otros verosímiles' [the construction of representations of the past, from different elements, with other resources and other probabilities.][37] The opening credits of *Lo que el tiempo nos dejó* unfold against a flickering sepia backdrop, where scratches and dark patches appear upon the screen, as if we are watching an old film reel. The following message then appears:

> 'El siguiente programa es una ficción basada en situaciones históricas, pero no documentales. Los personajes, las imágenes, los hechos y los argumentos no son reales, solo se utilizaron momentos de la historia argentina como contexto, y se versionaron, desde la ficción, algunos personajes de la vida real con fines dramáticos y argumentales, para representar diferentes sucesos de nuestra historia'.
>
> [The following programme is a fiction based upon historical occurrences, but not documentary sources. The characters, images, events and plots are not real, but rather they employ moments in Argentine history as context and they adapt, through fiction, certain specific figures from real life in order to create drama and plot and to represent different events from our history.]

Thus, from the outset, the programme explicitly recognizes its fictionality, informing the viewer that its characters, events and plots are not representative of an objective historical truth. As the opening disclaimer acknowledges, this is a fictional narrative that sacrifices 'objective' historical truth in the pursuit of an emotional connection between past and present.

This repudiation of objectivity is the final key element of the fictionscape of *Lo que el tiempo nos dejó*. That it is also a recurrent feature in the work of Felipe Pigna, who acted as historical consultant to the series, is notable. The best-selling author of more than fourteen works of national history and the presenter of numerous television and radio programmes, he has achieved 'una gran popularidad como historiador y narrador del pasado, al llevar a la pantalla chica el contenido plasmado en sus libros' [great popularity as a historian and as a narrator of the past, bringing to the small screen the subjects explored in his books.][38] In the introduction to his 2005 work, *Lo pasado pensado: entrevistas con la historia argentina (1955–1983)* [The Past Considered: Interviews with Argentine History (1955–1983)], he defines his historiographical approach, saying: 'Renuncio explícitamente a la declamada e hipócrita objetividad, proclamada y reclamada por los más obvios y subjetivos opinólogos y algunos pretendidos dueños de la historia' [I explicitly renounce that declaimed and hypocritical objectivity, proclaimed and demanded by the most obvious and subjective so-called experts and some alleged owners of history.][39] He continues, characterizing history as 'una propiedad social, colectiva, y que lo mejor que puede ocurrirnos es que mucha gente se interese por ella, la viva, la discuta, se la apropie, porque como venimos diciendo, es un patrimonio nacional' [a social, collective possession, and the best thing that can happen is that lots of people become interested in history, live history, argue over it, adapt it, because as we have been saying, it's part of our national heritage.]⁴⁰ There are significant parallels between Pigna's perspective and Samuel's notion of living history, not least the common focus on affective interpretation of the past and a shared recognition of history as a common good. In their common rejection of 'epic and grand narrative in favour of personal observation and local knowledge',⁴¹ both historians allude to the horizontalist inclinations of this form of history.

Furthermore, as the title of his 2004 work *Los mitos de la historia argentina 1* [The Myths of Argentine History 1] suggests, Pigna considers the role of the popular historian as that of truth-teller, unmasking the 'conspiracies' of orthodox historiographic narratives and presenting what has previously been occluded by hegemonic historical discourse. As Michael Goebel comments of *Algo habrán hecho por la historia argentina* [They Must Have Done Something for Argentine History], a historical docudrama co-presented by Pigna, 'one of the programme's opening statements held that "we live surrounded by lies" about Argentina's history, which the two presenters purported to rectify'.⁴² This approach and its attendant discourse of truth and revelation fits perfectly within the narrative *anagnorisis* of the *telenovela*, where, as previously discussed, the story arc is driven by movement from ignorance to knowledge. On a similar note, the final line of the opening disclaimer of *Lo que el tiempo nos dejó* describes the ultimate objective of the series as the representation of 'diferentes sucesos de nuestra historia' [different events from our history.] Within Pigna's alternative histories, the 'difference' here lies between hegemonic narratives of the past, disseminated by the state and the popular 'truth' of the past, constituted through and by the everyday lived experiences of ordinary Argentines. It is a thesis of history that has, within an Argentine context, come to be known as 'neo-revisionism' due to its echoes of the alternative school of historical thought that originated in the 1930s. Goebel summarizes this new revisionism as being

> nourished by many ideas central to revisionism, such as the notion of two Argentinas, the opinion that Argentina had been pillaged and indebted by a powerful 'oligarchy' in alliance with 'foreign', particularly British, interests or the view that Argentine history had been 'falsified' in order to 'silence' the nation's true soul and interests.⁴³

A reaction against the 'foundational fiction' of Domingo Faustino Sarmiento's 1845 text *Facundo: civilización y barbarie*, the original revisionist movement contested the dichotomous series of allegiances outlined within Sarmiento's text. In *Facundo*, as Doris Sommers explains, we see 'the initial dichotomy of civilization versus barbarism, and the ones that follow from it: the future versus the past; European versus Indians; settlers versus nomads; and generally, deliberation versus passion'.⁴⁴ From the 1930s onwards, as the national economic promise widely forecast failed to materialize, writers such as Arturo Jauretche and Manuel Gálvez began to repudiate the 'liberal' histories of statesmen such as Sarmiento and Bartolomé Mitre; instead they characterized the official institutions of state, along with the land-owning oligarchy and their confessors in the Catholic Church as the authors of the nation's decline. In the first decade of the twenty-first century, Pigna and other writers such as Mario 'Pacho' O'Donnell, incorporated some of the basic tenets of revisionism into their contemporary approach to Argentine history, creating a potent admixture of historical thought. In constructing contiguities of meaning between the civilizing project of the generation of 1837 and the Process of National Reorganization instigated by the military junta of 1976–1983, they sought to highlight the ongoing imposition of 'foreign' ideologies upon the Argentine body politic and the marginalization of what they considered as the true history of the nation.

Central to this neo-revisionist project was the creation, by presidential decree 1880/2011 on 17 November 2011, of the Instituto Nacional de Revisionismo Histórico Argentino e Iberoamericano Manuel Dorrego. According to its founding document, the Institute was established to disseminate a revitalized national history that would include the reappraisal of historical figures such as Dorrego, who had fought for and defended 'el ideario nacional y popular' in the face of 'el embate liberal y extranjerizante', that, 'en pro de sus intereses han pretendido oscurecerlos y relegarlos de la memoria colectiva del pueblo argentino' [a national and popular ideology in the face of a liberal and unpatriotic onslaught, that, in the pursuit of its own interests attempted to obscure and banish these historical figures from the collective memory of the Argentine people].[45] As one of the Institute's thirty-three honorary members, Pigna was unequivocal in his support for the organization, stating that: 'la neoacademica sigue dominada por la visión liberal, la historia oficial fundada por Bartolomé Mitre, que ignora los procesos populares. El instituto servirá para que la gente tenga otra visión de la historia' [the neo-academy continues to be dominated by a liberal vision, that of the official history established by Bartolomé Mitre, which ignores popular historical processes. The Institute will serve to provide the people with an alternative vision of history].[46] The Institute's objectives were far-reaching and highly controversial, in that it proposed a re-evaluation of which histories should be taught and represented not only in all educational institutions, but also in the realms of heritage and culture. According to the historian Camila Perochena, with the creation of the Institute Manuel Dorrego specifically, and in the broader general alignment of her government with historical neo-revisionism, President Cristina Fernández de Kirchner had three well-defined objectives: the first, to create a roadmap for action in the present that would define her term in office; secondly, 'estar al servicio de la construcción y consolidación de una identidad nacional' [to be at the service of the construction and consolidation of a national identity]; and the third, to define the Kirchner years in government as 'el mayor ciclo de desarrollo en 200 años de historia nacional' and a period of 'reparación de los daños después de tres décadas de neoliberalismo' [the most successful period of development in two hundred years of national history and as a period of redress for the damage inflicted by three decades of neoliberalism].[47]

However, this official intervention by the state in how public history should be shaped and communicated immediately generated intense controversy and prompted a flood of criticism from academics, intellectuals, and journalists. Whilst the debate often appeared to reinforce pre-existing polarizations between prominent figures from each side of the Peronist/anti-Peronist divide and to reanimate old intellectual grievances between the proponents of popular historiography, such as Pigna, and advocates of an academic approach to the past, amongst them Luis Alberto Romero and Hilda Sábato, it was also reflective of a more general, non-partisan concern around the imposition of a state-endorsed interpretation of history upon contemporary Argentine society. The risks that such a potential lack of plurality of thought and endeavour represented were highlighted in a statement by researchers at the Centro de Documentación e Investigación de la Cultura de Izquierdas (CeDInCI) [Archives and Research Centre of Cultures of the Left] in Buenos Aires, which declared that 'un Estado democrático no debería suscribir escuelas historiográficas, ni artísticas ni filosóficas, sino ser el garante de la pluralidad de todas ellas' [a democratic State should not endorse specific historiographical, artistic or philosophic schools of thought, but rather should act as guarantor of the plurality of all of them].[48]

Whilst the Institute Manuel Dorrego did organize a number of conferences and other events, it ultimately failed to achieve its ambitious objectives, and was officially closed in December 2015 by Pablo Avelluto, the incoming Minister of Culture in Mauricio Macri's newly-elected government. But the neo-revisionist approach to the national past which it espoused is highly visible in the fictionscape of *Lo que el tiempo nos dejó*, not least in the temporal structure of the series. All six episodes take place within the twentieth century, beginning in 1909 and ending in 1982. However, the series is not structured in ascending chronological order; the first episode depicts events surrounding the illness and death of Eva Perón in 1951–52, whilst the sixth and final episode narrates the assassination of Buenos Aires Chief of Police Ramón Falcón at the hands of Russian anarchist émigré Simón Radowitzky in 1909.[49] Only episodes two and three follow a linear chronology, set as they are in 1966 and 1977, during the respective dictatorships of Juan Carlos Onganía and the tripartite military junta. Episode four takes the viewer back to the 1930s and a depiction of the ill-fated love affair between the tango singer Ada Falcón and producer Francisco Canaro, a narrative which takes place during another dictatorship, the first of the twentieth century. The fifth episode is chronologically the most recent, documenting the epistolary friendship between a schoolboy and a soldier fighting in the Malvinas conflict with the United Kingdom in 1982, Each narrative is complete and self-contained and characters from one episode do not reappear in any other. The most pertinent explanation for this fractured chronology is that the series is ordered in this way in order to foster an idiosyncratically neo-revisionist fictionscape. Accordingly, the first and last episodes establish the chronological cornerstones of the historical imaginary that the series seeks to transmit. They act as a thematic frame for the series, demarcating in space and time the narrative boundaries of this historical imaginary, those watershed moments of the past which shape the present. Thus, the series begins during the apogee of the first Peronist interregnum, with Eva Perón at her most powerful politically yet ailing physically as she gradually succumbs to ovarian cancer.

Entitled 'Mi Mensaje', episode one depicts the last year of her life and her withdrawal as candidate for the vice-presidency and is focalized through the character of her nurse, Elena Campos Arrieta. Here, it is Elena's transition from apolitical daughter to radicalized independent woman that is foregrounded in the narrative, rather than the travails of Evita. As such, her experiences become a metonymic representation of the transformational potential of Peronism upon the Argentine body politic. Therefore, there is great significance in the selection of 'Mi Mensaje' as the opening episode of the serial. This is, the viewer should infer, a formative episode in the historiography of the nation and a moment in the past that continues to define the present. Likewise, the final episode 'Un mundo mejor' [A Better World], is of equal import. In its depiction of the experiences of just one amongst over four million immigrants who sailed to Argentina in search of a better life in the late nineteenth century, episode six presents an alternative vision of the birth of the modern nation.[50] Just as the old adage argues it was the Irish who built America, this narrative characterizes the masses who fled Europe in search of a better life as the creators of modern Argentina. In Radowitzky's autodidacticism and his involvement in the nascent struggle for workers' rights, we glimpse the pioneering spirit of these foreign-born Argentines who brought prosperity and hope to a nation hidebound by social hierarchies and inequality.

Returning to the material remnants of history that, as we have seen, are a central feature of the fictionscape of the series, the affective motifs of consumer ephemera, music and their placement within the home are visible in all six episodes of *Lo que el tiempo nos dejó*, to a greater or lesser degree. Each of the six episodes depicts its protagonists at home, either with their family or the network of a community. The homes featured vary widely in socio-economic status, ranging from the *conventillo*[51] of the early twentieth century to the comfortable apartments of the urban bourgeoisie of the early 1980s. Notably, in episodes one and six, the 'foundational fictions' of this particular historical fictionscape, the most prominent cultural artefacts are technological innovations that enable communication. In 'Mi mensaje', Eva Perón presents Elena with a typewriter, so that the nurse may type up the hand-written manuscript of the first lady's final memoirs. She must work on the project in secret, as her conservative parents would not approve. Eventually, her father discovers the machine and outraged at his daughter's growing independence, he destroys it. The method of destruction he employs is telling; rather than throw the typewriter out, he shoots it with a hunting rifle, obliterating the machine and destroying its communicative potential. This action attributes a cruelty and reactionary worldview to the oligarchy which Elena's father represents. In episode six, 'Un mundo mejor', Simón uses the mimeograph at the print shop where he is employed in order to produce multiple copies of a leaflet promoting a forthcoming union meeting. However, this machine is destroyed after a xenophobic gang of thugs in the pay of Colonel Falcón break into the print shop. In contrast to those who smash up these innovative machines, in both Elena and Simón, we are presented with characters who are proficient in their use and, as such, embody 'la modernidad, el desarollo y el dinamismo' [modernity, development and dynamism.][52] In the historicist fictionscape of the series, those who seek to free themselves from authoritarian structures, whether in the home or in society more generally, epitomize the true spirit of the nation.

In episode two, 'La ley primera' [The First Law], the consumer artefacts of 1960s counterculture are used to connote the intellectual utopianism that prevailed amongst the staff and students of the University of Buenos Aires, until the intervention of the military government in July 1966.[53] Leo, a young man from rural Junín, comes to the capital to study at the Faculty of Exact Sciences under the tutelage of Manuel Sadowsky, a world-renowned scientist and the creator of the country's first computer. On the first day of his studies, he encounters fellow students Nina and Mónica, dancing languorously to American pop music in the student common room. These are modern girls, dressed in the fashionable miniskirts and eyeliner of the era. They are confident, politically aware and avid readers of Jean-Paul Sartre and Arthur Rimbaud. Leo finds a similar confidence and inquisitorial spirit in the rest of his university peer group; they are all intelligent young people eager for knowledge and through their philosophical discussions, they articulate a faith in progress and modernization. From the clothes they wear to the texts they read, the students embody a new Argentina, an emerging generation of 'champions of modernity and privileged consumers of its products'.[54] Furthermore, academic texts are not the only tool these young people employ to broaden their perceptions. Recreational drugs are everywhere and in one comic scene, we see Leo and Nina attending a lecture high on LSD, wide-eyed and with an apparently heightened sensitivity to knowledge.

However, it quickly becomes apparent that the autonomous university is a utopian enclave, a 'democratic island in a country that was ever less so'.[55] The military government of Onganía, personified in the character of General Fontana, is increasingly concerned with the radical ideas disseminated by the institution and in a recreation of the incident that would become known as 'La noche de los bastones largos' [Night of the Long Sticks], armed forces storm the faculty.[56] Trapped in the library and fearful of the advancing soldiers, Mónica, Nina and other students attempt to defend themselves with the only weapons at hand, the books that surround them. In a melodramatic analogy of the struggle between reason and violence, the students bombard the soldiers with books but to no avail. Here books, and by extension knowledge and reason, become arms against the brutality and conservatism of the authoritarian regime. This scene gains further currency of meaning when considered alongside the innovative history of the publishing house Eudeba, established by the University of Buenos Aires in 1958.[57] As Luis Alberto Romero asserts, 'what was singular about Eudeba was its combination of a policy of aggressive marketing and innovation — cheap books sold at newsstands in the city streets — placed in the service of the dissemination of the latest advances in the sciences'.[58] Its success in this attempt to transmit the knowledge cultivated within the university to a wider public is demonstrated in the sales it achieved: three million books were sold in the period 1959 to 1962 alone. That these books now serve no other purpose than makeshift missiles is a portent of things to come, since the destruction of this utopian community was the first salvo in the campaign of censorship and repression that the Onganía regime would enforce. With censorship 'extended to all manifestations of new fashions, from the miniskirt to long hair',[59] the clothes so favoured by Nina and Mónica would become unwearable.

Therefore, in 'La ley primera', the material artefacts of the past become metonymic signifiers of a struggle between social freedom and an encroaching authoritarianism. As the episode concludes, in captions which overlay archive news footage of these events, Pigna asserts:

> La noche nefasta del 29 de Julio de 1966 fue ideada por el dictador Onganía y sus secuaces. Se llevaron a 200 personas detenidas, los prisioneros sufrieron vejaciones y simulacros de fusilamiento. Por órdenes de Washington comenzaba a impartirse en la Argentina y en América Latina la doctrina de la seguridad nacional, aceptada con mucho gusto por los gobernantes locales, intelectuales y financistas de turno. La lucha conjunta de trabajadores y estudiantes iba a dar resultados y a Onganía y sus socios se les iba a terminar su dictadura porque una sociedad harta de noches y bastones comenzó a destruir sus objetivos y a emplazarlo.
>
> [The terrible night of 29 July 1966 was devised by the dictator Onganía and his henchmen. Two hundred people were arrested, and the prisoners suffered ill-treatment and mock executions. On the orders of Washington and the White House, the doctrine of national security began to circulate in Argentina and in Latin America, and was accepted enthusiastically by the local politicians, intellectuals and financiers of the moment. The united struggle of workers and students would bear fruit and bring about the destruction of the dictatorship of Onganía and his associates, as a society tired of nights and sticks began to destroy the objectives of the regime and to organize itself collectively.]

Within the historicist fictionscape of *Lo que el tiempo nos dejó*, the social and cultural freedoms of the 1960s, epitomized by the miniskirts and eyeliner of Nina and Mónica and the philosophical texts of Sartre, are thwarted by a conservative and undemocratic establishment, in league with the Cold War ideologies of the United States. But according to the closing text, collective action by workers and students would eventually undermine the Onganía regime and precipitate a return to democracy. Thus, the material artefacts of this episode are symbolic of a watershed moment in the historical imaginary. Here the utopian ideals of progress and modernity espoused by the students are temporarily suppressed by a military regime dedicated to the preservation of traditional Christian values. In Pigna's closing comments, we glimpse the enduring resonance of 'la noche de los bastones largos' within the neo-revisionist fictionscape, as a historiographic reference point replete with meaning. But it is also a portent of things to come, as less than a decade later, the repressive ideologies enacted in this episode would return in the much more brutal incarnation of *el Proceso*.

It is significant then, that the episode which follows is set only eleven years later, during the second year of another military dictatorship. Such temporal proximity reflects a genealogy of meaning between the two historical periods, an inferred causality linking the repression of 1966 to the much greater cruelty that *el Proceso* would unleash upon the Argentine body politic. Furthermore, in episode three, entitled 'La caza del ángel' [The Angel's Hunt], we encounter another prominent example of the materialist leitmotif that embeds significance within the everyday artefacts of the past. Set in 1977, the episode depicts one of the most notorious acts of Task Force 3.3.2, a group of naval officers that operated out of the

Fig. 4.4. Still from the opening scenes of 'La caza del ángel'; the first time we see the mothers searching for their children. Image: Telefe Argentina.

Fig. 4.5. The mothers in their outdoor clothing. Image: Telefe Argentina.

clandestine detention centre at the ESMA.[60] Posing as the relative of a *desaparecido*, navy Lieutenant Alfredo Astiz infiltrated the nascent Madres de Plaza de Mayo organization, whose activities in raising awareness of the junta's human rights abuses were beginning to cause concern in military circles, particularly since the country was due to host the Football World Cup the following year. After gathering intelligence on key figures within the group, Astiz co-ordinated the abduction of twelve of its members from the Santa Cruz church in central Buenos Aires on

8 December 1977.⁶¹ This particular episode exemplifies the inherent historical subjectivity of the fictionscape of *Lo que el tiempo nos dejó*, in that, for the purposes of narrative affect and cohesion, the names of the protagonists have been changed and certain historical details altered.

We first see the mothers in a series of brief, close-up camera shots, pleading through the screen doors of different houses for any scrap of information the residents may have about their disappeared children (Fig. 4.4). They are dressed plainly, in cardigans, coats and scarves, with several of the women wearing their aprons and housecoats under their outdoor clothing. In their somewhat drab, workaday garments, their ordinariness is striking. These clothes are not high-fashion, nor the height of the distinctive chic of the 1970s. As the episode progresses, we see the same coats and cardigans being worn indoors and out, as the women trek from one meeting place to another and then home again (Fig. 4.5). Even when they meet inside, with Father Rogelio from the local church or in a café to discuss their progress, the women do not remove their outdoor clothing. Rather, they often gather their coats tightly around them, in what appears as a protective gesture against the pain and suffering that surrounds them. Indeed, even in the private space of the family home, the protagonist Mabel is only seen twice without her heavy cardigan; once in a flashback scene in conversation with her daughter and later, in her nightdress as she talks with her husband before bed.

Here, these everyday items of clothing are used to denote the arduous efforts of this group of women in their search for their lost children, a struggle that has become synonymous with the quest for 'memoria, verdad y justicia' in Argentina over the past four decades. They do not remove their outdoor clothing because, simply, they are always outdoors, in the streets and squares, in an incessant search for any clue to their relatives' whereabouts. Theirs are lives consumed by loss and their suffering is further compounded by the wall of silence that greets their enquiries. It is only through constant activity, knocking at doors, gathering names for a petition and meeting with the priest that they cope with this burden of absence. In the final scenes, we see Mabel, who only by chance escaped abduction at the church, now accompanied by numerous other women in the Plaza de Mayo, reading aloud a declaration of their mission to find their disappeared children. A police officer approaches and instructs the women to disperse. But instead of leaving the square, they begin to walk around the Pirámide de Mayo, continuing to read aloud as they do so. The camera focuses on their feet and the slow rhythm of their walk as they circle the monument. In a series of visual segues between this dramatic reconstruction and newsreel footage, it is the shoes of the women that are featured most prominently (Fig. 4.6).

Circling the monument in their comfortable footwear, these women are now recognizable as the Madres, commencing their 'caminatas semanales de vigilia alrededor de la plaza, en las que llevan pancartas con las fotografías de sus hijos desaparecidos y la inquietante pregunta «¿dónde están?»' [long weekly vigil walks around the square, in which they hold up placards featuring photographs of their disappeared children and the disturbing question, 'where are they?']⁶²

Fig. 4.6. The mothers begin their *ronda* of the Plaza de Mayo. Image: Telefe Argentina

The primary functionality of footwear is to facilitate movement. In the closing sequence of the episode, the shoes of the Madres are linked inextricably to the thousands of steps they have taken around the Plaza de Mayo, undeterred by the slander or threats of violence directed at them by the military junta. Their constant activity, which began as a search for disappeared loved ones during *el Proceso* and broadened into an epoch-defining movement for human rights following the transition to democracy, defines them, as Beatriz Sarlo has asserted, as 'sujetos en acción' [subjects in action.][63] Whilst it is usually their emblematic headscarves that are commonly used as visual shorthand for the campaigning work of the Madres, in this episode the women are not seen wearing the head garments until the final scene, set in 2010. This is historically anomalous, since it was during a pilgrimage to the shrine of the Virgin of Luján in late 1976, in their first organized denunciation of their children's abduction, that the group began the practice of wearing white headscarves.[64] Resembling the cloth nappies their children had used in infancy, the headwear symbolized both their loss and their status as mothers. However, what 'La caza del ángel' and its focus upon the unremarkable shoes and coats worn by the women seeks to recuperate is the inherent ordinariness of these mothers and their collective solidarity before they gained international support as the Madres de Plaza de Mayo. In his closing comments, Pigna discusses 'el secuestro y la desaparición de un grupo de valientes mujeres argentinas' [the kidnapping and disappearance of a group of brave Argentine women] and goes on to describe the women as 'un ejemplo de coraje, perseverancia y dignidad, reconocido en todo el mundo' [an example of courage, tenacity and dignity, recognized the world over]. In its portrayal of the origins of this group of 'brave Argentine women', who would come to symbolize resistance against the military dictatorship, this episode endows the events with a symbolic significance. Within the historicist fictionscape of *Lo que el tiempo nos dejó*, the 'courage, perseverance and dignity' of the Mothers is represented by the material artefacts they wore in enacting their resistance against death, silence and impunity.

Set in 1982, 'Los niños que escriben en el cielo' [The Children Who Write in the Sky], is the fifth episode and aesthetically the richest of the series in the volume of consumer ephemera it depicts. With often garishly bright camera filters, we see the early 1980s in all its technicolour glory. The clothes are vividly coloured, as is the interior decoration of the apartment where nine-year-old Javier lives with his parents. This is an aspirational family, whose living accommodation is bright and modern, decked out in primary colours. Javier's father is a record producer and his financial success is reflected in the modern gadgets of this family home, from the labour-saving devices of the kitchen to the audio-visual equipment of the living room. As the events of the Malvinas conflict between Argentina and the United Kingdom unfold, it is through these electronic artefacts, most prominently the television, that information on the conflict is diegetically inserted into the dramatic narrative. Through news bulletins, government information films and the 24-hour telethon organized to raise funds for Argentine troops in the theatre of conflict, we see the combined efforts of the military regime and the media to galvanize support for the war.

But it is the vinyl records and cassette tapes of the period that feature most prominently in the historicist meaning that episode five attempts to construct. Just as television is the favoured propaganda tool of the military junta, the record player in Javier's family home and his father's vinyl collection are objects which emit an alternative discourse of resistance and hope. As an industry professional, Javier's father Nicolás sees an opportunity to raise the profile of Argentine popular music following the banning of English-language songs on radio and television by the military junta. As Pablo Vila asserts, 'for *rock nacional* the seizure of the Malvinas and the consequent decision of the authorities not to transmit any more music in English meant the chance to secure massive coverage in the audio-visual media which until then had denied it space'.[65] Thus, the home-grown musical movement that had grown out of the folk boom of the mid-1960s provided artists such as Charly García, Luis Spinetta and León Gieco with a discursive arena in which to question the institutions of *el Proceso* and, latterly, its military incursions over the Malvinas.[66]

Javier, shocked by the limited musical tastes of a female classmate and eager to impress her, creates a compilation tape of classic songs from the *rock nacional* canon, and we see him lounging by the record player as he selects the tracks (Fig. 4.7.). His labours are accompanied by a soundtrack of the 1982 hit by Pedro y Pablo, 'La gente del futuro'. Its up-tempo drumbeat and general jaunty sound belie its lyrical indictment of the military regime and the values of consumerism and self-interest that it has engendered. In the first chorus, the song demands: '¿Y dónde están ahora los filósofos críticos/Tiñendo sus palabras de intereses políticos?' [And where are the critical philosophers now?/Tingeing their words with political concerns?] According to this musical narrative, the nation has become contaminated by the economic discourse of the corrupt military government and its privileging of material success over solidarity and compassion, leaving a generation of Argentines

Fig. 4.7. Javier puts together a compilation of his favourite *rock nacional* songs in episode 5 of *Lo que el tiempo nos dejó*. Image: Telefe Argentina.

with no future. In 'éste presente tan tan duro' [this present that's so hard], the song seeks out those who have the integrity and hope to lead the country out of its present crisis, since it states, 'Tenemos que hacernos un mundo mejor/ Porque éste está enfermo y nosotros no' [We have to make a better world for ourselves/ Because this one is sick and we are not.][67]

The lyrics articulate a common bond between singer and listener, who, it is inferred, share the same values. Indeed, it is this sense of opposition to a rotten status quo, present in each of the six episodes of *Lo que el tiempo nos dejó*, that rock *nacional* articulates so vividly. Vila describes the musical genre as a 'counter-cultural movement' which 'functions as an ideology of everyday life; it generates forms of participation which are alternative in character; [...] and it shapes its own identity in opposition to the authoritarian and anti-democratic powers which define it as one of their enemies'.[68] In the final moments of 'Los niños que escriben en el cielo', in his closing message, Pigna denounces the Malvinas conflict as 'una guerra por una causa justa liderada por los más injustos comandantes' [a war in support of a just cause, led by the most injust of commanders]. He continues, describing the legacy of *el Proceso* as 'una guerra perdida, un país en ruinas con decenas de miles de desaparecidos, el aparato productivo casi destruido, chicos con hambre y la deuda externa multiplicada por cinco' [a war lost, a country in ruins with tens of thousands of disappeared people, national manufacturing almost destroyed, hungry children and the national deficit increased five times over.] Here, the historian asserts an explicit connection between the injustices of the recent past and the inequalities of contemporary society, condemning the social and economic legacy of the dictatorship. Pigna concludes by saying: 'se llevaron todo, pero no pudieron robarnos la esperanza de volver a vivir dignamente y con libertad' [they took everything, but they couldn't rob us of the hope of living, once again, in dignity and freedom]. In other words, despite the atrocities of history, which the series has laid bare, the Argentine people will continue to oppose injustice and cruelty in the hope of creating a better future for themselves and the country. In its use of a *rock nacional* soundtrack and its depiction of the now obsolete cultural artefacts of popular music such as the record player, cassette tapes and vinyl discs 'Los niños que escriben en el cielo' reinforces the key elements of this broader historicist fictionscape, once again foregrounding the everyday and its subjective histories in its depiction of significant historical events.

The fourth episode in the series is also dominated by music, since it is set in the tango clubs of Buenos Aires in the 1930s and depicts the torrid love affair between singer Ada Falcón and producer Francisco Canaro. No history of the Argentine twentieth century would be complete without some reference to this quintessentially *porteño* musical genre and its mournful laments. Yet 'Te quiero' [I Want You] sits uneasily within the series, for two main reasons. Firstly, as certain commentators have noted, Pigna's closing description of the tango genre as 'un canal de expresión del sufrimiento y la lucha de las clases populares' [a conduit for the expression of suffering and the struggle of the working class][69] is at odds with the glamourous and apparently apolitical milieu of fame and celebrity in which the episode is set. Historian Daniel James, writing of the cultural significance of the tango during this decade, asserts that it was 'cada vez más una forma de arte comercializado cuya conexión con el 'barrio' de trabajadores era tenue' [an increasingly commercialized art form that had a tenuous connection with the 'barrio' and the workers.][70] Therefore, Pigna's closing assertions are rendered somewhat anomalous by the preceding dramatic narrative. More significantly, however, this episode is at odds with the historical imaginary that the rest of the series seeks to cultivate. It depicts a relationship between two famous tango artists, both of whom are wealthy and enjoy all the material trappings of success. They have little in common with the ordinary people on which the five other episodes focus. Given their financial status, the objects with which Falcón and Canaro surround themselves are luxury items: fast cars, furs and jewels rather than the common artefacts of everyday life. As Dadamo, Della Mora and Piccinelli highlight in their assessment of this episode, whilst Pigna's closing comments refer to 'gobiernos infames que se desentendían de los dramas de las mayorías' [odious governments that want nothing to do with the dramas of the population], there is little socio-political critique within the narrative.[71] Unlike the other episodes, 'Te quiero' is an unadorned romantic melodrama, which fails to connect the historical period it depicts to the broader thematic concerns of the historicist fictionscape that the series as a whole encodes. It resonates with the melodramatic sensibilities of the *telenovela*. But without the guiding quotidian ethos or the general neo-revisionist outlook that permeates the other episodes, 'Te quiero' appears isolated and contradictory.

A far more successful example of music as socio-political signifier appears in 'La ley primera', in its depiction of the assembled students' spontaneous rendition of the Argentine national anthem. Gathered together in a lecture theatre with their tutor Professor Sadowsky, the students await the latest developments in the conflict

Fig. 4.8. The students sing the national anthem in episode 2 of *Lo que el tiempo nos dejó*. Image: Telefe Argentina.

between the university and the military government. Realizing that a military takeover of the campus is imminent, having heard the footsteps of the approaching soldiers, they defiantly begin to sing the anthem, finding solace in this communal act. As they sing the opening lines, we hear the refrain familiar to all Argentines: 'Oíd, mortales, el grito sagrado: ¡Libertad! ¡Libertad! ¡Libertad!' [Mortals, hear the sacred cry! Freedom! Freedom! Freedom!] The students' rendition of the second line is almost crazed in its ferocity; they bellow the words with all their might, stamping their feet and gesticulating wildly (Fig. 4.8.).

For this generation of young people, their version of the anthem connotes freedom of thought and expression, contrary to the conservative and reactionary worldview of the Onganía regime. As they sing, we see the serried ranks of the troops assemble outside, awaiting their orders to storm the building and put down the student uprising. As with much of the narrative of this episode, this scene is a portent of the future to come: the revolutionary struggles of the late 1960s and early 1970s and the military response to the apparent threat of subversion, which will result in the disappearance, death or exile of many of this generation of Argentines. Yet in their singing of the national anthem, the students assert their own singular vision of *argentinidad*, in the face of violence and repression.

An interesting addendum to this scene is the fact that Charly García, one of the most iconic proponents of *rock nacional*, would in 1990 record the national anthem for his album 'Filosofía barata y zapatos de goma' [Cheap Philosophy and Rubber Shoes].[72] Responding to the controversy generated by his idiosyncratic cover version, García commented: 'Quiero decir que las tres libertades, una soy yo. No me excluyan más de las libertades. Soy parte de una generación que es libertad y que se la tiene bien ganada. Así que no me digan cómo hay que cantar el Himno'. [What

I mean is that of the three freedoms in the anthem, one is mine. They don't get to exclude me from these freedoms anymore. I'm part of a generation that is freedom and for whom that freedom was hard won. So, don't tell me how the national anthem should be sung.]⁷³ For García, as for the students of 'La ley primera', the anthem has a personal political significance of opposition and dissent, alongside its function as a hymn to collective national identity.

As we have seen the television mini-series *Lo que el tiempo nos dejó* is a text of living history which reconstructs the past for consumption in the present, privileging verisimilitude over historical objectivity in its affective depiction of several carefully-chosen events from the Argentine twentieth century. The selection of historical events narrated, the primacy of material artefacts and the adoption of the melodramatic *anagnorisis* of the *telenovela* all facilitate access to the wider system of historical meanings that the series assembles in its fictionscape. This epistemic infrastructure illuminates not only the past it seeks to represent, but also the present in which it was created, highlighting the broader structure of feeling that underlies its composition. Whilst *horizontalidad* is not pre-eminent in the narratives of *Lo que el tiempo nos dejó*, it is present in its ethos of living history, where an alternative historiography of ordinary Argentines is told through everyday settings, routines and possessions. As a work of living history, it is testament to 'the imaginative dislocations which take place when historical knowledge is transferred from one learning circuit to another'.⁷⁴

'Vile Bodies', the fifth and final chapter, examines the historicist sensibilities and the horizontalist potential of Carlos Gamerro's 2004 novel *La aventuras de los bustos de Eva*. It is a literary narrative that satirizes the earnest political militancy of the Argentine armed left in the period immediately preceding the 1976 coup d'état. In its grotesque representations of this chaotic period in history, the novel combines a revitalized historicism with a strident horizontalist impetus. Once again, it is the dialogue between these two discursive forces that is central to an interpretation of the novel.

## Notes to Chapter 4

1. As mentioned previously, the Kirchners were in government for three consecutive terms, beginning in 2003 with the election of Néstor Kirchner as President of Argentina. He served one term and in 2007, his wife, Cristina Fernández de Kirchner, was elected as president. She was re-elected in 2011 and stood again in 2015 but was defeated by Mauricio Macri. Néstor Kirchner died in 2010. On 27 October 2019, Cristina Fernández de Kirchner was elected as Vice-President of Argentina, with Alberto Fernández (no relation) as President, in a victory for the centre-left Peronist party Frente de Todos.
2. Marcelo Brodsky, *Nexo: un ensayo fotográfico de Marcelo Brodsky*, ed. by Marcelo Brodsky (Buenos Aires: La Marca, 2001), pp. 38–41.
3. Andreas Huyssen, 'The Mnemonic Art of Marcelo Brodsky', in Brodsky, *Nexo*, pp. 7–11.
4. Jens Andermann, 'Returning to the Site of Horror', *Theory, Culture & Society*, 29:1 (2012), pp. 76–98 (p. 83).
5. *Nunca Mas*, p. 17.
6. Cara Levey, *Fragile Memory, Shifting Impunity: Commemoration and Contestation in Post-dictatorship Argentina and Uruguay* (Oxford: Peter Lang, 2016), p. 157.
7. Testimony of the wife of Jorge Eduardo Alday, in *Nunca Mas*, p. 17.

8. Lila Pastoriza, 'El lugar de las cosas robadas', in Brodsky, *Nexo,* pp. 42–45 (p. 42).
9. Benjamin, *Arcades Project*, p. 9.
10. Pastoriza, 'El lugar', in Brodsky, *Nexo*, p. 43.
11. Brodsky, 'El pañol', in *Nexo*, p. 39.
12. *Nunca Mas*, p. 285.
13. Sosa, *Queering Acts of Mourning*, p. 22.
14. José Pablo Feinmann, cited in Nerea Arruti, 'Tracing the Past: Marcelo Brodsky's Photography as Memory Art', *Paragraph*, 30:1 (2007), 101–20, (p. 107).
15. Pastoriza, 'El lugar', in Brodsky, *Nexo*, p. 42.
16. Brodsky, Nexo, p. 44.
17. Joe Moran, 'History, Memory and the Everyday', *Rethinking History*, 8:1 (2004), 51–68, (p. 57).
18. Avelar, *Untimely Present*, p. 2.
19. For information on the ratings achieved by each episode of the mini-series, see Florencia Dadamo, Leandro Della Mora and Mariana Piccinelli, 'Historia, memoria y el recurso audiovisual: las narraciones del pasado en la televisión argentina actual', in *La ficción histórica en la televisión iberoamericana 2000–2012*, ed., María de los Ángeles Rodríguez Cadena (Leiden: Brill Rodopi, 2016), pp. 90–126, (p. 93).
20. José Carlos Rueda Laffond and Amparo Guerra Gómez, 'Televisión y nostalgia. *The Wonder Years* y *Cuéntame cómo pasó*', *Revista Latina de Comunicación Social*, 64 (2009), 396–409, (p. 397).
21. Williams, *Long Revolution*, p. 68.
22. Raphael Samuel, *Theatres of Memory: Past and Present in Contemporary Culture* (London: Verso, 2012), p. 196.
23. Ibid.
24. James Young, *The Texture of Memory: Holocaust Memorials and Meaning* (New Haven, CT: Yale University Press, 1993), p. 147.
25. Milly Buonanno, 'Conceptos clave para el story-telling televisivo. Calidad, mediación, ciudadanía'. *Diálogos de la Comunicación*, 64 (2002), 76–85, (p. 77).
26. Tobias Ebbrecht, 'Docudramatizing History on TV: German and British docudrama and historical event television in the memorial year 2005', *European Journal of Cultural Studies*, 10:1 (2007), 35–53, (p. 35).
27. Ibid., p. 45.
28. Jenny Amaya, 'La pantalla *nos* recuerda: la construcción de la memoria cultural en la telenovela cubana', in *La ficción histórica en la televisión iberoamericana*, ed. by María de los Ángeles Rodríguez Cadena (Leiden: Brill Rodopi, 2016), pp. 64–89, (p. 67).
29. For an examination of the *telenovela* genre and it relocation to the Iberian television marketplace, see Mar Chicharro Merayo, 'Telenovelas and Society: Constructing and Reinforcing the Nation through Television Fiction', *European Journal of Cultural Studies*, 16:2 (2012), 211–25.
30. Amaya, 'La pantalla', p. 69.
31. Rebecca J. Atencio, 'A Prime Time to Remember: Memory Merchandising in Globo's *Años Rebeldes*', in *Accounting for Violence: Marketing Memory in Latin America*, ed. by Ksenija Bilbija and Leigh A. Payne (Durham, NC: Duke University Press, 2011), pp. 41–68, (p. 42).
32. Martín Sueldo, '*Montecristo*: Telenovela y derechos humanos', *Studies in Latin American Popular Culture*, 30 (2012), 180–93, (p. 189).
33. Sueldo, '*Montecristo*', p. 189.
34. Ibid., p. 191
35. Ibid., p. 191.
36. Amaya, 'La pantalla', p. 68.
37. Amaya, 'La pantalla', p. 68.
38. Dadamo, Della Mora and Piccinelli, 'Historia', p. 94.
39. Felipe Pigna, *Lo pasado pensado: entrevistas con la historia argentina* (Buenos Aires: Planeta, 2011), p. 12.
40. Ibid.
41. Samuel, *Theatres*, p. 196.
42. Michael Goebel, *Argentina's Partisan Past: Nationalism and the Politics of History* (Liverpool: Liverpool University Press, 2011), p. 216.

43. Goebel, *Argentina's Partisan Past*, p. 216.
44. Doris Sommers, *Foundational Fictions: The National Romances of Latin America* (Berkeley: University of California Press, 1991), p. 63.
45. Decreto 1880/2011, Secretaria de Cultura — Créase el Instituto Nacional de Revisionismo Histórico Argentino e Iberoamericano Manuel Dorrego, Boletín Oficial 21/11/2011.
46. *Clarín*, Editorial, 'El Kirchnerismo impulsa una nueva corriente revisionista', 26 November 2011, accessed 21 October 2020 <https://www.clarin.com/politica/construccion-relato-traslada-hechos-historia_0_r14UZ4q3w7x.html>
47. Camila Perochena, 'La historia en la política y las políticas en la historia: Batalla cultural y revisionismo histórico en los discursos de Cristina Fernández de Kirchner (2007–2015), *Prohistoria*, 33 (2020) pp. 233–63 (p. 243; p. 260).
48. CeDInCI, Boletín electrónico, núm. 25, diciembre 2014. Cited in Perochena, 'La historia', p. 251.
49. For a general history of the twentieth century in Argentina and the events depicted in the series, see Luis Alberto Romero, *Argentina in the Twentieth Century* (University Park: University of Pennsylvania Press, 2002).
50. Eleni Kefala, 'Borges and Nationalism: Urban Myth and Nation-Dreaming in the 1920s', *Journal of Iberian and Latin American Studies*, 17:1 (2011), 33–58, (p. 35). As Kefala explains, 'in the period between 1857 and 1914, 3,300,000 immigrants entered Argentina through the port of Buenos Aires'.
51. The *conventillo* was a shared lodging house or tenement building, usually arranged around a central courtyard that was a common form of accommodation for the urban working-class of Buenos Aires in the nineteenth and early twentieth centuries. It was an affordable but basic type of lodging, where tenants lived in private rooms and shared the communal spaces of the courtyard, washing facilities and toilet and kitchen. A description of the *conventillos* can be found in Romero, *Argentina*, p. 11.
52. Dadamo, Della Mora and Piccinelli, 'Historia', p. 122.
53. See Romero, *Argentina*, pp. 173–75. The title of episode two, 'La ley primera', is of historicist significance, in that it is a quotation from Chapter 32 of José Hernandez's epic text *La vuelta de Martín Fierra*, first published in 1872.
54. Romero, *Argentina*, p. 164
55. Romero, *Argentinam*, p. 164.
56. Goebel, *Argentina's Partisan Past*, p. 147.
57. Romero, *Argentina*, p. 165.
58. Ibid.
59. Romero, *Argentina*, p. 165.
60. Levey, *Fragile Memory*, p. 157.
61. For a full account of these events, and of Astiz's role in these and other disappearances, see Uki Goñi, *El infiltrado: Astiz, las Madres y el Herald* (Buenos Aires: Ariel, 2018).
62. Federico Lorenz and Peter Winn, 'Las memorias de la violencia política y la dictadura militar en la Argentina: un recorrido en el año del Bicentenario', in *No hay mañana sin ayer: batallas por la memoria histórica en el Cono Sur*, ed. by Peter Winn (Santiago: Lom, 2014), pp. 19–120 (p. 67).
63. Beatriz Sarlo, *La audacia y el cálculo: Kirchner 2003–2010* (Buenos Aires: Sudamericana, 2011), p. 185.
64. Kaiser, *Postmemories of Terror*, p. 319.
65. Pablo Vila and Paul Cammack, 'Rock Nacional and Dictatorship in Argentina', *Popular Music* 6:2 (1987), 129–48 (p. 141).
66. Pablo Semán, Pablo Vila and Cecilia Benedetti, 'Neoliberalism and Rock in the Popular Sectors of Contemporary Argentina', in *Rockin' las Américas: The Global Politics of Rock in Latin/o America*, ed. by Deborah Pacini Hernández, Héctor Fernández L'Hoeste and Eric Zolov (Pittsburgh, PA: University of Pittsburgh Press, 2004), pp. 261–89 (p. 266).
67. For the complete lyrics of Pedro y Pablo, 'La gente del futuro', see <http://www.musica.com/letras.asp?letra=849703> [accessed 10 November 2016].
68. Vila and Cammack, 'Rock Nacional and Dictatorship in Argentina' pp. 129–30.

69. Dadamo, Della Mora and Piccinelli, 'Historia', p. 109.
70. Daniel James, *Resistencia e integración: el Peronismo en la clase trabajadora, Argentina 1946–1976* (Buenos Aires: Sudamericana, 1990), p. 107.
71. Dadamo, Della Mora and Piccinelli, 'Historia', p. 109
72. Mara Favoretto, *Charly en el país de las alegorías: un viaje por las letras de Charly García* (Buenos Aires: Gourmet Musical, 2014), p. 146.
73. Favoretto, *Charly*, p. 146.
74. Samuel, *Theatres*, p. 8.

CHAPTER 5

# Vile Bodies:
# The Grotesqueries of History

Eva Péron, señores, está más viva que nunca.
[Eva Péron, gentleman, is more alive than ever.]
— Copi

As observed in earlier chapters, much of the historicist discourse to emerge in the cultural realm following the *Argentinazo* centred around the primacy of space, the built environment and material artefacts. In these topographical and haptic traces of the past, the potentiality of history is to be found in landscapes, buildings and objects, since these tangible remnants encode a palpable contiguity between the past and the present. The final chapter of this thesis will examine another text which centres its historicist explorations around the material: the 2004 satirical novel *La aventura de los bustos de Eva* by Carlos Gamerro. Set in 1975, against the backdrop of social unrest and political violence which dominated the short-lived administration of Isabel Perón, Gamerro's text is a carnivalesque romp which narrates the efforts of a hapless business executive to satisfy the outlandish ransom demands of the leftist urban guerrillas who have kidnapped his employer. Replete with grotesque iterations of the populist socio-political imaginary of the 1970s, the novel destabilizes the sacralized notions of the past that had come to proliferate in the years immediately before and after the 2001 Crisis. By employing recent interpretations of Mikhail Bakhtin's concepts of grotesque realism and the carnivalesque, Chapter 5 probes the significance of this little-studied novel in the post-Crisis period and its contribution to the foundation of a new form of ludic historicist discourse, pregnant with the emancipatory potential of horizontalism.

In *La aventura de los bustos de Eva*, our unlikely hero and narrator is Ernesto Marroné, chief of procurement at the large industrial conglomerate of Tamerlán and Sons.[1] The year is 1975 and the company is in a state of disarray following the kidnapping of its president, Fausto Tamerlán, by revolutionary Peronist guerrillas, the Montoneros. It is Marroné who is assigned with obtaining a crucial part of the ransom demanded by the revolutionaries in exchange for the safe release of their captive: namely, ninety-two plaster busts of their political muse and former first lady of Argentina, Eva Perón. According to the guerrillas' demands, in tribute to her, the sculptures are to be placed in prominent positions throughout each of the company's factories and offices. However, from the outset, Marroné's quest is frustrated by the internecine conflict between various Peronist factions from across the broad political spectrum of the Justicialist movement, a struggle which threatens to engulf civil society. Unwittingly, he becomes embroiled in industrial action at the plasterworks he visits to procure the busts, triggering a chain of events that render him a fugitive from justice. Along the way, he seeks refuge in an adjacent *villa miseria*, stumbles upon an Eva Perón-themed brothel for oligarchs and finally finds the statues he seeks in a collection maintained by a kindly old Peronist in a town designed in Evita's own image. Thus, *Los bustos de Eva* is a picaresque tale of adventure and self-enlightenment, in which our narrator's faith in free-market capitalism is constantly challenged by his encounters with the militant cadres of revolutionary Peronism.

However, despite its iconoclastic ethos and the high comedy of its prose, this text, as with the four other novels that constitute Gamerro's literary corpus, is relatively neglected amongst studies of contemporary Argentine fiction, with much recent scholarship focusing instead upon the autofictional narratives of the generation of authors whose parents were disappeared or exiled during the last military dictatorship. In a recent monograph on the autofictional turn in post-dictatorship cultural production, Jordana Blejmar asserts that Gamerro's novels present a limited historicist focus, in comparison with autofictional texts such as Mariana Eva Perez's *Diario de una princesa montonera — 110% Verdad* [Diary of a Montonera Princess — 110% True](2012) and Ernesto Semán's *Soy un bravo piloto de la nueva China* [I Am a Brave Pilot from New China] (2011), both of which, she argues, engage with the totality of 'the rites and institutions of post-dictatorship memory and reparation'.[2] Echoing previous assertions by Martín Kohan,[3] Blejmar classifies Gamerro's works alongside the comedy of Bombita Rodríguez and his alter-ego 'El Palito Ortega Montonero' and the satirical magazine *Barcelona*, as texts which privilege 'parodies and the sarcastic treatment of the political imaginary of the 1970s', the target of which is 'always the political militant'.[4] However, for Blejmar, whilst this group of cultural texts employ satire to 'displace, destabilize and disarticulate epic or overly solemn narratives of the revolution', the historiographical specificity of their subject matter undermines their relevance to wider issues of historical memory in a contemporary milieu.[5]

Indeed, *Los bustos de Eva* does centre around political naïf Ernesto Marroné's encounters with the politics and praxis of the revolutionary Peronism of the 1970s, yet a close reading of the novel reveals a historicist interrogation of the national past which reaches far beyond the chronological specificities of its plot. By focussing upon its grotesque realism, this analysis will highlight how, not unlike the later autofictional narratives of the post-dictatorship generation, *Los bustos de Eva* seeks a re-evaluation of the recent past beyond the hegemonic narratives of political militancy espoused by the human rights community and, latterly, successive Kirchner administrations, from 1996 onwards. By visualizing the social disintegration of mid-1970s Argentina through the comic prism of the grotesque, Gamerro's novel elicits a horizontalist reconsideration of the complicity of wider society in the normalization of violence that preceded the 1976 military *coup d'état* and the subsequent atrocities of *el Proceso*.

Chronologically the penultimate of the author's five novels to date, in the fictional timescape of Gamerro's narrative corpus *Los bustos de Eva* is the earliest of four related works which are set over a period of three decades, from the mid-1970s to the early 1990s.[6] The misadventures of Ernesto Marroné continue in *Un yuppie en la columna del Che Guevara* [A Yuppie in Che Guevara's Army] (2010). These two novels constitute a prequel to what is perhaps Gamerro's best-known work, *Las islas* [The Islands] (1998), a text which centres around the legacy of the 1982 Malvinas conflict between Argentina and the United Kingdom. *El secreto y las voces* (2002) is, within Gamerro's historicist chronotope, the most recent work, chronicling a journalist's 1997 investigation into the disappearance of a political militant in a rural town two decades earlier.[7] Thus, throughout his literary corpus, Gamerro constructs a social network of characters, interactions and locations which reflects the socio-political context of the last three decades of Argentine history. The discrete stories of each of these four novels conjoin to present the reader with a coherent narrative whole, in which fragments of the past are gathered together and fashioned into a new and innovative historicist totality. Just as, twenty years after the disappearance of Darío Ezcurra in 1977, the journalistic narrator of *El secreto y las voces* can uncover the unspeakable truth of this crime, so the self-reflexive network of character interactions and events in Gamerro's corpus steadily gives up its secrets. Through their narratological intricacy and prominent satiric impulse, the texts combine to confect a historicist fictionscape that consistently problematizes the past, defying received historiographies.

Moreover, it is in the grotesque realism which dominates much of Gamerro's fiction, and upon which this evaluation of *Los bustos de Eva* will focus, that we find further indications of a new and innovative historicist discourse which challenges pre-existing modes of representing the past. As Blejmar asserts, that parody and intertextuality are prominent within the novel is irrefutable. The motivational argot of corporate self-improvement manuals, the earnest propaganda of Montonero publications such as *Evita Montonera*, and the constant parallels between our narrator's travails and those of Cervantes's Don Quixote are a few examples of the parodic interplay within the text. However, these intertextual allusions are always enacted within a somatic framework, since it is the grotesque and its attendant carnivalesque sensibilities which form the dominant narrative sensibility of the novel. The body, its orifices, appendages and excrescences reign supreme in Gamerro's narrative universe, informing all aspects of the text. The title of the novel, itself a double entendre that aligns the sculptural with the anatomical, is the first indication of the grotesque predilections of *Los bustos de Eva*. In contrast to the sacralized portrayal of a beatific Eva Perón in *Lo que el tiempo nos dejó*, Gamerro's incarnations of the former first lady destabilize the cult of Eva. 'Debasement [...] the fundamental artistic principle of grotesque realism' is everywhere here,[8] from Ernesto's chronic constipation to the extravagant orgy of the oligarchs at the specialist brothel La Fundación de Ayuda Sexual Eva Perón [The Eva Perón Sexual Assistance Foundation].[9] In his ornate prose, the author establishes a discourse of viscerality and disgust that centres around the human body, from which no one is exempt.

In his seminal exploration of the grotesque, *Rabelais and his World*, Bakhtin established the potential of the form, declaring that 'the grotesque conception of the body is interwoven not only with the cosmic but also with the social, utopian and historic theme, and above all with the theme of the change of epochs and the renewal of culture'.[10] According to Bakhtin, the grotesque is possessed of a potential far greater than parody, and exists as a potent cultural force which invokes social and material change beyond the text, eliciting contemporary reappraisals of the past. In doing so, it broadens the limits of the possible in historicist discourse. In her appraisal of Bakhtin's work, Frances Connelly reaffirms the grotesque as an agent of cultural change, describing the form as 'an action, not a thing — more like a verb than a noun'. She continues, asserting that the grotesque 'creates meaning by prying open a gap, pulling us into unfamiliar, contested terrain'.[11] In his own elaborations on the Bakhtinian grotesque, Michael Holquist evinces the horizontalist potential of the form, a force which he characterizes as 'exploring the interface between a stasis imposed from above and a desire for change from below, between old and new, official and unofficial'.[12] Here, the grotesque is a levelling impetus, rupturing the boundaries of the social through its scandalizing narrative formulations of the high and the low. In place of hierarchy and division, grotesque realism and its carnivalesque proclivities promote the emancipatory potential of a holistic and unified society, in which 'each man belongs to the immortal people who create history'.[13] It is within these specific interpretations of Bakhtin's grotesque as a mobilizing agent of change that Gamerro's novels are grounded.

Indeed, there are significant parallels between such descriptions of the transformational power of the grotesque and Marina Sitrin's analysis of the profound change brought about by the *Argentinazo*. Focussing on the cleavage that these events enacted within popular conceptions of established power structures, she states: 'It was a rupture with the past. It was a rupture with obedience. […] The 19th and 20th was a crack in history upon which vast political landscapes unfolded. Revolutions were created — revolutions of everyday life'.[14] As we saw in Chapter One, horizontalism was not a product of the 2001 Crisis. It existed previously in nascent form, in the organizing principles and praxis of activists such as the *piqueteros* and H.I.J.O.S. But the momentum of the *Argentinazo* propelled this new form of socio-political consciousness into wider circulation. Sitrin's characterization of the *Argentinazo* as a rupturing of the boundaries of the status quo mirrors Connelly's description of the grotesque, in that both assessments describe a kinetic force which encodes a profound potential for change. Moreover, as 'a social relationship which implies, as its name suggests, a flat plane upon which to communicate', *horizontalidad* resonates with the same disdain for hierarchical structures as the grotesque.[15] This unremitting disrespect of power and status is central to grotesque realism and, as we shall see, it is everywhere in *Los bustos de Eva*. A joyful and egalitarian mode of seeing the world, it conceptualizes all life as reducible to its material components and, in particular, the human body as a collection of somatic processes.

Moreover, in Bakhtin's conceptualization of the grotesque as an artistic modality inextricably linked to cultural renewal, and in Holquist and Connelly's subsequent affirmations of the destabilizing potential of the grotesque, there is a cognitive parallel to be drawn with Raymond William's writings on the evolution of an emergent structure of feeling. As discussed in Chapter One, Williams describes his concept as the 'felt sense of the quality of life at particular place and time: a sense of the ways in which the particular activities combined into a way of thinking and living'.[16] It is, he asserts, a social dynamic that is most visible at times of great change or transition. He describes how 'conventions — the means of expression which find tacit consent — are a vital part of this structure of feeling. As the structure changes, new means are perceived and realised, while old means come to appear empty and artificial'.[17] Here, the emergence of innovative artistic practices destabilizes the hegemony of established modes of cultural expression, precipitating new approaches to what was once fixed in the popular imaginary. Whilst the grotesque is not, by any approximation, a new means of expression, Gamerro's application of the form to the realm of historical memory, and in particular the contested terrain of 1970s Argentina, is pioneering. Firstly, in its irreverent depictions of the Montoneros, many of whom were disappeared during el Proceso, Los bustos de Eva challenged contemporaneous narratives of victimhood, and attendant issues of guilt and innocence, in relation to the recent past. In addition, in the character of Ernesto, a narrator entirely lacking in ideological convictions, Gamerro interrogates the complicity of civil society during this turbulent period.

This ludic sense of historicity is significantly different to the sense of the past articulated within the other texts explored in this monograph. When questioned in an interview on the bawdy irreverence of his fictions, Gamerro explained his approach, declaring that 'cuando la política de derechos humanos y la Estatal confluyen, aunque no sean las mismas, liberan a la literatura para decir otra cosa' [when the politics of human rights and those of the state converge, even though they may not be in absolute harmony, this frees literature to talk about other things.][18] This statement can be interpreted as a reference to the strategic alignment of successive Kirchner administrations with the memory work of the human rights community. In bringing the 'state terrorism and justice narratives into the executive policymaking considerations', Kirchnerismo reinstalled the primacy of the past within the popular imaginary.[19] On 24 March 2004, at the site of the former ESMA, Néstor Kirchner made one of the defining speeches of his presidency, in which he described himself as part of a generation of activists who had, in the 1970s, fought for a more just and equal society. Asserting his identity as both 'compañero' to those political militants and 'presidente de la nación argentina', Kirchner affirmed his affiliative bond with the disappeared, their families and the survivors of state terrorism, and moreover, his commitment to securing justice for this community.[20] It was, as Beatriz Sarlo states, the 'acto fundador' [foundational act] of the Kirchner era, a statement of intent that signalled a paradigmatic shift in the way the recent past was perceived.[21] As Gamerro suggests, with the state adopting the historicist impetus of human rights discourse, cultural narratives of the past were endowed with a new potential, freed from the testimonial impulse and able to explore the events of recent history in innovative and diverse ways.

In its divergence from this newly-installed official discourse of historicity through the horizontal sensibilities of the grotesque, *Los bustos de Eva* signals a shift in the structure of feeling. The novel begins in the early 1990s, when, returning home after a round of golf at his country club, Ernesto notices a poster of his namesake, the revolutionary icon Ernesto 'Che' Guevara, on the wall of his teenage son's bedroom. Troubled by this discovery, he ruminates on his son's possible Marxist leanings, stating:

> una generación entera se había inmolado en el altar de dudosos ídolos, una generación de la cual él, Marroné, era un sobreviviente. ¿Y para qué había sobrevivido, si no para contar la historia y contándola, conjurar su repetición, y volver al descanso de la tumba a los inquietos fantasmas del pasado?[22]
>
> [a whole generation had sacrificed itself on the altar of dubious idols — a generation of which, he, Marroné, was a survivor. But what had he survived for if not to tell his story, and in the telling to prevent it being repeated and lay the unquiet ghosts of the past to rest in the slumber of the grave?[23]

Therefore, from the outset, his purpose in retelling his revolutionary adventures from 1975 is to lay the past to rest, consigning it to oblivion. But in the topsy-turvy world of the grotesque, this purpose is inverted. Ernesto's intransigence about his personal past and his determination to adhere to a single fixed narrative of history serves only to highlight the folly of historicist orthodoxy. Thus, from the opening pages of the novel onwards, Gamerro asserts literature's potential for challenging hegemonic versions of the past.

Ernesto's name is also significant and is indicative of a significant grotesque trope that Gamerro employs. In *Rabelais and his World*, Bakhtin refers to the leitmotif of 'praise-abuse' in the use of proper nouns within the author's works. He describes how each proper noun used by Rabelais has 'a clear etymological meaning that characterizes its owner', and thus becomes a nickname rather than a conventional form of address.[24] He continues, averring that 'a nickname can never be neutral, since its meaning always includes an element of evaluation, positive or negative'.[25] Therein lies the 'praise-abuse'. Gamerro's characters embody this element of the grotesque in that their names are informed by their personal characteristics, habits and worldview. In Ernesto's case, his first name is, as previously mentioned, an allusion to his revolutionary compatriot which hints at his repressed self-aggrandizing fantasies of fame. His surname, a version of the colour 'marrón' [brown] with added vowel and the accent transposed, has a dual meaning in that it refers to both Ernesto's true identity and his recurrent digestive problems. Adopted from a poor family and raised by wealthy parents, his comparatively darker skin colour and his perceived 'sangre plebeya' [plebeian blood] has troubled Ernesto throughout his life not least because, in a fit of rage at the ten-year old boy, his father once angrily chided him as the 'hijo de negros'.[26] It is this knowledge of his biological origins that causes the protagonist to feel like an impostor in his comfortable middle-class existence, fuelling his desires for new and exciting experiences. Furthermore, in a comic aside, as the colour of human faeces, his surname also alludes to his chronic constipation, a problem which can only be ameliorated by reading corporate self-help literature whilst on the toilet. By reducing Ernesto to the content of his bowels, the narrative deflates the protagonist's egotism and undermines the social hierarchy to which he aspires. It is an initial indication of the horizontalist impulse implicit within the grotesque ethos of Gamerro's text.

The scatological allusions of Ernesto's name are merely the opening salvo in the barrage of grotesqueries with which Gamerro bombards the reader throughout *Los bustos de Eva*. As Connelly affirms, 'the carnivalesque works with the material world, and especially with the body. This is not the body as our minds conceive it, but as our own mortal bodies experience it'.[27] In foregrounding corporeality and sensation, the carnivalesque is both material and sensorial, a form of narrating the interactions between the body and the world it inhabits. As the protagonist, it is Ernesto's body, and its relations with the material world that form the dominant subjectivity within the novel. As mentioned previously, he suffers from chronic constipation and his narration of events is punctuated by frequent unsuccessful trips to the toilet. The cause of Ernesto's bowel problems and the character whose abduction by armed revolutionaries forms the narrative motor of the novel is Fausto Tamerlán, owner and Chief Executive of Tamerlán & Sons. His unusual moniker is probably a Hispanicized version of his birth name, as he is a German immigrant who arrived in Argentina on the historic date of 17 October 1945, when a popular uprising forced the release from prison of then Colonel Juan Perón. As his name suggests, Fausto is a man without scruples, and his meteoric rise to power in the corporate world has been facilitated by his willingness to set aside moral considerations in the pursuit of power and economic success. Like his namesake, the Mongol warlord, he is a merciless tyrant who rules over his 'subjects', in this case his employees, with a rod of iron. His idiosyncratic recruitment process provides just one example of the power and cruelty for which he is renowned. As Ernesto painfully recalls, Fausto insists on digitally penetrating all prospective employees in the anus in order to assess their true potential. The reason for this violation is, as Fausto reveals to Ernesto during his own job interview, because the human soul is situated in the rectum. Whilst inserting his finger into Ernesto's sphincter, he embarks upon a rambling critique of the failure of philosophers throughout history to pinpoint the location of the human soul, before declaring:

> Ese orificio es nuestro más delicado órgano de percepción del error, y no hay mejor antídoto contra cualquier estúpida tentación de independencia o rebeldía que un culo bien fruncido. A partir de ahora, Marroné, cuando se le presente alguna duda, consúltelo con su culo, y él le dirá lo que debe hacer. Recuérdelo: su culo es su mejor amigo.[28]

> [That orifice is our most sensitive organ for perceiving errors, and there's no better antidote for idiotic leanings towards independence or rebellion than a nicely puckered arse. From now on, Marroné, when you're in any doubt, consult your arse and it'll tell you what to do. Remember: your arse is your best friend.][29]

In penetrating his employees and violating their trust on the pretext of a job interview, Fausto asserts his absolute power over them and it is from this point on that Ernesto's stomach ailments begin, his intestines becoming 'un nudo gordiano que sólo podía cortar a fuerza de poderosos laxantes' [a perverse Gordian knot that he could only cut with the aid of powerful laxatives.][30] This monstrous violation and its subsequent impact on the narrator, detailed in the opening chapter, come to define our impressions of both characters. This is, of course, an articulation of the grotesque and of the 'many-centuries-old link of laughter with the images of the body's lower stratum'.[31] And whilst Fausto is initially the humiliator, he is himself emasculated by his kidnap, during which he is captured during a sexual encounter with a male revolutionary posing as a sex worker, who has been trained by 'un pederasta chino para trabajar las nalgas como un cepo y retener al Señor Tamerlán, a la manera del abotonamiento perruno, hasta que sus cómplices llegaran a llevárselo' [a Chinese pederast to clamp his buttocks shut doggy-style and keep Señor Tamerlán there until his accomplices could take him away.][32] Thus, he too is debased, and his position of authority in the corporate hierarchy is undermined. That both characters are humiliated through non-consensual acts of anal penetration demonstrates once again the levelling impulse of the grotesque, as despite their differences in social status, Ernesto and Fausto are both forced to undergo a similarly degrading experience.

While Ernesto represents the vacillations of the Argentine middle class during the political instability of the mid-1970s, and Fausto the unscrupulous attitude of the captains of industry, so there are two further characters who can be seen to represent specific sections of the body politic. Paddy Donovan, alias Colorado, is a former schoolmate of Ernesto's at the prestigious bilingual school St Andrew's College. Handsome, athletic and academically successful, he was idolized by his classmates. But now, disillusioned with his former life as scion of a wealthy upper-class family, Paddy has found his vocation as an urban guerrilla and is one of the most prominent organizers of the occupation at the Sansimón plasterworks. As he explains to his bemused former schoolmate, he has embarked upon a process of 'proletarización', leaving behind the trappings of his haute bourgeois lifestyle to join the impending political revolution. In the entryist praxis typical of Montonero activists, he has come to work in the factory in order to convert the workers to the revolutionary cause. Within the social-political topography of the novel, Paddy represents what David Rock describes as the 'pronounced middle-class character' of the Montoneros and the revolutionary Peronist movement in general. Recruits like Paddy, he asserts, were 'propelled to the barricades by a guilt-ridden perception of the extremes of social injustice in their midst, and the pervasive atmosphere of moral stagnation and political collapse surrounding them.'[33]

This bourgeois angst is apparent in Paddy's recollection of his visit to a brothel with his comrades from the factory. He is reluctant to go along and his hesitation results in him being paired with the last remaining prostitute, a dark-skinned young woman from the north. As with Ernesto's biological family, here once again ethnicity is closely aligned with economic status and social class. Confronted by the woman's haggard appearance, her goitre and her rotten teeth, Paddy struggles to become aroused and so, as he recalls: 'trataba de pensar en su pueblo, que había sufrido casi cinco siglos de opresión, y en las condiciones infrahumanos de hambre y miseria en la que habría crecido, la explotación feudal que habría sufrido en su tierra y la sexual de acá' [and I forced myself to think of her people, who've suffered nearly five centuries of oppression, and of the subhuman conditions of hunger and poverty she must have grown up in, the feudal exploitation in her land and the sexual exploitation here in the capital.][34] Anxious not to humiliate himself in front of his comrades, he forces himself to think of his former girlfriend Monique, a beautiful blonde model, in order to perform sexually. This incident highlights the gulf between his political ideologies and the material reality of Argentine society. In his utopian aspirations and his repudiation of his privileged upbringing, Paddy displays a naivete which, the novel suggests, was prevalent throughout the ranks of the revolutionary Peronist movement. Here, Gamerro mocks him as the archetypal 'useful idiot', a deluded pawn in the increasingly militaristic struggle between the Montoneros and the paramilitary squads of the Triple A (Alianza Anticomunista Argentina), mobilized by Isabel Perón's Minister of Social Welfare, José López Rega.[35] Ever the eager proselytiser, it is Paddy who urges Ernesto to read the propaganda organ *Evita Montonera*. For it is in the symbolic figure of Evita Montonera that the guerrillas enunciate their revolutionary mission. Their heroine is 'la Evita revolucionaria por excelencia, militante, peronista fanática, sectaria, implacable, que anunciaba a voz en cuello su compromiso incondicional con la justicia social' [the Evita who was a revolutionary par excellence, a militant, a fanatical Peronist, sectarian, relentless, who announced at the top of her voice her unconditional commitment to social justice.][36] In propaganda such as this magazine and in the popular Montonero chant of 'Si Evita viviera, sería Montonera' [If Evita was alive, she'd be a Montonera] we see the bespoke Eva of this guerrilla discourse. In pillorying Paddy, Gamerro interrogates the revindication of political militancy espoused by the human rights community, in particular the activists of H.I.J.O.S, which, as we have seen, emerged in the late 1990s.

The final character which we will examine as a social signifier within the grotesque universe of the novel is el Tuerto, a worker at the Sansimón plasterworks who lives in the nearby *villa miseria*. In the Lunfardo argot, the descriptor tuerto signifies a person with one eye or with a generally crooked physical demeanour. This character, 'el gordo de casco marrón y ojo velado al que todos llamaban el Tuerto' [the fat man in the brown helmet and milky white eye that everyone called El Tuerto],[37] assumes the role of Ernesto's guide and helper during the Factory occupation. In the Quixotic intertext of the novel, el Tuerto is the Sancho Panza to Ernesto's knight errant, and his pragmatism and practicality provide a balancing counterpoint to the narrator's outlandish fantasism. For Bakhtin, corpulence and excesses of appetite 'convey a powerful carnivalesque spirit'.[38] Connected to alimentary processes and the realm of the lower body, obesity denotes a clownish and vital worldview. Accordingly, el Tuerto is often described in relation to the preparation of food. During the worker's asado at the factory, 'como un cíclope sonriente, con largos cubiertos de asador en la mano, presidía el Tuerto el general holocausto de los animales parrilleros' [and there, wielding the long knife and fork of the *asador*, stood El Tuerto, presiding like a grinning cyclops over this general holocaust of roasting animal flesh.][39] As the grotesque conductor of the feast, he supervises the culinary proceedings with an unrestrained glee. However, el Tuerto is not entirely committed to the revolutionary cause. He is motivated by a general sense of self-preservation and follows what appears to be the course of action most beneficial to himself. But he is highly susceptible to external influence, as we see in the incident with his wife Pipota. El Tuerto returns home with Ernesto and, embarrassed by Pipota's constant nagging in the presence of his friend and the three local gangsters who have come to visit, he feels compelled to rebuke her publicly. She is frying milanesas and so, in a grotesque act of culinary mimesis, he forcibly bastes her hand in breadcrumbs and egg yolk and pushes it into the scalding oil of the hot pan. We see here how the broader social discourse of violence permeates everyday life at the granular level, becoming an accepted form of social relations.

Therefore, through these four central characters and their grotesque idiosyncrasies, Gamerro constructs a metonymic tableau of Argentine society in the mid-1970s. Ernesto is torn between the comforts of his bourgeois existence and his delusions of fame and grandeur, and it is in the militancy of the factory occupation that he finds a potential outlet for the latter aspirations. His former school friend Paddy is consumed by the revolutionary fervour of the Montonero cause, having eagerly imbibed the earnest and humourless propaganda that he now distributes. In contrast, Tamerlán, with his rapacious urge for world domination, is committed only to the pursuit of wealth and power and is willing to do business with whomever will prove most useful to his ambitions. Finally, el Tuerto is a model of self-serving acquiescence, content to coast along and follow the majority. In their own distinct way, each of these characters is equally culpable in perpetuating the chaotic status quo, as they accommodate the violence and instability that surrounds them, seeking to turn it to their own advantage. Moreover, in his equally grotesque depictions of each of the four men, Gamerro devalues the social hierarchies by which they are defined, rendering them equal through their shared corporality. Each character is as grotesque as the last in the horizontalist plane of their physical existence.

Within this grotesque social topography, the central narrative motif of kidnapping is particularly appropriate. That Tamerlán's abduction is a fictionalized account of an actual crime further cements the historicist potential of *Los bustos de Eva*. It is based upon the kidnapping of the Born brothers by the Montoneros in September 1975, in the twilight months of the Peronist administration.[40] Such kidnappings, along with frequent bank robberies and the assassinations of right-wing Peronists and police personnel were part of the typical *modus operandi* of the militarized wing of the Argentine left during the mid-1970s, as the leftist guerrillas of the Montoneros and Marxist fellow travellers the ERP (Ejército Revolucionario del Pueblo) sought to consolidate power and influence, following the death of President Juan Perón.[41] The Born kidnapping of 1975 represented the apogee of this trend in kidnapping and was a spectacular propaganda coup for the Montoneros (Fig. 5.1).

Furthermore, the $60 million ransom collected for the release of the Born brothers secured the financial future of the organization in a very difficult political climate, since by this point the government of Isabel Perón, assisted by the paramilitary squads of the Triple A, was actively engaged in hunting down and eliminating the armed Left.

Fig. 5.1. Jorge Born, the Argentine businessman kidnapped by the Montoneros in 1974. The ransom paid for the release of Born and his twin brother was reputed to be $60 million. Image: www.elmundo.es.

To evaluate fully the significance of the kidnapping in *Los bustos de Eva* and its prominence in the Argentine historical imaginary of the 1970s, it is pertinent to mention another similar incident five years earlier, in late May of 1970. It was then that the nascent Montoneros organization first came to public prominence, with a kidnapping so audacious that it irrevocably transformed the political landscape, ushering in a new era of popular armed struggle during which politics and violence became inextricably intertwined. The kidnapping of General Aramburu, codenamed 'Operation Pindapoy', was carried out by the founding members of the Montonero organization, a group which at that time numbered no more than twelve recruits.[42] Aramburu, a prominent participant in the *Revolución libertadora* which ousted Perón in 1955 and enforced the 'deperonization' of Argentine society, was held captive by the group for three days, subjected to 'a revolutionary trial' and executed shortly afterwards, on 1 June 1970.[43] His participation in the capture and secret burial of Eva Perón's embalmed body following her widower's flight in 1955, a procedure codenamed 'Operation Cadaver', constituted another motivation for his kidnapping.[44] But it was not until 1974 and the kidnapping of the deceased General's corpse, once again by the Montoneros, that the body of Evita was finally returned to Argentina.

For Sarlo, the execution of Aramburu signalled a watershed moment in the recent past of the nation. Argentina, she posits, 'no iba a ser la misma a partir de los hechos de mayo y junio de 1970' [would never be the same following the events of May and June 1970].[45] Much more than a single politically-motivated abduction, for Sarlo the Aramburu kidnapping was the 'manifestación de una sensibilidad colectiva' [manifestation of a collective sensibility],[46] an epoch-defining declaration of intent. In effect, it raised the curtain on a period that witnessed the advent of what Sebastián Carassai has termed 'la naturalización de la violencia' [the naturalization of violence], during which extreme brutality and sudden violent death became part of the backdrop of everyday life. As Carassai highlights, it was incidents such as the Aramburu kidnapping that prompted the Argentine current affairs magazine *Panorama* to declare terrorism as their 'Personality of the Year' in 1970.[47] Explaining his decision, the magazine's editor Tomás Eloy Martínez asserted that 'la gelinita, la metralla, los secuestros, los robos políticos eran sumados [...]: también habían marcado a fuego la historia argentina' [gelignite, shrapnel, kidnappings, all of these things added up [...] moreover Argentine history had been marked by fire.][48] Significantly, for Sarlo, 1970 was the year which saw violence emerge not only as the physical manifestation of political conflict but also as literary discourse. She cites the publication of a new short story by Jorge Luis Borges, his first since 1953 and one of eleven short fictions that constituted the forthcoming selection *El informe de Brodie* [Brodie's Report], in the literary magazine *Los Libros* in August 1970, as a textual parallel to the endemic social violence of the period. Entitled 'El otro duelo' [The Other Duel], the story narrates the tale of two soldiers, 'prisioneros de uno de esos encontronazos desprolijos de las guerras civiles del Río de la Plata' [prisoners in one of those untidy skirmishes during the civil wars of the River Plate], who are sentenced to death by their captors.[49] Aware of the mutual enmity between the two men, the captain supervising their execution provides them with a final opportunity to settle their rivalry. But the contest has a grotesque twist: they will both have their throats slit open from ear to ear and, in their final seconds of sentient existence, forced to run a race to establish which man is physically superior. From this coincidence of the literary and the social, Sarlo draws no more than one conclusion, that 'Borges y los hechos que se producen en ese año 1970 definieron, de diverso modo, los años que vendrían' [Borges and the incidents that occurred in 1970 defined, in different ways, the years to come.][50]

Therefore, in siting the kidnapping of a business executive in 1975 at the narrative core of *Los bustos de Eva*, Gamerro evokes a seminal series of events in the national imaginary which are, as Nóe Jitrik suggests, 'indudablemente trascendentes y en los que una comunidad se reconoce porque definen el curso y el sentido de su historia' [undoubtedly significant and in which a community recognizes itself, because these events define the course and the sense of history.][51] In their convoluted grotesquery, this series of kidnappings conveys the violent sensibilities of the period. In addition, through their fictionalized re-enactment in the grotesque milieu, the novel augments the representation of these histories, debasing the hegemonic narratives of the past in the present. In doing so, it magnifies the horizontalist potential of the past, invoking collective notions of the social and calling upon the body politic to recognize its own participation in history.

As we have observed, characterization is central to the grotesque realism of *Los bustos de Eva*. Likewise, the carnivalesque spatio-temporalities of the narrative constitute a rich discourse of the grotesque. Here, two aspects of Bakhtin's analysis are key; firstly, how the form is conjured through topography and, secondly, the feast as the *sine qua non* of grotesque realism. Regarding the former, he asserts that 'mountains and abysses, such is the relief of the grotesque body; or speaking in architectural terms, towers and subterranean passages'. Just as, in its somatic incarnations, the grotesque is concentrated around the extremities, 'the confines of the body and the outer world', so in architectural representations, it is manifested in extremes of height and depth.[52] The novel contains numerous such locations and the first we encounter is the cavernous bunker constructed to Tamerlán's specifications underneath his office building on the Paseo Colón. Called to a meeting with Govianus, the company's accountant and acting CEO in Tamerlán's absence, Ernesto describes the site as the 'subterráneo complejo de oficinas que el presidente de la compañía había bautizado con el poético y valquiriano nombre de *Nibelheim*, pero que todos sus empleados denominaban, más familiarmente, el búnker de Tamerlán' [the subterranean office complex that the company's president had christened with the poetic, Valkyrian name 'The Nibelheim,' but which all of his employees had more familiarly christened 'Tamerlán's Bunker']. Equipped with its own power station and weapons store, the bunker was built by a team of engineers from the Soviet Union. Its facilities and the vastness of its size are indicative of Tamerlán's megalomaniac tendencies. As the narrator tells us, 'si la revolución llegaba a triunfar en la Argentina, el capitalismo podría atrincherarse allí y desde la clandestinidad resistir durante meses' [If a communist revolution was ever victorious in Argentina, capitalism could hole up here and hold out for months.][53] From this fortified basement complex, the chairman confects his plans of world domination and administers his corporate empire with the ruthlessness of a warlord. Here, capitalism is bellicose and merciless. Yet these intimidating surroundings are undermined by the events of Ernesto's meeting, during which Govianus shows him a package sent to the company by the kidnappers. The envelope contains Tamerlán's severed finger. The digit's appearance has 'algo amenazador, como esos amuletos hechos de garra de animal' [a menacing air about it, like one of those amulets made out of animal claws], and it provokes such disgust in the narrator that he drops the digit on the floor.[54] Both men must then crawl around the office on their hands and knees in search of the missing finger. This comedic flourish underlines the inefficacy of the subterranean fortress that Tamerlán has created, since it is of no use to him, as he languishes in a makeshift dungeon beneath a Montonero safehouse.

The second spatio-temporality which adheres to Bakhtin's architectural specifications of the grotesque is the Sansimón plasterworks, the factory that Ernesto visits to arrange the purchase of the ninety-two busts. Its exterior is, for the most part, unremarkable, save for the fact that the plaster dust which issues constantly from the factory has coated the surrounding yard and its vegetation with a thick layer of white dust. The area appears petrified, deformed by this blanket of fine dry powder. Inside, the plasterworks are a model of Taylorist efficiency. Teams of workers in colour-coded helmets scurry to and fro, focussed on the efficient execution of their particular aspect of the manufacturing process. On its upper floor, glass-fronted offices house the administrative staff, along with numerous managers. In order to monitor the productivity of his workers in this 'verdadera catedral del trabajo humano' [a true cathedral to human labour], Sansimón has installed a network of chairlifts which hang from the ceiling of the factory.[55] This bizarre surveillance system is staffed by foremen who observe the workers' progress from their vertiginous viewpoints, shouting at the employees below through a megaphone when they observe any errors or other general signs of inefficiency. Inspired by a recent visit to the United States, the enterprising factory owner is determined to extract the maximum production value from his employees. In the grotesque spatio-temporality of this 1970s workplace, we glimpse the future of capitalism, as seen from the past.

There are several other notable architectural incarnations of the grotesque within the novel, not least the swamp like *villa miseria* that El Tuerto calls home, and which Ernesto describes drily as 'esta Venecia de cartón y lata' [this mock Venice of cardboard and tin.][56] The Peronist kitsch of the Fundación de Ayuda Sexual Eva Perón is also noteworthy, although it does not feature towers or subterranean passages. Rather, it is significant as the site of one of the great carnivalesque episodes of the novel and it is this notion of the communal celebration of the feast to which we will now turn our attention. Bakhtin highlights the carnivalesque sensibilities of the feast, saying: 'the whole speaks in all carnival images; it reigns in the very atmosphere of this feast, making everyone participate in its awareness'. Here, the term is used to denote all forms of celebration, culinary or otherwise, as Bakhtin clarifies, stating that 'the feast means liberation from all that is utilitarian, practical. It is a temporary transfer to the utopian world'.[57] There are several such communal celebrations that take place within the novel. For example, in the first day of the worker's occupation, as part of an elaborate ruse to distract their captors, the management succeed in arranging a minor orgy in the offices to which they are confined. This grotesque spectacle culminates in an enraged soliloquy from Sansimón, who, dressed in lingerie, beseeches the employee guarding him: 'La vida es para vivirla ahora Baigorrita. A fin de cuentas, todos queremos lo mismo: una vida digna. ¿Y qué se necesita para tener una vida digna? Plata, Baigorrita, nada más que plata. Lo demás son cuentos' [Life's for living now, Baigorrita. Think about it, we're all after the same thing: a decent life. And what do you need for a decent life? Money, Baigorrita, nothing but money. The rest is fairy tales.][58] This grotesque spectacle is comic, but it also reflects the desperation of the factory boss in the face of the worker's insurrection and the unadorned lust for capital that motivates him. It is this rampant materialism that forms the most grotesque element of this lascivious tableaux, rather than the sexual acts themselves.

There are two central feast-like celebrations within the novel and their juxtaposition reveals a grotesque oppositionality resonant with horizontalist meaning. The first is a lavish *asado* organized by the workers following a triumphant assembly in which their commitment to the occupation is reaffirmed. Held in the grounds of the factory, the feast is open to the striking employees and the local community and is lavish in scale. As previously mentioned, it is El Tuerto who presides over the cooking of mountainous quantities of meat and poultry, including 'medias reses enteras, orladas de guirnaldas de morcillas, chorizos y chinchulines, ejércitos de pollos cuyas pieles se volvían a la vista come cuero lustrado y parecían sonreír de pensar los deliciosos que quedarían' [whole sides of beef trimmed with garlands of black puddings, pork sausages and chitterlings; armies of chickens whose skins crisped and goldened; whole suckling pigs, butterflied and gleaming like polished leather, smiling at the thought of how delicious they'd taste.][59] Alongside, there are 'dos pirámides de apiladas damajuanas, una de vino blanco y otro de vino tinto' [two tall pyramids of demijohns — one of white, one of red] and baskets of bread so large that two men are needed to carry them.[60] In an ironic allusion to the officious organizational tendencies of the militant Left, 'un comité ensaladero' [a salad committee] is formed to take charge of vegetable cutting, whilst a similar delegation is engaged in the preparation of sausages. Yet there is a genuinely joyful sense of celebration present here, as 'comenzaran a llegar contingentes de delegados obreros, estudiantes, simpatizantes, vecinos y colados a pasearse entre las parrillas húmedas' [the contingents of worker delegates, students and sympathisers, all of whom began milling about among the smoking grills.][61] In the communal celebrations of the feast, there is an affirmation of the liberating potential of the social. As Bakhtin propounds, 'man's encounter with the world in the act of eating is joyful, triumphant; he triumphs over the world, devours it without being devoured himself'.[62]

However, the celebrations are halted by the arrival of Miguel, a Montonero leader who orders the termination of the feast due to the security risk it poses. He chides Paddy for permitting the *asado* to take place, decrying the feast as 'una típica desviación pequeño-burguesa y liberal' [a typical petty-bourgeois and liberal deviation].[63] In Miguel's pompous moralizing, we see once again the dislocation between revolutionary rhetoric and social praxis, a development that would ultimately result in the loss of previously widespread popular support for the Montoneros amongst the working class. The guerrillas became, in the words of Rodolfo Walsh, a 'lost patrol',[64] an increasingly militarized revolutionary vanguard whose ideological intransigence alienated the community which it proposed to liberate. Here, Gamerro lampoons the armed Left as personified by the killjoy Miguel, since, in denying the carnivalesque celebrations of the feast, he denies the revistalising potential of the social itself.

The antithetical celebration to the workers' *asado* takes place at the Fundación de Ayuda Sexual Eva Perón, the idiosyncratic brothel of the oligarchs which Ernesto stumbles upon during his attempt to escape an armed skirmish in the *villa miseria*. An ersatz re-creation of the centre for social assistance created by Eva Perón, the Fundación of *Los bustos de Eva* is also in the business of realizing dreams through an encounter with Evita, albeit those of a purely sexual nature. It is a Peronist themed brothel, where wealthy clients come to enjoy the favours of women dressed as different incarnations of Eva Perón. As with many of Ernesto's exploits, his visit to the Foundation is unplanned. Attempting to find his way out of the *villa miseria* he escaped to after the raid on the Sansimón Plasterworks, he glimpses what he presumes to be the ghost of Eva gliding through the mud and filth of the shanty town. Captivated by this glamourous phantasm, he follows her to the Foundation. After entering, he is greeted with the sight of another Eva, seated behind a large mahogany desk. In her appearance and demeanour, she resembles the real Eva Perón, the only distinction being that this woman is, save for her ostentatious jewellery, completely naked. Ernesto joins the queue of men awaiting an audience and, when his moment arrives, the woman greets him by saying 'Bienvenido a la Fundación de Ayuda Sexual Eva Perón. Todos tus deseos serán satisfechos. ¿Trajiste la carta?' [Welcome to the Eva Perón Sexual Aid Foundation. All your desires will be satisfied. Did you bring your letter?] He lacks the requisite letter of introduction but is admitted anyway, as he declares that he is looking for the busts of Eva. He then enters the Foundation proper, 'un vasto salón decorado en un kitsch peronista, mezcla de constructivismo soviético blando y estilo provenzal californiano, con toque de yesería neoclásica, fuentes y palmeras en maceta' [a vast lounge decorated in the official Peronist style: a soft blend of Soviet Constructionism and Californian Provençal, with touches of neoclassical stucco.][65]

In this description of the interior decoration of the brothel, the stylized *mise-en-scène* of the salon reflects the diverse aesthetics of the Peronist imaginary. This mélange of decorative styles amidst which the prostitutes mingle with their clients is a material recreation of the propagandistic imagery of Peronism. In his essay entitled 'La construcción imaginaria de un mundo', Daniel Santoro describes the Peronist aesthetic as an admixture of two visual discourses. Firstly, he cites the influence of 'la propaganda soviética de la década del treinta al cincuenta; aquí detectamos rasgos del Constructivismo, el Cubismo, incluso el Futurismo italiano de Depero' [Soviet propaganda of the 1930s to 1950s: here we can see features of Constructivism, Cubism, and even the Italian Futurism of Depero]. The second element, he asserts, is composed of 'imágenes tributarias de la propaganda del confort norteamericano de postguerra, pero a través de una visión moderada y lejos del desenfreno consumista' [spinoffs of the post-war US propaganda of comfort, but moderated and a far cry from unfettered consumerism].[66] Just as the political discourse of Peronism enshrined the virtues of a 'third way', an ideological stance 'between individual capitalism and its opposite and necessary consequence, collectivist communism',[67] so in its aesthetic narratives, it combined the spatial signifiers of these two antagonistic political ideologies to produce a syncretic visual form. Gamerro's description raises, once again, the populist inconsistencies of Peronism in its promise to be all things to all people. As a movement led by an all-powerful *caudillo*, the political subjectivities of the Peronist movement are anathema to the horizontalist impulse of the grotesque.

Furthermore, by recreating the aesthetic idiosyncrasies of the Peronist imaginary in the physical environment of the brothel, the text invokes a distinctly carnivalesque sensibility. In mocking the kitsch furnishings of the salon, the novel destabilizes the sacralized Peronist political imaginary. Additionally, in the flesh and blood incarnations of Eva Perón, it imbues this political discourse with a grotesque materiality, stripping the heroine of revolutionary Peronism of her

FIG. 5.2. *Evita Montonera*, one of several regular publications produced by the Montoneros. Image: *Página12*.

mythic aura. As the women perform their diverse characterizations of Eva amidst the ostentatious décor, we see the levelling power of the grotesque once more. As Gamerro describes,

> por este decorado de fantasía se paseaban, en todas sus variantes, hasta una docena y media de Evas. Las había de *chignon* y traje príncipe de Gales, de velo y sombrero, de vestido de verano y cabello suelto; una reina de Dior enjoyada de pies a cabeza, alguna envuelta en suntuosas pieles, otra enteramente enfundada en vinilo negro, una sin otra ropa que el portaligas y las medias, otra sin siquiera eso, ambas de riguroso rodete.[68]

> [around this fantastic decor strolled as many as a dozen and a half Evas. There were Evas with chignons and Prince of Wales check suits; Evas in veils and hats; Evas in summer dresses with their hair down; a Dior queen bejewelled from head to toe; another wrapped in sumptuous furs; another encased entirely in black vinyl; one wearing nothing but stockings and suspenders, and another not even that, both with stern-looking buns.][69]

Here, the denizens of the Argentine upper classes come to satiate their masochistic fantasies of the former First Lady. In life, they despised her and, here, they can defile her image by acting out their deepest fantasies with sex workers styled in her image. These acts of myth-desecration epitomize the innate horizontalism of the grotesque and its disdain for all the pretensions of status and power.

The Foundation also caters for the wealthy trade union barons of the Peronist Right, whose nostalgia for the heady days of the first Peronato draws them to

Fig. 5.3. Ciudad Evita, the town in greater Buenos Aires built in the image of Eva Perón's profile. Image: Google Earth.

this kitsch sexual tableaux of *Justicialismo*. Fetishists fondle items of clothing that purportedly once belonged to Evita, masochists are willingly beaten by belligerent Evas and transvestite Evas are also available for those so inclined. The sexual services on sale are representative of a discourse made flesh, a corporeal manifestation of the all-pervasive Peronist imaginary. Ironically, the only Eva that is not available in the Foundation is the version that Ernesto has most recently encountered in the pages of *Evita Montonera* (Fig. 5.2).

The absence of this most politicized of Evas is, the establishment's manager explains, due to market forces, since there is little appetite for the revolutionary Eva amongst the brothel's clientele. Just as the propaganda of the Montoneros enunciates its idiosyncratic symbolism of Eva to fortify militants in their armed struggle against capitalism and the Argentine establishment, so the consumer diktats of the marketplace inform the range of Evas on offer to clients in search of sexual fulfilment. Politics and sex, violence and pleasure, all are enacted through the discursive medium of Eva, a symbol of all meaning and none. Here, the grotesque sexual bean feast of the brothel is ultimately a denial of the carnivalesque since, unlike the workers' *asado*, it is organized according to the principles of the capitalist marketplace. Participation is not open to all but rather limited to those with the economic wherewithal to purchase the services on offer.

In the final section of the novel, spatial tropes of the grotesque align with the carnivalesque conceit of the feast in the parodic environs of Ciudad Evita. Yet, unlike the fictional spatio-temporalities of the factory and the Foundation, this most unlikely of spaces is a topographical reality. Planned and constructed under the auspices of the Eva Perón Foundation from 1948, this is a town in Greater Buenos Aires designed in the model of an English garden city. However, from above, its boundaries have been shaped to the profile of its benefactress.[70] Ben Bollig describes the settlement as 'a vast 1940s suburban development, made up of model units for Peronist workers, designed with a curving street pattern at odds with the grid found in the rest of Buenos Aires'.[71] In the spatial idiosyncrasies of the city, Eva Peron is etched upon the landscape. Just as the built structures of *La multitud* and *Elefante blanco* speak of the historical specificities of their origins, so Ciudad Evita underlines the hegemonic narratives of the first Peronato (Fig. 5.3).

Ernesto comes here in search of a sculptor named Rogelio García, whom he believes can help him fulfil his mission to obtain the ninety-two busts. As he searches for García's home, the increasingly disorientated Ernesto wanders around the leafy streets. Eventually, he is given some directions by various passing children, in a surreal chorus of advice: 'No, por ahí te vas para la nariz. No, para el rodete seguís derecho por acá, y después…Vas a ver una plaza grande, que vendría a ser por la mejilla' [No, you're heading for the nose that way. No, if you want the bun, you go straight on down here, and then... You'll see a big square, somewhere around the cheek.][72] The streets and squares of the city are moulded around the physiognomy of Eva Perón and, consequently the contours of her face, as imposed upon the landscape, are used by inhabitants as a navigational tool. The geographical idiosyncracy of Ciudad Evita epitomizes the horizontalist allegiances of the grotesque. According to Sitrin's spatial analogy, *horizontalidad* transforms social relations by creating a 'a flat plane upon which to communicate'.[73] Here, on the flat plains of the pampas, a town has been constructed to resemble the facial profile of Eva Perón. The inhabitants of Ciudad Evita literally walk over this physical recreation of her body, specifically her face, every day. Whilst the design and creation of the town was intended as a celebratory tribute to the First Lady, the hubristic ostentation of the concept is rendered comical by its physical reality. Ciudad Evita is the ultimate iteration of the grotesque, in that 'it brings low that which is high and revitalizes the high by appropriating the low'.[74]

There is also one final feast that takes place here. Fittingly, it is in the carnivalesque citadel of Ciudad Evita that Ernesto finally obtains the treasure he has spent the entire novel seeking, in the sculptures of Eva Perón that Rogelio and his friends saved from the proscription of Peronism by the *Revolución libertadora* of 1955. Ernesto is welcomed warmly by the sculptor, who invites him to bathe and rest, and then to join him in an *asado*. Exhausted and filthy, Ernesto accepts and sits down to eat with Rogelio and his friend Rodolfo. The atmosphere is relaxed and convivial, and the two men regale their visitor with stories of their exploits as Peronist militants in the hostile political environment of the 1950s. It is, in the true spirit of Bahktin's conceptualization of the feast as joyous act. Yet Ernesto is immune to the collegiality of the occasion. Outwardly simulating enjoyment and interest, he is inwardly fixating upon how to steal the busts that Rodolfo has hoarded away. Unwittingly, with a slip of the tongue, he betrays his true intentions

Fig. 5.4. A bust of Eva Perón, in the vestibule of the Museo Evita in Buenos Aires. Image: https://turismo.buenosaires.gob.ar/

and his two companions realise their mistake in assuming their visitor was a fellow Peronist. Rodolfo becomes angry and suspicious, refusing to give up his collection of busts to the now-unmasked impostor. But Rogelio counsels him, saying, 'nosotros queremos ser mejores, ¿o no? Escúchame. Todo lo que perdimos... Todo lo que perdiste... No va a volver porque te aferres a unos ídolos. Son figuritas de piedra y madera. No son Perón y Eva. Dejá que se los lleve' [we want to be better than them, don't we? Listen to me. Everything we lost... Everything you lost... you won't bring it back by clinging on to idols. They're just figurines of wood and stone. They aren't Perón and Eva. Let him have them.][75] Unlike the Montoneros and the oligarchs of the Foundation, both of whom fetishize Eva, albeit in very different ways, Rogelio does not place all his faith in material representations of his beliefs.

But Ernesto, in denying himself the pleasure of participation in the feast and subsequently stealing the required number of busts, rejects the pleasure of this horizontalist celebration. His deluded fantasies of self-advancement take precedence over the opportunity for genuine social interaction and he eschews the collective in favour of the individual. Here, it is Ernesto's ruthless quest for self-advancement in the rigidly hierarchical structures of power and influence which is truly grotesque. Yet, in the moralistic universe of the novel, his egotistical endeavours do not go unpunished, since after transporting the busts to Tamerlán & Sons, he learns that his employer has been killed in a rescue attempt and so, his precious cargo of sculptures is now surplus to requirements (Fig. 5.4).

As this chapter has discussed, *Los bustos de Eva* employs grotesque realism and the carnivalesque to rupture official versions of the recent past, crafting a narrative fictionscape in which all sectors of society are complicit in the normalization of violence in the period preceding the military coup of 1976. By situating his narrative of political militancy and its excesses within the egalitarian environs of the grotesque, Gamerro weaves together an innovative and distinctly horizontalist tale of the recent past. In doing so, he redraws the boundaries of historicist representation, mocking the earnest militancy of revolutionary Peronism, the rapacious impulses of an emergent neoliberalism, and the self-serving acquiescence of the working class in equal measure. In demolishing the totems of the historicist discourse established by the human rights community during the late 1990s, the text articulates an alternative vision of this violent period of Argentine history. Here, the horizontalist impulse of the grotesque explodes hegemonic tropes of historicist agency, invoking notions of collective responsibility and reinvigorating the potential of the past as a common endeavour.

Indeed, following the general elections of 2015 in Argentina, and throughout the Macri administration of 2015–2019, cultural narratives of historicity and horizontalism were frequently mobilized collectively against the neoliberal policies of the Cambiemos government. In one example, on 7 May 2019, a little over five months before the forthcoming presidential elections, a small group of performers and activists staged an arresting performance of protest and commemoration in the centre of Buenos Aires. In a celebration of the one hundredth anniversary of the birth of Eva Perón, Les Muchaches Peronistas, an anti-Macrist collective of artists and political activists, organized a march of one hundred 'Evitas' through the centre of the capital, comprising women from all walks of life dressed as the former first lady.[76] Inspired by an idea from the Rosario-based Colectiva Mixta de Culturas, the Buenos Aires group described the demonstration as a repudiation of the conservative ideologies of Cambiemos, asserting that:

> la Evita del presente estaría a favor del derecho al aborto legal, seguro y gratuito, con sus párpados llenos de glitter, seria trans y negra, lesbiana, futbolista, maestra, jubilada, y cada sector que hoy pelea por sus derechos ante el atropello de la Alianza Cambiemos.[77]

> [the Evita of the present would be in favour of the right to free, legal and safe abortion, with her eyelids covered in glitter, she would be trans and black, lesbian, a female footballer, teacher, retiree, part of every sector that today struggles for their rights against the abuses of the Cambiemos coalition government]

Anyone who wanted to become Eva for a day was encouraged to come along and be transformed into their preferred version of Eva by the volunteer hairdressers and make-up artists who had assembled at the starting point of the demonstration. Actors staged recreations of significant scenes from Evita's life alongside the march, while the '100 Evitas' distributed flyers imprinted with her image and words. The purpose of the event, according to Pacha, a spokeperson for the collective, was to 'disputar desde lo simbólico y desde lo artístico algo que nos atraviesa a todos y todas [...], disputar el espacio público para romper con algunas creencias y prejuicios' [challenge, in a symbolic and artistic form, something which affects all of us, to stage an intervention in public space, in order to break with certain beliefs and prejudices].[78] The historicist corporality of this horizontalist action goes beyond what could be characterized as the unremitting iconicity of Eva Perón; rather, it is an articulation of the continued potency of these two discursive forces in Argentine society, almost two decades after the transformative events of December 2001. In constructing a genealogy of meaning between Eva Perón's historical demands for economic equality and social justice, and contemporary pressure for change and democratic renewal, '100 Evitas CABA' weaponized historicity through the praxis of horizontalidad. From the presence of the protestors in the streets of the *microcentro*, to the period clothes they wore, and the glitter painted on their eyelids: history was manifest in spatial, material and somatic terms. The past was present in the here and now of the everyday as a clamour for equality and a celebration of difference and diversity.

Likewise, in *Los bustos de Eva*, *horizontalidad* is a potent discursive force, which intersects with the historicist subjectivities of the novel to produce new ways of thinking about both the past and the present. As such, it represents a significant evolution in the structure of feeling that emerged after the *Argentinazo*. The afterword which follows considers what conclusions can be drawn from the various texts explored within this book, and how they illuminate the dialogic relation between historicity and *horizontalidad* in the post-Crisis era.

## Notes to Chapter 5

1. From this point onwards, the name will be referred to by the abbreviated title *Los bustos de Eva*, for purposes of brevity. All English translations of text from the novel are taken from Ian Barnett's 2015 translation of the novel: Carlos Gamerro, *The Adventures of the Busts of Eva Perón*, trans. by Ian Barnett (London: And Other Stories, 2015).
2. Jordana Blejmar, *Playful Memories: The Autofictional Turn in Post-Dictatorship Argentina* (Cham: Palgrave Macmillan, 2016), p. 39. Contrary to grammatical convention, Perez's surname does not feature a tilde on the second vowel.
3. Blejmar cites Kohan's argument from his essay 'Pero bailamos', *Katatay–Revista Crítica de Literatura Latinoamericano* 9:11/12 (2014), 23–27 (p. 24).
4. Blejmar, *Playful Memories*, p. 39
5. Ibid., p. 69.
6. *El sueño de Señor Juez* [The Dream of Señor Juez], published in 2000, has the earliest historical setting. It narrates the founding of the fictional rural town of Malihuel in 1877.
7. The novel *El secreto y las voces* is available in an English translation, entitled *An Open Secret*. See Carlos Gamerro, *An Open Secret*, trans. by Ian Barnett (London: Pushkin Press, 2011).
8. Mikhail Bakhtin, *Rabelais and his World* (London: Midland, 1984), p. 395.
9. The name of the brothel satirizes the title of the Fundación de Ayuda Social María Eva Duarte de Perón, a charitable organization established by the Argentine First Lady in 1948. It was through this Foundation that Eva Perón co-ordinated the distribution of money, household goods and other items to the poorest in society. See Nicholas Fraser and Marysa Navarro, *Evita: The Real Lives of Eva Perón* (London: Andre Deutsch, 2003), pp. 114–33.
10. Navarro, *Evita: The Real Lives of Eva Perón*, p. 394.
11. Frances S. Connelly, *The Grotesque in Western Art and Culture: The Image at Play* (Cambridge: Cambridge University Press, 2012), pp. 2–3.
12. Michael Holquist, 'Prologue', in Bakhtin, *Rabelais*, p. 11.
13. Bakhtin, *Rabelais*, p. 391.
14. Sitrin, *Everyday Revolutions*, p. 2.
15. Sitrin, *Everyday Revolutions*, p. 8.
16. Williams, *Long Revolution*, p. 68.
17. Raymond Williams and Michael Orrom, *A Preface to Film* (London: Film Drama, 1954), p. 22.
18. Carlos Gamerro, cited in Martin Lojo, 'La Argentina, una violenta invención de la literatura. Martin Kohan y Carlos Gamerro', *La Nación*, 31 August 2015 <http://www.lanacion.com.ar/1814885-la-argentina-una-violenta-invencion-de-la-literatura-martin-kohan-y-carlos-gamerro> [accessed 15 April 2017].

19. Lessa, *Memory*, p. 129.
20. For a full analysis of Kirchner's 2004 speech at the ESMA, and the significance of the event, see Elizabeth Jelin, *La lucha por el pasado: cómo construimos la memoria* social (Buenos Aires: Siglo Ventiuno, 2017), pp. 206–12. The full speech is also available to view on YouTube, at <https://www.youtube.com/watch?v=vr3ayB5xeyc> [accessed 14 February 2018].
21. Beatriz Sarlo, *La audacia y el cálculo: Kirchner 2003–2010* (Buenos Aires: Sudamericana, 2011), p. 189.
22. Carlos Gamerro, *La aventura de los bustos de Eva* (Buenos Aires: Edhasa, 2012), p. 14.
23. Carlos Gamerro, *The Adventures of the Busts of Eva Perón*, trans. by Ian Barnett (London: And Other Stories, 2015), pp. 9–10.
24. Bakhtin, *Rabelais*, p. 459.
25. Ibid., p. 459.
26. This translates literally as 'the son of blacks'. It is a racist epithet that links skin colour with social class.
27. Connelly, *The Grotesque*, p. 84.
28. Gamerro, *Los bustos de Eva*, p. 33
29. Gamerro, *The Busts of Eva*, pp. 25–26.
30. Gamerro, *Los bustos de Eva*, p. 41. Gamerro, *The Busts of Eva*, p. 32.
31. Bakhtin, *Rabelais*, p. 55.
32. Gamerro, *Los bustos de Eva*, p. 92. Gamerro, *The Busts of Eva*, p. 75.
33. David Rock, 'Revolt and Repression in Argentina', *The World Today*, 33:6 (1977), pp. 215–22 (p. 217, 218).
34. Gamerro, *Los bustos de Eva*. p. 150. Gamerro, *The Busts of Eva*, p. 124.
35. José López Rega, nicknamed 'El brujo' due to his interest in the occult, was a powerful figure in Isabel Perón's government and the death squads of the Triple A operated out of his Ministry of Social Welfare. See Gillespie, *Soldiers*, p. 153.
36. Maryssa Navarro, 'Evita, historia y mitología', *Caravelle*, 98 (2012), 113–33 (p. 131).
37. Gamerro, *Los bustos de Eva*, p. 212. Gamerro, *The Busts of Eva*, p. 175.
38. Bakhtin, *Rabelais*, p. 220
39. Gamerro, *Los bustos de Eva*, p. 236. Gamerro, *The Busts of Eva*, p. 195.
40. In the mid-1970s, the Born brothers were the heirs to 'the largest grain-exporting houses in Buenos Aires', according to historian David Rock. For further information, see Rock, *Argentina*, p. 363. A full account of the kidnapping operation and the political reverberations of the crime over the next two decades, see Maria O'Donnell, *El secuestro de los Born* (Buenos Aires: Sudamericana, 2015).
41. For a full account of the complex composition and varying ideologies of the numerous guerrilla groups in operation during this period, see Gillespie, *Soldiers*. More recently, the most comprehensive evaluation of the Argentine armed left during the 1970s can be found in the three volumes of Eduardo Anguita and Martín Caparrós's *La voluntad*. For example, *La voluntad: una historia de la militancia revolucionaria en la argentina, tomo 1 — 1966–1973* (Buenos Aires: Planeta, 2013).
42. For a detailed account of both the reasons for and the consequences of the kidnapping of Aramburu, see Gillespie, *Soldiers*, pp. 89–96.
43. Ibid.
44. For details of the often-bizarre peregrinations of the corpse of Eva Peron, see Nicholas Fraser and Marysa Navarro, *Evita: The Real Lives of Eva Perón* (London: Andre Deutsch, 2003). The 1995 novel *Santa Evita* by Tomás Eloy Martínez is a fictionalized account of the First Lady's final days, 'Operation Cadaver' and of her afterlife as myth and icon.
45. Beatriz Sarlo, *La pasión y la excepción: Eva, Borges y el asesinato de Aramburu* (Buenos Aires: Siglo Veintiuno, 2004), p. 136.
46. Ibid., p. 136.
47. Sebastián Carrasai, *Los años setenta de la gente común: la naturalización de la violencia* (Buenos Aires: Siglo Veintiuno, 2013), p. 66.
48. Cited in ibid.

49. Sarlo, *La pasión*, p. 9.
50. Sarlo, *La pasión*, p. 10
51. Noé Jitrik, *Historia e imaginación literaria: posibilidades de un género* (Buenos Aires: Editorial Biblos, 1995), p. 55.
52. Bakhtin, *Rabelais*, p. 317, 319.
53. Gamerro, *Los bustos de Eva*, p. 16, 36. Gamerro, *The Busts of Eva*, p. 11, 28.
54. Gamerro, *Los bustos de Eva*, p. 21. Gamerro, *The Busts of Eva*, p. 16.
55. Gamerro, *Los bustos de Eva*, p. 85.
56. Gamerro, *Los bustos de Eva*, p. 309. Gamerro, *The Busts of Eva*, pp. 253–54.
57. Bakhtin, *Rabelais*, p. 256, 276.
58. Gamerro, *Los bustos de Eva*, p. 112. Gamerro, *The Busts of Eva*, p. 91.
59. Gamerro, *Los bustos de Eva*, pp. 236–37. Gamerro, *The Busts of Eva*, p. 195.
60. Gamerro, *Los bustos de Eva*, pp. 236–37. Gamerro, *The Busts of Eva*, p. 195.
61. Gamerro, *Los bustos de Eva*, p. 237. Gamerro, *The Busts of Eva*, p. 196.
62. Bakhtin, *Rabelais*, p. 281.
63. Gamerro, *Los bustos de Eva*, p. 243.
64. Cited in María José Moyano, *Argentina's Lost Patrol: Armed Struggle, 1969–1979* (New Haven, CT: Yale University Press, 1995), p. 1.
65. Gamerro, *Los bustos de Eva*, pp. 329–30. Gamerro, *The Busts of Eva*, p. 271.
66. Daniel Santoro, 'La construcción imaginaria de un mundo', in *Perón mediante: Grafica peronista del periodo clásico*, ed. by Guido Indiij (Buenos Aires: La Marca Editora, 2012), pp. 21–23 (p. 22).
67. Mariano Ben Plotkin, *Mañana es San Perón: A Cultural History of Peron's Argentina* (Wilmington, DE: Scholarly Resources, 2003), p. 23.
68. Gamerro, *Los bustos de Eva*, p. 330.
69. Gamerro, *The busts of Eva*, p. 271.
70. Detailed information on the origins of Ciudad Evita is scarce. Plotkin mentions it briefly. Some general information is available on the local authority website of La Matanza, the district in which it is now located. <http://lamatanza.org.ar/ciudad-evita/> [accessed 15 April 2017].
71. Ben Bollig, 'Carlos Gamerro's Historical Fiction Reveals Stories of Facts Once Hidden', *The Guardian*, 10 July 2012 < https://www.theguardian.com/books/2012/jul/10/carlos-gamerro-open-secret-islands> [accessed 15 April 2017].
72. Gamerro, *Los bustos de Eva*, p. 359. Gamerro, *The Busts of Eva*, p. 294.
73. Sitrin, *Everyday Revolutions*, p. 8
74. Connelly, *The Grotesque*, p. 82.
75. Gamerro, *Los bustos de Eva*, p. 381. Gamerro, *The Busts of Eva*, p. 313.
76. Anccom, 'Evitas 100 x 100', 8 May 2019, <https://anccom.sociales.uba.ar/2019/05/08evitas-100-x100/> [accessed 5 August 2020].
77. '100 Evitas, 100 Mujeres, 100 Años', Mariano Quiroga, *Kranear*, 5 May 2019 <https://kranear.com.ar/2019/05/05/100-evitas-100-mujeres-100-anos> [accessed 9 July 2019].
78. '100 Evitas'.

# AFTERWORD

> Art reflects its society [...] but also art creates, by new perceptions
> and responses, elements which the society, as such, is not able to realise
> — RAYMOND WILLIAMS

The purpose of a historicist critical evaluation of cultural forms is, as Raymond Williams writes, 'to relate them to the particular traditions and societies in which they appeared'.[1] Accordingly, the purpose of this book has been to examine the cultural specificities of historicity and *horizontalidad* in the post-Crisis period in Argentina, and to consider the wider pattern of the ebb and flow of both discourses as symptomatic of a new structure of feeling. As we have seen, the historicist impulse was present before the *Argentinazo*, as was the theory and praxis of *horizontalidad*. However, in the years after the Crisis, these two discursive forces gained strength and momentum, pervading all aspects of social and cultural life. The critical excavation of a structure of feeling is not an exact science, not least since, as Williams asserts, 'it operates in the least tangible parts of our activity'.[2] Consequently, the corpus evaluated here comprises multiple, and often divergent narratives of historicity and *horizontalidad*. Frequently, as with the novel *El cantor de tango* and the documentary *La multitud*, historicism is the pre-eminent subjectivity, and the possibility of an alternative concept of the present and future is tacit, if not conspicuous in its absence.

Paradoxically, at times the utopian potentiality of horizontalism has made its presence felt in the least likely of locations, such as within the mainstream feature film *Elefante blanco* and Carlos Gamerro's rambunctious re-evaluation of political militancy in the 1970s, *Las aventuras de los bustos de Eva*. In the syncretic narratives of *Mu*, which combine complex historical allusions with non-vertical activism, we see the two discourses inextricably intertwined. In the popular historiography of the television series *Lo que el tiempo nos dejó,* the ability of ordinary people to organize themselves autonomously against the authoritarian structures of the state reveals a horizontalist aspiration. But in each text, both discourses are visible, even if only, as in *La multitud*, in the empty space they demarcate. In these collisions of past and present, the spectre of the *Argentinazo* is always present, shaping the ways each text articulates its vision of the world. While historicity may be the more dominant of the two discourses, without the tempering influence of *horizontalidad*, the past is merely past, lacking the positive impetus to effect change in the present.

Writing in 2017, Verónica Garibotto likened the revelatory potential of cultural texts to the personal articulations of a patient engaged in psychoanalysis, asserting that 'in an era that has survived unthinkable historical catastrophes, texts — much like patients undergoing treatment –– bear witness to the crisis'.[3] Describing works of culture as 'precocious modes of accessing history', Garibotto highlights the ability of such texts to 'decipher historical truths that are unspoken'.[4] As the preceding chapters have highlighted, the cultural narratives that emerged in the post-2001 period foretold an impending societal shift in how a sense of the past was conceptualized and enacted. Through a process of active historicization, the past once again became a radical tool for reshaping the future, beyond its earlier configurations as the source of trauma and injustice in the present. This transformation in historicist discourse was facilitated in no small part by the horizontalist praxis that flourished in the period immediately after the *Argentinazo*. The discursive force of *horizontalidad* informed how history was viewed and used to alter lived experience in the present. Indeed, even as economic conditions improved and horizontalism receded as a political force, its presence within the cultural sphere remained undiminished, as we see in the communitarian narrative of the most recent text considered in this study, the 2012 feature film *Elefante blanco*.

In their evolution through a range of cultural modalities, the texts analysed here demonstrate how narratives of historicity, aided and abetted by the horizontalist impulse, have developed during the decade after the *Argentinazo*, moving from the spectral exigencies of the hauntological turn, to the more concrete historiographical interruptions of spatial and material signifiers into the everyday routines of the urban, and finally to a literal embodiment of the past in the somatic demands of the body itself. Each of these historicist iterations is underpinned ever more firmly by a horizontalist praxis which not only informs the way the past is conceptualized and articulated but also, crucially, declaims the imperative to view 'the present as history'.[5] *Horizontalidad* brought about an emancipation of the past, facilitating individual and collective interactions with the cultural minutiae of history through innovative and inclusive activism and representation.

In 2015, Cristina Fernández de Kirchner was succeeded as President of the Nation by Mauricio Macri, of the centre-right coalition party Cambiemos. This change of administration appeared to signal the quietus of the forms of historicity and horizontalism which permeated the Kirchner era. A new epoch, it seemed, had begun, in which the sense of the past observed in the texts featured here no longer flourished unchallenged.[6] New versions of history began to emerge, not all of them positive or even benign. In an interview with Buzzfeed on 10 August 2016, in referring to the state terrorism of the 1970s as a 'guerra sucia', Macri publicly reanimated the long-refuted concept of 'the two demons' and appeared to marginalize issues of memory and human rights in favour of 'los derechos humanos del siglo XXI, como la salud, la educación, lo que necesita la gente para ser feliz' [the human rights of the twenty-first century, such as health, education, the things people need to be happy].[7] These remarks signalled the beginning of a new political approach to memory, and to historicity more broadly. As Crenzel writes, Macri 'rejected the role of human rights organizations and their demands' through rhetoric and policy changes that sought to curtail the influence of the human rights movement on Argentine society.[8]

However, paradoxically, throughout Macri's single term in power, just as hegemonic discourses of historicity appeared to recede in strength, new forms of *horizontalidad* surfaced to become once again a powerful mobilizing force in Argentine society. In the mass-demonstrations of the feminist movement of Ni una menos and the subsequent non-verticalist campaigns for causes such as the legalization of abortion, traces of the exigent potential of the *Argentinazo* make their presence felt.[9] What remains to be seen is how the discursive forces of historicity and horizontalidad will adapt within the new political context in Argentina, following the election of Frente de Todos in October 2019, a Peronist coalition government headed by Alberto Fernández, with Cristina Fernández de Kirchner as Vice-President. Perhaps some indication can be gleaned from a public ceremony which took place at the former Ministerio de Obras Públicas in central Buenos Aires on 12 December 2019, where two large steel murals that had adorned the building since 2010 were reilluminated after a period of disuse. Depicting Eva Perón in two contrasting poses, the murals were originally erected during the bicentenary year and would light up every evening at 8.25pm, her official time of death. However, from December 2015 onwards, this historicist installation was left unused and gradually fell into disrepair, a massive white elephant adrift amidst the city skyline. Four years later, with several new government ministers and a large and enthusiastic crowd looking on, the murals were illuminated once again. Commenting on the spectacle, the Minister of Culture Tristán Bauer enthused: 'es una noche de profunda emoción, [...] quisieron apagar la luz de Evita, pero esa era una tarea imposible' [it is a night of deep emotion, [...] they wanted to extinguish the light of Evita, but this proved an impossible task].[10] As a metaphorical declaration of intent by the Fernández government, this reclamation of the image of Evita, that historicist signifier *par excellence*, could not have been clearer.

This book has uncovered the contiguities and divergences present within the dialogic relations between historicity and *horizontalidad* in the post-Crisis era, in the decade following the *Argentinazo*. In its analyses of a range of cultural texts from the period, it has affirmed how the pre-eminence of these two discursive forces constituted a new structure of feeling, in the cultural sphere and beyond. In the light of the evolving socio-political context in Argentina, these findings may be used as the foundations for further investigation into the ongoing relationship between historicity and horizontalism. For, just as cultural texts enunciate the unspoken truths of the past, so further study may reveal how the documentary culture of the post-2015 period contains the nascent truths of a radically different present and future.

### Notes to the Afterword

1. Williams, *Long Revolution*, p. 61.
2. Williams, *Long Revolution*, p. 69.
3. Verónica Garibotto, 'Pitfalls of Trauma: Revisiting Postdictatorship Cinema from a Semiotic Standpoint', *Latin American Research Review*, 52: 4 (2017), 654–67 (p. 654).
4. Ibid.
5. Jameson, *Postmodernism*, p. 284.

6. Carlos E. Cué, 'Polémica en Argentina por las cifras de desaparecidos de la dictadura', *El País*, 26 January 2016 <https://elpais.com/internacional/2016/01/27/argentina/1453931104_458651.html> [accessed 15 May 2018].
7. For a summary of Macri's televised interview with Buzzfeed, see: <https://www.infobae.com/politica/2016/08/10/22-definiciones-de-macri-en-su-entrevista-en-buzzfeed/> [accessed 23 February 2020].
8. Emilio Crenzel, 'Four cases under examination: Human Rights and Justice in Argentina under the Macri Administration', *Modern Languages Open*, 20: 1 (26), pp. 1–13 (p. 2).
9. *La Nación*, 'Masiva convocatoria en contra de los femicidios', 19 October 2016, <https://www.lanacion.com.ar/1948483-ni-una-menos-miles-de-mujeres-se-concentran-en-el-obelisco-en-contra-de-los-femicidios> [accessed 15 May 2018].
10. Melisa Molina, 'El mural de Evita de nuevo illuminado', *Pagina 12*, 12 December 2019, <https://www.pagina12.com.ar/236289-el-mural-de-evita-de-nuevo-iluminado> [accessed 5 August 2020].

# BIBLIOGRAPHY

Acuña, Claudia, Diego Rosemberg, Juditha Gociol and Patricia Rojas, '19 y 20 de diciembre de 2001: Los días en que todo cambió', in *Grandes crónicas periodísticas*, ed. by Graciela Pedraza (Cordoba: Editorial Comunicarte, 2008), pp. 163–66
Aguilar, Gonzalo, *Other Worlds: New Argentine Film* (Basingstoke: Palgrave Macmillan, 2008)
—— 'Shantytowns: Buenos Aires, the Shattered City' in *World Film Locations: Buenos Aires*, ed. by Santiago Oyarzabal and Michael Pigott (Bristol: Intellect Books, 2014), pp. 48–49
Amaya, Jenny, 'La pantalla *nos* recuerda: la construcción de la memoria cultural en la telenovela cubana', in *La ficción histórica en la televisión iberoamericana 2000–2012*, ed. by María de los Ángeles Rodríguez Cadena (Leiden: Brill Rodopi, 2016), pp. 64–89
Andermann, Jens, *New Argentine Cinema* (London: Tauris, 2012)
—— 'Returning to the Site of Horror: The Recovery of Clandestine Concentration Camps in Argentina', *Theory, Culture & Society*, 29:1 (2012), 76–98
Andermann, Jens and Álvaro Fernández Bravo, eds, *New Argentine and Brazilian Cinema: Reality Effects* (Basingstoke: Palgrave Macmillan, 2013)
—— 'Introduction', in *New Argentine and Brazilian Cinema: Reality Effects*, ed. by Jens Andermann and Álvaro Fernández Bravo (Basingstoke: Palgrave Macmillan, 2013), pp. 1–9
Andersen, Martin Edward, *Dossier Secreto: Argentina's Desaparecidos and the Myth of the "Dirty War"* (Oxford: Westview Press, 1993)
Anderson, Benedict, *Imagined Communities* (London: Verso, 2006)
Anguita, Eduardo, and Martín Caparrós, *La voluntad, una historia de la militancia revolucionaria en la Argentina, tomo 1: 1966–1973* (Buenos Aires: Planeta, 2013)
—— *La voluntad, una historia de la militancia revolucionaria en la Argentina, tomo 2: 1973–1976* (Buenos Aires: Planeta, 2013)
—— *La voluntad, una historia de la militancia revolucionaria en la Argentina, tomo 3: 1976–1978* (Buenos Aires: Planeta, 2015)
Arenillas, María Guadalupe, 'Towards a Nondiscursive Turn in Argentine Documentary Film', in *Latin American Documentary Film in the New Millennium*, ed. by María Guadalupe Arenillas and Michael J. Lazzara (New York: Palgrave Macmillan, 2016), pp. 275–90.
Arias, Lola, *Audición para una manifestación*, online video and project summary, <http://lolaarias.com/proyectos/audicion-para-una-manifestacion/?lang=es> [accessed 21 October 2020]
Roberto Arlt], *Los siete locos* (Madrid: Cátedra, 2011)
Arruti, Nerea, 'Tracing the Past: Marcelo Brodsky's Photography as Memory Art', *Paragraph*, 30:1 (2007), 101–20
Atencio, Rebecca J., 'A Prime Time to Remember: Memory Merchandising in Globo's Años Rebeldes', in *Accounting for Violence: Marketing Memory in Latin America*, ed. by Ksenija Bilbija and Leigh A. Payne (Durham, NC: Duke University Press), pp. 41–68
Attwood, Feona, Vincent Campbell, I. Q. Hunter and Sharon Lockyer, eds, *Controversial Images: Media Representation on the Edge* (Basingstoke: Palgrave Macmillan, 2013)

AVELAR, IDELBER, *The Untimely Present: Postdictatorial Latin American Fiction and the Task of Mourning* (Durham, NC: Duke University Press, 1999)
AUYERO, JAVIER, *Poor People's Politics: Peronist Survival Networks and the Legacy of Evita* (Durham, NC: Duke University Press, 2000)
BADENES, DANIEL, *Editar sin patrón: La experiencia política-profesional de las revistas culturales independientes* (Buenos Aires: Club Hem, 2017)
BAKHTIN, MIKHAIL, *Problems of Dostoevsky's Poetics*, trans. and ed. by Caryl Emerson (Manchester: Manchester University Press, 1984)
—— *Rabelais and his World* (London: Midland, 1984)
BAL, MIEKE, JONATHAN CREWE and LEO SPITZER, *Acts of Memory: Cultural Recall in the Present* (Hanover: University Press of New England, 1999)
BAUMAN, ZYGMUNT, *Globalization: The Human Consequences* (Cambridge: Polity Press, 1998)
BELINCHÓN, GREGORIO, 'Pablo Trapero contra la hipocresía', *El País*, 27 June 2012 <http://cultura.elpais.com/cultura/2012/06/27/actualidad/1340812132_977262.html> [accessed 21 October 2020]
BENJAMIN, WALTER, *The Arcades Project* (Cambridge, MA: University of Harvard Press, 1999)
—— *Berlin Childhood Around 1900* (Cambridge, MA: Harvard University Press, 2006)
—— *Illuminations* (London: Pimlico, 1999)
BERNADES, HORACIO 'Elefante blanco, social y masivo', *Pagina12*, 17 May 2012, <http://www.pagina12.com.ar/diario/suplementos/espectaculos/subnotas/25232-6708-2012-05-17.html> [accessed 21 October 2020]
BEWES, TIMOTHY, *Reification, or, The Anxiety of Late Capitalism* (London: Verso, 2002)
BIDDISS, MICHAEL, 'Thatcherism: Concepts and Interpretations', in *Thatcherism: Personality and Politics*, ed. by Kenneth Minogue and Michael Biddiss (Basingstoke: Macmillan, 1987), pp. 1–20.
BILBIJA, KSENIJA and LEIGH A. PAYNE, eds, *Accounting for Violence: Marketing Memory in Latin America* (Durham, NC: Duke University Press, 2011)
—— 'Introduction: Time is Money, The Memory Market in Latin America', in *Accounting for Violence: Marketing Memory in Latin America*, ed. by Ksenija Bilbija and Leigh A. Payne (Durham, NC: Duke University Press, 2011), pp. 2–40.
BLAUSTEIN, EDUARDO, *Prohibido vivir aquí* (Buenos Aires: Punto de encuentro, 2006).
BLEJMAR, JORDANA, *Playful Memories: The Autofictional Turn in Post-Dictatorship Argentina* (Cham: Palgrave Macmillan, 2016)
BÖHMER, MARTIN, 'An Oresteia for Argentina: Between Fraternity and the Rule of Law', in *Law and Democracy in the Empire of Force*, ed. by Jefferson Powells and James Boyd White (Ann Arbor, MC: University of Michigan Press, 2009), pp. 89–124.
BOLLIG, BEN, 'Carlos Gamerro's historical fiction reveals stories of facts once hidden', *The Guardian*, 10 July 2012 <https://www.theguardian.com/books/2012/jul/10/carlos-gamerro-open-secret-islands> [accessed 21 October 2020]
BORG, RUBEN, PAUL FAGAN and WERNER HUBER, eds, *Flann O'Brien: Contesting Legacies* (Cork: Cork University Press, 2014)
BORGES, JORGE LUIS 'Autobiographical Essay', in *The Aleph and Other Stories 1933–1969*, trans. and ed. by Norman di Giovanni (London: Lowe and Brydone, 1971), pp. 203–60.
—— *The Aleph and Other Stories 1933–1969*, trans. and ed. by Norman di Giovanni (London: Lowe and Brydone, 1971)
—— *Obras completas* (Buenos Aires: Emecé, 1974)
—— 'Del rigor en la ciencia', in *Obras completas* (Buenos Aires: Emecé, 1974), p. 847
BRANDIST, CRAIG, *The Bakhtin Circle: Philosophy, Culture and Politics* (London: Pluto Press, 2002)

BRODSKY, MARCELO, *Nexo: un ensayo fotográfico de Marcelo Brodsky* (Buenos Aires: La Marca, 2001)

BRUHN, JORGEN, 'Seeing without Understanding: Mediality Aspects of Literature and Memory in Vladimir Nabokov's "Spring in Fialta"', *Orbis Litterarum*, 70:5 (2015), 380–404

BUONANNO, MILLY, 'Conceptos clave para el story-telling televisivo. Calidad, mediación y ciudadanía', *Diálogos de la Comunicación*, 64 (2002), 76–85

CABAÑAS BRAVO, MIGUEL, *El arte foráneo en España: presencia e influencia* (Madrid: CSIC, 2005)

CARA-WALKER, ANA, 'Cocoliche: The Art of Assimilation and Dissimulation among Italians and Argentines', *Latin American Research Review*, 22:3 (1987), 37–67

CARRASAI, SEBASTIÁN, *Los años setenta de la gente común: la naturalización de la violencia* (Buenos Aires: Siglo Veintiuno, 2013)

CERRUTTI, MARCELA and ALEJANDRO GRIMSON, 'Neoliberal Reforms and Protests in Buenos Aires', in *Neoliberalism Interrupted: Social Change and Contested Governance in Contemporary Latin America*, ed. by Mark Goodale and Nancy Postero (Stanford, CA: Stanford University Press, 2013), pp. 109–36

CHAKARS, MELISSA and STUART ANDERSON, eds, *Modernization, Nation-Building, and Television History* (New York: Routledge, 2015)

CHICHARRO MERAYO, MAR, 'Telenovelas and Society: Constructing and Reinforcing the Nation through Television Fiction', *European Journal of Cultural Studies*, 16:2 (2012), 211–25.

CHURCHWELL, SARAH, 'Roy Lichtenstein: From Heresy to Visionary', *The Guardian*, Saturday 23 February 2013 <https://www.theguardian.com/artanddesign/2013/feb/23/roy-lichtenstein-heresy-to-visionary> [accessed 21 October 2020]

CLEMENT, ALEXANDER, *Brutalism: Post-War British Architecture* (London: Crowood Press, 2011)

*Clarín*, Editorial, 'El Kirchnerismo impulsa una nueva corriente revisionista', 26 November 2011<https://www.clarin.com/politica/construccion-relato-traslada-hechos-historia_0_r14UZ4q3w7x.html> [accessed 21 October 2020]

COLAS, SANTIAGO, *Postmodernity in Latin America: The Argentine Paradigm* (Durham, NC: Duke University Press, 1994)

—— 'The Third World in Jameson's *Postmodernism or the Cultural Logic of Late Capitalism*', *Social Text: Third World and Colonial Issues*, 31/32 (1992), 258–70

COLLECTIVA SITUACIONES, *19 & 29: Notes for a New Social Protagonism*, trans. by Nat Holdren and Sebastian Tanza (Brooklyn, NY: Autonomedia, 2012)

COLOMER, JULIETA, *Escrache: Imágenes de una generación que nos devolvió a la historia* (Buenos Aires: Mónadanomada + el zócalo, 2015)

CONNELLY, FRANCES, S., *The Grotesque in Western Art and Culture: The Image at Play* (Cambridge: Cambridge University Press, 2012)

CRENZEL, EMILIO, 'Present Pasts: Memory(ies) of State Terrorism in the Southern Cone of Latin America', in *The Memory of State Terrorism in the Southern Cone: Argentina, Chile and Uruguay*, ed. by Francesca Lessa and Vincent Druliolle (New York: Palgrave Macmillan, 2011), pp. 1–14.

—— *Memory of the Argentina Disappearances: The Political History of Nunca Más* (Abingdon: Routledge, 2011)

—— 'Toward a History of the Memory of Political Violence and the Disappeared in Argentina', in *The Struggle for Memory in Latin America*, ed. by Eugenia Allier-Montaño and Emilio Crenzel (New York: Palgrave, 2015), pp. 15–34

—— 'Four Cases Under Examination: Human Rights and Justice in Argentina under the Macri Administration', *Modern Languages Open*, 26:1 (2020), 1–13

CROSS, GARY, *Consuming Nostalgia: Memory in the Age of Fast Capitalism* (New York: Columbia University Press, 2015)
CUÉ, CARLOS E, 'Polémica en Argentina por las cifras de desaparecidos de la dictadura', *El País*, 26 January 2016 <https://elpais.com/internacional/2016/01/27/argentina/1453931104_458651.html> [accessed 21 October 2020]
DADAMO, FLORENCIA, LEANDRO DELLA MORA and MARIANA PICCINELLI, 'Historia. memoria y el recurso audiovisual: las narraciones del pasado en la televisión argentina actual', in *La ficción histórica en la televisión iberoamericana 2000–2012*, ed. by María de los Ángeles Rodríguez Cadena (Leiden: Brill Rodopi, 2016), pp. 90–128
DE CERTEAU, MICHEL, 'Practices of Space', in *On Signs*, ed. by Marshal Blonsky (Baltimore: John Hopkins University Press, 1985), pp. 122–45
Decreto 1880/2011, Secretaria de Cultura –– Créase el Instituto Nacional de Revisionismo Histórico Argentino e Iberoamericano Manuel Dorrego, Boletín Oficial 21/11/2011
DENTITH, SIMON, *Bakhtinian Thought: An Introductory Reader* (London: Routledge, 1995)
DERRIDA, JACQUES, *Specters of Marx: The State of the Debt, the Work of Mourning and the New International* (Abingdon: Routledge, 1994)
DINARDI, CECILIA, 'Assembling the Past, Performing the Nation: The Argentine Bicentenary and Regaining of Public Space in the Aftermath of the 2001 Crisis', in *Argentina since the 2001 Crisis: Recovering the Past, Reclaiming the Future*, ed. by Cara Levey, Daniel Ozarow and Christopher Wylde (Basingstoke: Palgrave Macmillan, 2014), pp. 215–32.
DINERSTEIN, ANA CECILIA, 'Disagreement and Hope: The Hidden Transcripts in the Grammar of Political Recovery in Postcrisis Argentina', in *Argentina Since the 2001 Crisis: Recovering the Past, Reclaiming the Future*, ed. by Cara Levey, Daniel Ozarow, and Christopher Wylde (Basingstoke: Palgrave Macmillan, 2014), pp. 115–33
DONALD, JAMES, 'Metropolis: The City as Text', in *The Social and Cultural Forms of Modernity*, ed. by Robert Bocock and Kenneth Thompson (London: Polity Press/Open University, 1992), pp. 417–70
DRAPER, SUSANA 'The Question of Awakening in Postdictatorship Times: Reading Walter Benjamin with Diamela Eltit', *Discourse: Benjamin in Winter*, 32 (2010), 87–116
DRULIOLLE, VINCENT, 'Remembering and its Places in Postdictatorship Argentina', in *The Memory of State Terrorism in the Southern Cone: Argentina, Chile, and Uruguay*, ed. by Francesca Lessa and Vincent Druliolle (Palgrave Macmillan: Basingstoke, 2011), pp. 15–41
EBBRECHT, TOBIAS, 'Docudramatizing History on TV: German and British Docudrama and Historical Event Television in the Memorial Year 2005', *European Journal of Cultural Studies*, 10:1 (2007), 35–53
ECHEVERRÍA, ESTEBAN ANTONIO, 'El matadero', in *The Argentina Reader*, ed. by Gabriela Nouzeilles and Graciela Montaldo (Durham, NC: Duke University Press, 2002), pp. 107–14
Edinburgh International Film Festival 2008, <http://www.edfilmfest.org.uk/films/2008/the-appeared/full-details#>
EILITTÄ, LEENA, LILIANE LOUVEL and SABINE KIM, eds, *Intermedial Arts: Disrupting, Remembering and Transforming Media* (Newcastle upon Tyne: Cambridge Scholars, 2012)
ELLESTROM, LARS, ed., *Media Borders, Multimodality and Intermediality* (Basingstoke: Palgrave Macmillan, 2010)
ELOY MARTÍNEZ, TOMÁS, *El cantor de tango* (Buenos Aires: Planeta, 2004)
––– *La novela de Perón* (Madrid: Alianza, 1989)
––– *La pasión según Trelew* (Buenos Aires: Alfaguara, 2009)
––– *Réquiem por un país perdido* (Buenos Aires: Alfaguara, 2003)

―― *Santa Evita* (Barcelona: Seix Barral, 1995)
―― *The Tango Singer*, trans. by Anne McLean (Bloomsbury: London, 2007)
ESQUIVADA, GABRIELA, *Noticias de los Montoneros: la historia del diario que no pudo anunciar la revolución* (Buenos Aires: Sudamericana, 2009)
FAULKNER, WILLIAM, *Requiem for a Nun* (New York: Vintage, 1996)
FEATHERSTONE, DAVID, *Solidarity: Hidden Histories and Geographies of Internationalism* (London: Zero Books, 2012)
FAVORETTO, MARA, *Charly en el país de las alegorías: un viaje por las letras de Charly García* (Buenos Aires: Gourmet Musical, 2014)
FEITLOWITZ, MARGUERITE, *A Lexicon of Terror: Argentina and the Legacies of Torture* (New York: Oxford University Press, 2011)
FINKIELMAN, JORGE, *The Film Industry in Argentina: An Illustrated Cultural History* (Jefferson, North Carolina: McFarland, 2004)
FISHER, JO, *Mothers of the Disappeared* (Boston: South End, 1999)
FISHER, MARK, *Capitalist Realism* (Winchester: Zero Books, 2008)
―― *Ghosts of My Life: Writings on Depression, Hauntology and Lost Futures* (London: Zero Books, 2013)
FORSTER, RICARDO, *La anomalía argentina: Aventuras y desventuras del tiempo kirchnerista* (Buenos Aires: Sudamericana, 2012)
FRASER, NICHOLAS and NAVARRO, MARYSA, *Evita: The Real Lives of Eva Perón* (London: Andre Deutsch, 2003)
FREITAG, FLORIAN '"Like Walking into a Movie": Intermedial Relations between Theme Parks and Movies', *Journal of Popular Culture*, 50:4 (2017), 704–22
GALÁN FAJARDO, ELENA and JOSÉ CARLOS RUEDA LAFFOND, 'Como contar la historia. Estrategias de proximidad en la televisión argentina', *Athenea Digital*, 14:3 (2014), 23–47.
GALOTTA, NAHUEL, 'Ciudad Oculta por dentro, la villa que se revela en el cine' *Clarín*, 27 May 2012 <http://www.clarin.com/capital_federal/Ciudad-Oculta-dentro-villa-revela_0_707929263.html> [accessed 21 October 2020]
GAMBETTA CHUK, AÍDA NADI, 'Soma y sema: *El cantor de tango* (2004) de Tomas Eloy Martínez *Graffylia*, Spring (2007), 40–45
GAMERRO, CARLOS, *La aventura de los bustos de Eva Perón* (Buenos Aires: Edhasa, 2012)
―― *Las islas* (Buenos Aires: Edhasa, 2012)
―― *El secreto y las voces* (Buenos Aires: Edhasa, 2011)
―― *Un yuppie en la columna del Che Guevara* (Buenos Aires: Edhasa, 2011)
―― *The Adventure of the Busts of Eva Perón*, trans. by Ian Barnett (London: And Other Stories, 2015)
―― *An Open Secret*, trans. by Ian Barnett (London: Pushkin Press, 2011)
GARAVELLI, CLARA, 'White Elephant/Elefante blanco', in *World Film Locations: Buenos Aires*, ed. by Santiago Oyarzabal and Michael Pigott (Bristol: Intellect Books, 2014), pp. 120–21.
GARCÍA CANCLINI, NÉSTOR, *Consumers and Citizens: Globalization and Multicultural Conflicts* (Minneapolis: University of Minnesota Press, 2001)
GARIBOTTO, VERÓNICA, 'Pitfalls of Trauma: Revisiting Postdictatorship Cinema from a Semiotic Standpoint', *Latin American Research Review*, 52: 4 (2017), 654–67
―― *Rethinking Testimonial Cinema in Postdictatorship Argentina: Beyond Memory Fatigue* (Bloomington, IN: Indiana University Press, 2019)
GIAMBARTOLOMEI, MAURICIO, 'El Parque de la Ciudad, olvidado y arruinado como una fantasma', *La Nación*, 31 May 2013 <http://www.lanacion.com.ar/1587106-el-parque-de-la-ciudad-olvidado-y-arruinado-como-una-feria-fantasma> [accessed 21 October 2020]
GIAMBARTOLOMEI, MAURICIO, 'Ciudad Oculta: Un nuevo ministerio en el predio que ocupaba el Elefante Blanco', *La Nación*, 23 June 2019 <https://www.lanacion.com.ar/

buenos-aires/ciudad-oculta-nuevo-ministerio-predio-ocupaba-elefante-nid2260576> [accessed 21 October 2020]
GERAGHTY, NIALL H. D., and MASSIDDA, ADRIANA LAURA, eds, *Creative Spaces and Urban Marginality in Latin America* (London: University of London Press, 2019)
——, 'The Spatiality of Desire in Martín Oesterheld's *La multitud* and Luis Ortega's *Dromómanos* (2012)', in *Creative Spaces and Urban Marginality in Latin America*, eds, Niall H.D. Geraghty and Adriana Laura Massidda, (London: University of London Press, 2019), pp. 201–40
GILBERT, JEREMY, *Anticapitalism and Culture* (Oxford: New York: Berg, 2008)
GILLESPIE, RICHARD, *Soldiers of Perón: Argentina's Montoneros* (Oxford: Clarendon, 1982)
GOBELLO, JOSÉ, *Nuevo diccionario lunfardo* (Buenos Aires: Corregidor, 2014)
GOEBEL, MICHAEL, *Argentina's Partisan Past* (Liverpool: University of Liverpool Press, 2011)
GOÑI, UKI, *El infiltrado: Astiz, las Madres y el Herald* (Buenos Aires: Ariel, 2018)
GONZÁLEZ ECHEVARRIA, ROBERTO, ed., *Cervantes' Don Quixote: A Casebook* (Oxford: Oxford University Press, 2005)
GOODALE, MARK and NANCY POSTERO, eds, *Neoliberalism Interrupted: Social Change and Contested Governance in Contemporary Latin America* (Stanford, CA: Stanford University Press, 2013)
GORDILLO, GASTÓN, R., *Rubble: The Afterlife of Destruction* (Durham, NC: Duke University Press, 2014)
GORDON, AVERY, *Ghostly Matters: Ghosts and the Sociological Imagination* (Minneapolis: University of Minnesota Press, 2008)
GORELIK, ADRIÁN, and GRACIELA SILVESTRI, 'The Past as Future: A Reactive Utopia in Buenos Aires', in *The Latin American Cultural Studies Reader*, ed. by Ana del Sarto, Alicia Rios and Abril Trigo (Durham, NC: Duke University Press), pp. 427–40
——'Buenos Aires is (Latin) America Too', in *City/Art: The Urban Scene in Latin America*, ed. by Rebecca E. Biron (Durham, NC: Duke University Press, 2009), pp. 61–84
——'A Metropolis in the Pampas: Buenos Aires 1890–1940', in *Cruelty and Utopia: Cities and Landscapes of Latin America*, ed. by Jean-Francois Lejeune (New York: Princeton University Press, 2003), pp. 146–59
——*Miradas sobre Buenos Aires: historia cultural y crítica urbana* (Buenos Aires: Siglo Veintiuno, 2004)
GRAY, ANN and ERIN BELL, *History on Television* (London: Routledge, 2012)
GUTMAN, DANIEL, 'Un símbolo porteño', *Clarín*, 17 May 2011, <https://www.clarin.com/ciudades/Buenos-Aires-vista-mirador-elevado_0_BJDWe8faw7g.html> [accessed 21 October 2020]
HARTE, LIAM and MICHAEL PARKER, eds, *Contemporary Irish Fiction: Themes, Tropes, Theories* (Basingstoke: Macmillan, 2000)
HARVEY, DAVID, 'Neoliberalism as Creative Destruction', *The Annals of the American Academy of Political and Social Science*, 610 (2007), 22–44
——*Spaces of Capital* (Edinburgh: Edinburgh University Press, 2001)
HATHERLEY, OWEN, *A Guide to The New Ruins of Great Britain* (London: Verso, 2011)
——*Militant Modernism* (Winchester: Zero Books, 2008)
HIRSCH, MARIANNE, 'Family Pictures: *Maus*, Mourning and Post-Memory', *Discourse: Journal for Theoretical Studies in Media and Culture*, 15: 2 (1992), 3–29
——'Projected Memory: Holocaust Photographs in Personal and Public Fantasy', in *Acts of Memory: Cultural Recall in the Present*, ed. by Mieke Bal, Jonathan Crewe and Leo Spitzer (Hanover: University Press of New England, 1999), pp. 3–23
HOBSBAWM, ERIC, *On History* (London: Abacus, 1998)
HOLDSWORTH, AMY, *Television, Memory and Nostalgia* (Basingstoke: Palgrave Macmillan, 2011)

HOLQUIST, MICHAEL, 'Prologue', in Mikhail Bakhtin, *Rabelais and his World* (London: Midland, 1984), pp. xiii–xxiii
HUTCHEON, LINDA, *The Politics of Postmodernism* (London: Routledge, 2002)
HUYSSEN, ANDREAS, *Present Pasts: Urban Palimpsests and the Politics of Memory* (Stanford, CA: Stanford University Press, 2003)
—— 'The Mnemonic Art of Marcelo Brodsky', in *Nexo: un ensayo fotográfico de Marcelo Brodsky* (Buenos Aires: La Marca, 2001), pp. 7–11
INDIIJ, GUIDO, ed., *Perón mediante: Grafica peronista del periodo clásico* (Buenos Aires: La Marca editora, 2012)
JAMES, DANIEL, *Resistance and Integration: Peronism and the Argentine Working Class* (Cambridge: Cambridge University Press, 1988)
JAMESON, FREDRIC, 'Marx's Purloined Letter', in *Ghostly Demarcations: A Symposium on Jacques Derrida's Specters of Marx*, ed. by Michael Sprinker (London: Verso, 1999)
—— *The Political Unconsciousness: Narrative as a Socially Symbolic Act* (London: Methuen, 1981)
—— *Postmodernism, or, The Cultural Logic of Late Capitalism* (Durham, NC: Duke University Press, 1991)
JELIN, ELIZABETH, *La lucha por el pasado: como construimos la memoria social* (Buenos Aires: Siglo Veintiuno, 2017)
—— *State Repression and the Struggles for Memory* (London: Latin American Bureau, 2003)
JITRIK, NÓE, *Historia e imaginación literaria: posibilidades de un género* (Buenos Aires: Editorial Biblos, 1995)
JONES, STEVE, 'The Lexicon of Offence: The Meanings of Torture, Porn, and "Torture Porn"', in *Controversial Images: Media Representation on the Edge*, ed. by Feona Attwood, Vincent Campbell, I. Q. Hunter and Sharon Lockyer (Basingstoke: Palgrave Macmillan, 2013), pp. 186–201
KAPUR, JYOTSNA and KEITH B. WAGNER, eds, *Neoliberalism and Global Cinema: Capital, Culture and Marxist Critique* (New York: Routledge, 2011)
—— 'Introduction: Neoliberalism and Global Cinema', in *Neoliberalism and Global Cinema: Capital, Culture and Marxist Critique*, ed. by Jyotsna Kapur and Keith B. Wagner (New York: Routledge, 2011), pp. 1–18
KAISER, SUSANA, 'Memory Inventory: The Production and Consumption of Memory Goods in Argentina', in *Accounting for Violence: Marketing Memory in Latin America*, ed. by Ksenija Bilbija and Leigh A. Payne (Durham: Duke University Press, 2011)
—— *Postmemories of Terror* (London: Palgrave Macmillan, 2005)
KEELING, DAVID, J., BUENOS AIRES: GLOBAL DREAMS, LOCAL CRISES (Chichester, NY: Wiley, 1996)
KEFALA, ELENI, 'Borges and Nationalism: Urban Myth and Nation-dreaming in the 1920s', *Journal of Iberian and Latin American Studies*, 17:1 (2011), 33–58
—— *Peripheral (Post)Modernity: The Syncretist Aesthetics of Borges, Piglia, Kalokyris and Kyriakidis* (New York: Peter Lang, 2007)
KING, ANTHONY D., ed., *Re-presenting the City: Ethnicity, Capital and Culture in the 21st Century Metropolis* (Basingstoke: MacMillan Press, 1996)
KING, JOHN, '"Ya nunca más seríamos lo que éramos": Tomás Eloy Martínez and *Primera Plana* in the 1960s', *Bulletin of Latin American Research*, 31: 4 (2012), 426–44.
KLEIN, NAOMI 'Out of the Ordinary', *The Guardian*, Saturday 25 January 2003, <https://www.theguardian.com/world/2003/jan/25/argentina.weekend7> [accessed 21 October 2020]
—— *The Shock Doctrine* (London: Penguin, 2007)
KOHAN, Martín, 'Pero bailamos', *Katatay–Revista Critica de Literatura Latinoamericano* 9:11/12 (2014), 23–27

LANDSBERG, ALISON, *Engaging the Past: Mass Culture and the Production of Historical Knowledge* (New York: Columbia University Press, 2015)
*lavaca*, '20 de diciembre de 2001: la batalla que nos pario', 20 December 2005 <http://www.lavaca.org/notas/20-de-diciembre-de-2001-la-batalla-que-nos-pario> [accessed 21 October 2020]
*La Nación*, 'Masiva convocatoria en contra de los femicidios', 19 October 2016, <https://www.lanacion.com.ar/1948483-ni-una-menos-miles-de-mujeres-se-concentran-en-el-obelisco-en-contra-de-los-femicidios>
LESSA, FRANCESCA, *Memory and Transitional Justice in Argentina and Uruguay: Against Impunity* (New York: Palgrave Macmillan, 2013)
——, and VINCENT DRULIOLLE, eds, *The Memory of State Terrorism in the Southern Cone: Argentina, Chile, and Uruguay* (Palgrave Macmillan: Basingstoke, 2011)
LEVEY, CARA, DANIEL OZAROW and CHRISTOPHER WYLDE, eds, *Argentina Since the 2001 Crisis: Recovering the Past, Reclaiming the Future* (Basingstoke: Palgrave Macmillan, 2014)
—— 'Revisiting the Argentine Crisis a Decade On: Changes and Continuities', in *Argentina Since the 2001 Crisis: Recovering the Past, Reclaiming the Future*, eds, Cara Levey, Daniel Ozarow, and Christopher Wylde (Basingstoke: Palgrave Macmillan, 2014), pp. 1–19
LEVEY, CARA, *Fragile Memory, Shifting Impunity: Commemoration and Contestation in Post-Dictatorship Argentina and Uruguay* (Oxford: Peter Lang, 2016)
LEWIS, DANIEL K., *The History of Argentina* (New York: Palgrave Macmillan, 2003)
LOJO, MARTÍN, 'La Argentina, una violenta invención de la literatura. Martin Kohan y Carlos Gamerro', *La Nación*, 31 August 2015 <http://www.lanacion.com.ar/1814885-la-argentina-una-violenta-invencion-de-la-literatura-martin-kohan-y-carlos-gamerro> [accessed 21 October 2020]
LÓPEZ LEVY, MARCELA, *We Are Millions: Neo-Liberalism and New Forms of Political Action in Argentina* (London: Latin American Bureau, 2004)
LORENZ, FEDERICO and PETER WINN, 'Las memorias de la violencia política y la dictadura militar en la Argentina: un recorrido en el ano del Bicentenario', in *No hay mañana sin ayer: batallas por la memoria histórica en el Cono Sur*, ed. by Peter Winn (Santiago: Lom, 2014), pp. 19–120
——, *Cenizas que te rodearon al caer* (Buenos Aires: Sudamericana, 2017)
LYNCH, KEVIN, *The Image of the City* (Cambridge, MA: MIT Press, 1960)
LYNCH, MICHAEL, *Scotland: A New History* (London: Pimlico, 1992)
LYOTARD, JEAN FRANÇOIS, *The Postmodern Condition: A Report on Knowledge* (Minneapolis: University of Minnesota Press, 1984)
MAC ADAM, ALFRED, 'Introduction', in *Jorge Luis Borges, On Argentina* (London: Penguin Classics, 2010)
MAGUIRE, GEOFFREY, *The Politics of Postmemory: Violence and Victimhood in Contemporary Argentine Culture* (Cham: Palgrave Macmillan, 2017)
MARTÍN-Cabrera, Luis, *Radical Justice: Spain and the Southern Cone Beyond Market and State* (Lewisburg, PA: Bucknell University Press, 2011)
MARX, KARL, 'The Eighteenth Brumaire of Louis Bonaparte', in *The Communist Manifesto* (London: Penguin, 2013)
MASIELLO, FRANCINE, *The Art of Transition: Latin American Culture and Neoliberal Crisis* (Durham, NC: Duke University Press, 2001)
MCGUIGAN, JIM, ed., *Raymond Williams on Culture and Society: Essential Writings* (London: Sage Publications, 2014)
MCGUIRE, JAMES, W., *Peronism Without Peron: Unions, Parties and Democracy in Argentina* (Stanford, CA: Stanford University Press, 1997)
MEADES, JONATHAN, *Museums Without Walls* (London: Unbound, 2013)
——, 'Yesterday's tomorrows', *New Statesman*, 30 April 2009

MEE, LAURA and JOHNNY WALKER, eds, *Cinema, Television and History: New Approaches* (Newcastle-upon-Tyne: Cambridge Scholars Publishing, 2014)

MIESSEN, MARKUS and CHANTAL MOUFFE, *The Space of Agonism* (Berlin: Sternberg Press, 2012)

MILOWICKI, EDWARD J. and ROBERT RAWDON WILSON, 'A Measure for Menippean Discourse: The Example of Shakespeare', *Poetics Today* 23:2 (2002), 291–326

MOLINA, MELISA, 'El mural de Evita de nuevo iluminado', *Pagina 12*, 12 December 2019, <https://www.pagina12.com.ar/236289-el-mural-de-evita-de-nuevo-iluminado>

MORAN, JOE, 'History, Memory and the Everyday', *Rethinking History*, 8:1 (2004), 51–68

MOUFFE, CHANTAL, *Agonistics: Thinking the World Politically* (London: Verso, 2013)

MOYANO, MARÍA JOSÉ, *Argentina's Lost Patrol: Armed Struggle, 1969–1979* (New Haven, CT: Yale University Press, 1995)

*Mu*, Issue 1, December 2006

———, Issue 4, May 2007

———, Issue 7, September 2007

———, Issue 21, December 2008

———, Issue 29, October 2009

——— 'El fiolo que te parió: las mil y unas formas de proxenetismo', Issue 4, May 2007, p. 3

——— 'Una nueva generación de derechos humanos: la segunda desaparición de Julio López', Issue 1, December 2006, p. 6

———, cover matter, Issue 4, May 2007

———, cover matter, Issue 21, May 2007

———, cover matter, Issue 29, October 2009

———, cover matter, Issue 4, May 2007

NAVARRO, MARYSA, 'Evita, historia y mitología', *Caravelle*, 98 (2012), 113–33

——— *Evita: The Real Lives of Eva Perón* (London: Andre Deutsch, 2003)

NOUZEILLES, Gabriela, and Graciela Montaldo, eds, *The Argentina Reader* (Durham, NC: Duke University Press, 2002)

*Nunca Mas: A Report by Argentina's National Commission on Disappeared People* (London: Faber and Faber, 1986).

OESTERHELD, MARTIN, DIR., *La Multitud*, 2012

ONUCH, OLGA, ' "It's the Economy, Stupid," or Is It? The Role of Political Crises in Mass Mobilization: The Case of Argentina in 2001', in *Argentina Since the 2001 Crisis: Recovering the Past, Reclaiming the Future*, eds, Cara Levey, Daniel Ozarow, and Christopher Wylde (Basingstoke: Palgrave Macmillan, 2014), pp. 89–114

O'DONNELL, MARIA, *El secuestro de los Born* (Buenos Aires: Sudamericana, 2015)

PACHECO, MARIANO, *Cabecita negra: ensayos sobre literatura y Peronismo* (Buenos Aires: Punto de Encuentro, 2016)

PACINI HERNÁNDEZ, DEBORAH, HÉCTOR FERNÁNDEZ L'HOESTE and ERIC ZOLOV, eds, *Rockin' las Americas: The Global Politics of Rock in Latin/o America* (Pittsburgh, PA: University of Pittsburgh Press, 2004)

PAGE, JOANNA, *Crisis and Capitalism in Contemporary Argentine Cinema* (Durham, NC: Duke University Press, 2009)

PAGE, MAX, ED. *Memories of Buenos Aires: Signs of State Terrorism in Argentina* (Amherst and Boston, MA : University of Massachusetts Press, 2013)

——— 'Introduction', in *Memories of Buenos Aires: Signs of State Terrorism in Argentina*, ed. Max Page (Amherst and Boston, MA: University of Massachusetts Press, 2013), pp. xvii–xxii

PASTORIZA, LILA, 'El lugar de las cosas robadas', in *Nexo: un ensayo fotográfico de Marcelo Brodsky* (Buenos Aires: La marca, 2001), pp. 42–45

PEROCHENA, CAMILA 'La historia en la política y las políticas en la historia: Batalla cultural y revisionismo histórico en los discursos de Cristina Fernández de Kirchner (2007–2015), *Prohistoria*, 33 (2020) pp. 233–63

PETRELLA, IVÁN, *The Future of Liberation Theology: An Argument and Manifesto* (London: SCM Press, 2006)

PIGLIA, RICARDO, *Crítica y ficción* (Barcelona: Penguin Random House, 2014)

—— *Cuentos morales: antología personal (1961–1990)* (Buenos Aires: Planeta, 1998)

—— *El último lector* (Barcelona: Anagrama, 2005)

PIGNA, FELIPE, *Lo pasado pensado: entrevistas con la historia argentina (1955–1983)* (Buenos Aires: Planeta, 2005)

PLOTKIN, MARIANO BEN, *Mañana es San Perón: A Cultural History of Peron's Argentina* (Wilmington, DE: Scholarly Resources, 2003)

PODALSKY, LAURA, *Specular City: Transforming Culture, Consumption, and Space in Buenos Aires 1955–1973* (Philadelphia, PA: Temple University Press, 2004)

RADWAY, JANICE, 'Foreword', in Avery Gordon, *Ghostly Matters: Ghosts and the Sociological Imagination* (Minneapolis: University of Minnesota Press, 2008), p. xvi

REYNOLDS, SIMON, *Retromania* (London: Faber and Faber, 2011)

RIBEIRO DE MENEZES, ALISON, '¿Una agonía esperpéntica? Shifting Memory Horizons and Carnivalesque Representations of the Spanish Civil War and Franco Dictatorship, *Bulletin of Spanish Studies*, 91:1–2 (2014), 239–53

ROCK, DAVID, *Argentina 1516–1982: From Spanish Colonization to the Falklands War* (London: Tauris, 1986)

—— 'Revolt and Repression in Argentina', *The World Today*, 33 (1977), 215–22.

RODRÍGUEZ CADENA, MARÍA DE LOS ÁNGELES, ed., *La ficción histórica en la televisión iberoamericana (2000–2012)* (Leiden: Brill, 2016)

ROMERO, LUIS ALBERTO, *Argentina in the Twentieth Century* (University Park, Pennsylvania: University of Pennsylvania, 2002)

ROSANO, SUSANA, 'En definitiva, en Argentina todos caemos en el barroco fúnebre: reportaje a Tomas Eloy Martínez', *Revista Iberoamericana*, 72 (2006), 657–62

RUEDA LAFFOND, JOSÉ CARLOS and AMPARO GUERRA GÓMEZ, 'Televisión y Nostalgia. The Wonder Years y Cuéntame cómo pasó', *Revista Latina de Comunicación Social*, 64 (2009), 396–409

RUEDA LAFFOND, JOSÉ CARLOS, '¿Reescribiendo la historia? Una panorámica de la ficción histórica televisiva española reciente', *Alpha*, 29 (2009), 85–104

SALVIA, SEBASTIÁN P., 'La caída de la Alianza. Neoliberalismo, conflicto social y crisis política en Argentina', *Colombia Internacional*, 84 (2015), 107–38

SALZANI, CARLOS, 'The City as Crime Scene: Walter Benjamin and the Traces of the Detective', *New German Critique*, 100: Winter (2007), 165–87

SAMUEL, RAPHAEL, *Theatres of Memory: Past and Present in Contemporary Culture* (London: Verso, 1996)

SANTORO, DANIEL, 'La construcción imaginaria de un mundo', in *Perón mediante: Grafica peronista del periodo clásico*, ed. by Guido Indiij (Buenos Aires: La Marca editora, 2012), pp. 21–23

SARLO, BEATRIZ, *La audacia y el cálculo: Kirchner 2003–2010* (Buenos Aires: Sudamericana, 2011)

—— *Escenas de la vida posmoderna: intelectuales, arte y videocultura en la Argentina* (Buenos Aires: Ariel, 1994)

—— *La pasión y la excepción: Eva, Borges y el asesinato de Aramburu* (Buenos Aires: Siglo Veintiuno, 2003)

—— *Tiempo pasado: cultura de la memoria y giro subjetivo — una discusión* (Buenos Aires: Siglo Veintiuno, 2005)

SASSEN, SASKIA, 'Rebuilding the Global City', in *Re-presenting the City: Ethnicity, Capital and*

*Culture in the 21st Century Metropolis*, ed. by Anthony D. King (Basingstoke: MacMillan Press, 1996), pp. 23–42

SCORER, JAMES, *City in Common: Culture and Community in Buenos Aires* (Albany: State University of New York Press, 2016)

SDRIGOTTI, FERNANDO, 'Pizza, Beer and Cigarettes/Pizza, birra, faso', in *World Film Locations: Buenos Aires*, ed. by Santiago Oyarzabal and Michael Pigott (Bristol: Intellect Books, 2014), pp. 48–49

SEMÁN, PABLO, PABLO VILA and CECILIA BENEDETTI, 'Neoliberalism and Rock in the Popular Sectors of Contemporary Argentina', in *Rockin' las Americas: The Global Politics of Rock in Latin/o America*, ed. by Deborah Pacini Hernández, Héctor Fernández L'Hoeste and Eric Zolov (Pittsburgh, PA: University of Pittsburgh Press, 2004), pp. 261–89

SHAVIRO, STEVEN, *The Cinematic Body* (Minneapolis: University of Minnesota Press, 1993)

SHUMWAY, NICOLAS, *The Invention of Argentina* (Berkeley: University of California Press, 1991)

SITRIN, MARINA, '*Horizontalidad* and Territory in the Occupy Movements', *Tikkun* 27:2 (2012), 32–63

—— *Horizontalism: Voices of Popular Power in Argentina* (Edinburgh: AK Press, 2006)

—— *Everyday Revolutions: Horizontalism and Autonomy in Argentina* (London: Zedbooks, 2012)

SOMMERS, DORIS, *Foundational Fictions: The National Romances of Latin America* (Berkeley: University of California Press, 1991)

SOSA, CECILIA, 'Food, conviviality and the work of mourning, the *asado* scandal at Argentina's ex-ESMA', *Journal of Latin American Cultural Studies*, 25:1 (2016), 123–46

—— *Queering Acts of Mourning in the Aftermath of Argentina's Dictatorship: Performances of Blood* (Woodbridge: Tamesis, 2014)

SUELDO, MARTÍN, '*Montecristo*: Telenovela y derechos humanos', *Studies in Latin American Popular Culture*, 30 (2012), 180–93

SVAMPA, MARISTELLA, *Cambio de época: movimientos sociales y poder político* (Buenos Aires: Siglo Veintiuno, 2012)

—— 'Revisiting Argentina 2001–2013: From "¡Que se vayan todos!" to the Peronist decade', in *Argentina Since the 2001 Crisis: Recovering the Past, Reclaiming the Future*, ed. by Cara Levey, Daniel Ozarow and Christopher Wylde (Basingstoke: Palgrave Macmillan, 2014), pp. 155–76

TAYLOR, DIANA, *Disappearing Acts: Spectacles of Gender and Nationalism in Argentina's "Dirty War"* (Durham, NC: Duke University Press, 2005)

TEDESCO, LAURA, *Democracy in Argentina: Hope and Disillusion* (London; Portland: Frank Cass, 1999)

TELEFE ARGENTINA, *Lo que el tiempo nos dejó*, 2010

TRAPERO, PABLO, DIR., *Elefante blanco*, 2012

TREACY, MIA E.M., *Reframing the Past. History, Film and Television* (Basingstoke: Routledge, 2016)

QUIROGA, MARIANO, '100 Evitas, 100 Mujeres, 100 Años', *Kranear*, 5 May 2019 <<https://kranear.com.ar/2019/05/05/100-evitas-100-mujeres-100-anos>> [accessed 9 July 2019]

URRACA, BEATRIZ, 'Transactional Fiction: (Sub)urban Realism in the Films of Trapero and Caetano', in *New Trends in Argentine and Brazilian Cinema*, ed. by Cacilda Rego and Carolina Rocha (Bristol: Intellect, 2011), pp. 147–61

VALLEJOS, SOLEDAD, 'Arruga, una causa que mantiene muchas dudas', *Página 12*, Saturday 18 October 2014, <https://www.pagina12.com.ar/diario/sociedad/3-257810-2014-10-18.html> [accessed 21 October 2020]

VARELA, MIRTA, 'Memory and Childhood in the Melodrama of the Malvinas War: The

Children Who Write on the Sky', *Critical Arts: A South-North Journal of Cultural and Media Studies*, 29:5 (2015), 644–57

VERBITSKY, HORACIO, 'De Mugica a Carrara', *Pagina 12*, 11 May 2014 <https://www.pagina12.com.ar/diario/elpais/subnotas/1-67895-2014-05-11.html>

—— *Confessions of an Argentine Dirty Warrior* (London: The New Press, 2005)

VEZZETTI, HUGO, *Pasado y presente: guerra, dictadura y sociedad en la argentina* (Buenos Aires: Siglo Veintiuno, 2002)

—— *Sobre la violencia revolucionaria: memorias y olvidos* (Buenos Aires: Siglo Veintiuno, 2013)

VILA, PABLO and PAUL CAMMACK, 'Rock Nacional and dictatorship in Argentina', *Popular Music* 6:2 (1987), 129–48

WAINWRIGHT, OLIVER, 'Wayne Hemingway's "pop-up plan" sounds the death knell for legendary Balfron Tower', *The Guardian*, 26 September 2014 <http://www.theguardian.com/artanddesign/architecture-design-blog/2014/sep/26/wayne-hemingways-pop-up-plan-sounds-the-death-knell-for-the-legendary-balfron-tower> [accessed 21 October 2020]

WEINBROT, HOWARD, *Menippean Satire Reconsidered* (Baltimore, MD: John Hopkins University Press, 2005)

WHEATLEY, HELEN, *Re-viewing Television History: Critical Issues in Television History* (London: Tauris, 2007)

WILLIAMS, RAYMOND and MICHAEL ORROM, *A Preface to Film* (London: Film Drama, 1954)

WILLIAMS, RAYMOND, *The Long Revolution* (Cardigan: Parthian, 2011)

—— *Marxism and Literature* (Oxford: Oxford University Press, 1977)

—— *Television: Technology and Cultural Form* (Abingdon: Routledge Classics, 1970)

—— 'Culture is Ordinary', in *Raymond Williams on Culture and Society: Essential Writings*, ed. by Jim McGuigan (London: Sage Publications, 2014), pp. 1–18

WILSON, JASON, *Buenos Aires: A Cultural and Literary History* (London: Signal Books, 2007)

WINN, PETER, ed., *No hay mañana sin ayer: batallas por la memoria histórica en el Cono Sur* (Santiago: Lom, 2014)

WOLFREYS, JULIAN, *Writing London, Vol. 2: Materiality, Memory, Spectrality* (Basingstoke: Palgrave Macmillan, 2004)

WorkhouseEngland <http://www.workhouse-england.co.uk/workhouse-england--our-story.html> [accessed 21 October 2020]

WYLDE, CHRISTOPHER, 'Continuity and Change in the Interpretation of Upheaval: Re-examining the Argentine Crisis of 2001–02', in *Argentina Since the 2001 Crisis: Recovering the Past, Reclaiming the Future*, ed. by Cara Levey, Daniel Ozarow and Christopher Wylde (Basingstoke: Palgrave Macmillan, 2014), pp. 23–43

YOUNG, JAMES, *The Texture of Memory: Holocaust Memorials and Meaning* (New Haven: Yale University Press, 1993)

ZIBECHI, RAÚL, *Territories in Resistance: A Cartography of Latin American Social Movements* (Oakland: AK Press, 2012)

# INDEX

Abuelas de Plaza de Mayo (human rights organization) 19, 20, 107
Ackroyd, Peter 44
Acuña, Claudia 26
*afectados* (those directly affected by state terrorism) 20
agonism 91–92, 93–94
Aguilar, Gonzalo 76, 77, 80
*Algo habrán hecho por la historia argentina* [They Must Have Done Something for Argentine History], historical docudrama 109
Alianza government, Argentina 2
Almirón, Fernando 25
Amadori, Luis César 77
Amaya, Jenny 106, 107
*anagnorisis* 106, 109
*Años Rebeldes* [Rebel Years], telenovela 106–07
*Aparecidos* [The Appeared] (dir. Paco Cabezas) 4, *14*, 14–16, 17, 19
Aramburu, Pedro Eugenio 136–37
architecture and built environment:
    Balfron and Trellick towers, London 42
    Buenos Aires in literature 44–49
    business districts 72, 73–74
    Castle Market, Sheffield 51–52
    Ciudad Evita *143*, 143–44
    *cocoliche* style, Buenos Aires 51, 54
    Goldfinger, Ernő 42
    grotesque architecture 138–39, 143–44
    Hatherley, Owen 41–42, 43, 51–52
    historicity and 41–42
    Mies van der Rohe, Ludwig 66
    modernist architecture 41–42, 43, 50–51, 51–52
    Obelisk, Buenos Aires 50–51, 80
    Park Hill housing estate, Sheffield 42
    Prebisch, Alberto 50, 51
    suburbs 5, 80–81
    theme parks and leisure parks 66, 69–73, 74–75
    Torre Espacial, Villa Lugano 69–70, 72, 74–75, *75*, 80
    utopianism 41–42, 43, 44, 51–52, 82–87
    *villas miseria* (shanty towns) 5–6, 66, 74, 75–76, 77–79
    Waterworks Palace, Buenos Aires 54, *55*, 56
Arenillas, María 69
Argentina:
    Alianza government 2
    Cambiemos government 146, 152–53
    CONADEP (Comisión Nacional para la Desaparición de Personas), *Nunca más* report 16, 100–01, 102
    *Cordobazo* uprising 22
    *corralito* legislation 2, 22, 89
    Frente de Todos, coalition government 122 n. 1, 153
    Justicialist movement 84, 127
    military coups 2
    national anthem 120–22
    'La noche de los bastones largos' [Night of the Long Sticks] 113–14
    'Obediencia Debida' legislation 16
    'Punto Final' legislation 16
    *Revolución libertadora* [Liberating Revolution] 84, 136
    *Rodrigazo* uprising 22
    *see also Argentinazo* (2001 Crisis, Argentina); *el Proceso* [Process of National Reorganization, 1976–1983]
'Argentina's Dirty War', television documentary 102
*Argentinazo* (2001 Crisis, Argentina) 1–3, 22–26, 151, 153
    *Elefante blanco* 89
    Eloy Martínez's *El cantor de tango* 59–60
    horizontalism 129
    *lavaca* collective and *Mu* (periodical) 7, 25–26
    social class 26
    term 22–23
    theatrical interpretation by L. Arias 8
Arias, Lola, *Audición para una manifestación* 8–9
Arlt, Roberto 46, 89
Arruga, Luciano 33
Astiz, Alfredo 115–16
autofictional narratives 127
Avelar, Idelber 13, 40, 104
Avelluto, Pablo 111

Bakhtin, Mikhail 129, 131, 134, 139, 140, 144
*baldosas* (commemorative paving stones) 18, *18*, 24
Balfron Tower, London 42
*Barcelona* (periodical) 127
Bauer, Tristán 153
Bauman, Zygmunt 87
Benasayag, Miguel 27
Benedetto, Gustavo 25
Benjamin, Walter 41, 42, 101
    *The Arcades Project* 49
    *Berlin Childhood Around 1900* 50
Berman, Marshall 44
Blaustein, Eduardo 85
Blejmar, Jordana 127, 128

# 168 INDEX

Boca Juniors football club 72
bodies, and the grotesque 128, 129, 132–33, 138, 152
Bollig, Ben 144
Bombita Rodríguez (comedy character) 127
*El Bonaerense* (dir. Pablo Trapero) 80
Borges, Jorge Luis 47
  'El aleph' 49
  'Del rigor en la ciencia' 67
  'La muerte y la brújula' 49, 59
  'El otro duelo' [The Other Duel] 137
Born brothers kidnapping 135, *136*
Brodsky, Fernando 101
Brodsky, Marcelo 6
  'El pañol' *99*, 100–04, *103*
Buenos Aires:
  architecture 44–45, 50–51, 54
  Avenida de Mayo 25, 51
  Borges and 47
  Calle Libertad *45*
  Calle Pasteur 58
  Casa Rosada 23
  Central Térmica Costanera Sur 72
  Centro Cultural San Martín 8
  Ciudad Deportiva de La Boca 71, 72
  Ciudad Evita *143*, 143–44
  civilization/barbarism binary 48
  Club Atlético, clandestine prison 58, *58*
  *conurbano bonaerense* (Greater Buenos Aires) 5–6
  Escuela Mecánica de la Armada [Navy Mechanics School] clandestine prison 17, 18, 100–02, 107, 115, 130
  hauntology and 44–49
  Interama/Parque de la Ciudad theme park, 66, 69, 69–70, *70*, 72, 74–75
  Jewish community 57
  La Boca district 83
  Liniers district 57
  Lomas de Mirador 33
  murals depicting Eva Perón 153
  Museo Evita *145*
  Obelisk on Avenida 9 de Julio 50–51, *53*, 80
  Pirámide de Mayo 116
  Plaza de Mayo 23, *24*, 25, 116, *117*
  Puerto Madero 72, 73–74, 77
  Puerto Nuevo 77–78
  Santa Cruz church 115
  San Telmo district 18
  'sites of repression' 17–19
  Vasena metalworks 58
  Villa 20: 74
  Villa 31: 76, 85
  Villa Rodrigo Bueno 76, 77
  Waterworks Palace 54, *55*, *56*
  *see also* Ciudad Oculta, Buenos Aires; Villa Lugano, Buenos Aires
*Buenos Aires* (dir. David José Kohon) 79
Buonanno, Milly 105

Cabandié, Juan 107
Cabezas, Paco, *Aparecidos* (dir.) 4, 14, *14*, 14–16, 17, 19
Caetano, Adrián 80
Cage, John 69
Cambiemos government 146, 152–53
Canaro, Francisco 111, 120
capitalism, *see* neoliberalism/late capitalism
capitalist realism 91
Capote, Truman 59
*Carancho* (dir. Pablo Trapero) 80
Carassai, Sebastián 137
Cardel, Luis 46
carnivalesque 132, 134, 139, 141–43
Castle Market, Sheffield 51–52
Cavallo, Domingo 23
Central Térmica Costanera Sur, Buenos Aires 72
Centro Cultural San Martín, Buenos Aires 8
Centro de Documentación e Investigación de la Cultura de Izquierdas (CeDInCI) [Archives and Research Centre of Cultures of the Left] 111
Centro de Estudios Legales y Sociales (CELS) (human rights organization) 20
Certeau, Michel de 84
Chicharro, Mar 106
Churchwell, Sarah 31
cinema, Argentine:
  *Aparecidos* (dir. Paco Cabezas) 4, *14*, 14–16, 17, 19
  *El Bonaerense* (dir. Trapero) 80
  *Buenos Aires* (dir. David José Kohon) 79
  *Carancho* (dir. Pablo Trapero) 80
  *Detrás de un largo muro* (dir. Lucas Demare) 79
  *La hora de los hornos* (dir. Fernado Solanas) 79
  *La multitud* (dir. Martín Oesterheld) 5, 66, *68*, 69, 69–75, *70*, 80, 81
  *Mundo Grúa* (dir. Pablo Trapero) 80
  and neoliberalism 79–80
  New Argentine Cinema 76, 79–81
  *Pizza, Birra, Faso* (dir. Caetano and Stagnaro) 80
  *Puerto Nuevo* (dir. Soffici and Amadori) 77–79, *78*
  suburbs in 80–81
  *villas miseria* in 77–79
  *see also* Elefante blanco [White Elephant] (dir. Pablo Trapero)
Ciudad Deportiva de La Boca, Buenos Aires 71, 72
Ciudad Evita *143*
Ciudad Oculta, Buenos Aires 5–6, 75–76, 79, 81–83
  chapel, and Liberation Theology 84–87
  no-go zones and criminality 88
  ruined hospital *83*, 83–84
*Clarín* (newspaper) 79
Club Atlético, clandestine prison 58, *58*
*cocoliche* architectural style 51, 54
cognitive mapping 5, 67–69
  Elefante blanco 76, 81, 87, 90, 94, 95
  *La multitud* 74
Colectiva Mixta de Culturas 146
Colectivo Situaciones 38

Colomer, Julieta 19–20
CONADEP (Comisión Nacional para la Desaparición de Personas) *Nunca más* report 16, 100–01, 102
Connelly, Frances 6, 129, 132
*conurbano bonaerense* (Greater Buenos Aires) 5–6
*conventillos* 112
Copi (Raúl Damonte Botana) 126
*Cordobazo* uprising 22
*corralito* legislation 2, 22, 89
Cortázar, Julio, *Rayuela* 58
Crenzel, Emilio 152
criminality and illegal drugs 88–89
culture, Raymond Williams on 3, 4, 7
Cumbernauld, new town 42
*curas villeros* (priests in shanty towns) 85, 88

Dadamo, Florencia 120
Darín, Ricardo 76
Della Mora, Leandro 120
Demare, Lucas 79
Derrida, Jacques 5, 43
*desaparecidos* ('disappeared' persons) 15
  Abuelas de Plaza de Mayo (human rights organization) 19, 20, 107
  appropriated children of 107
  Arruga, Luciano 33
  *baldosas* (commemorative paving stones) 18, *18*, 24
  Brodsky, Fernando 101
  Brodsky, Marcelo, 'El pañol' 100–04
  CONADEP report 16, 100–01, 102
  ESMA and 100–02, 114–18
  execution at Obelisk, 1976 52
  López, Jorge Julio 27
  Madres de Plaza de Mayo (human rights organization) 19, 20, *115*, 115–18
  television and 107
detention centres, clandestine 33
  Club Atlético 58, *58*
  Escuela Mecánica de la Armada [Navy Mechanics School] 17, 18, 100–02, 107, 115, 130
*Detrás de un largo muro* (dir. Lucas Demare) 79
Dinerstein, Cecilia 2
docudrama genre 106
Dorrego, Manuel 110
drugs, illegal 88–89
Druliolle, Vincent 18

Ebbrecht, Tobias 106
Echeverría, Esteban Antonio, 'El matadero' [The Slaughterhouse] 48, 57
Edelstein, David 14
*Elefante blanco* [White Elephant] (dir. Pablo Trapero) 4, 5–6, 7, 81–94, *86, 91, 93*
  building site as space of agonism 76, 91–94
  chapel and Liberation Theology 85–87
  cognitive mapping 76, 81, 87, 90, 94, 95

horizontalism 76, 91–94
narcotics business 87–90
ruined hospital as failed utopia 82–84
spatial historicity 66–67, 75–77, 81–94
Eloy Martínez, Tomás, *El cantor de tango* [The Tango Singer] 4, 5, 7, 40–62
  *Argentinazo* in 59–60
  Buenos Aires in literature 44–49
  hauntology 40–41, 44–50, 60–62
  Liniers district episode 57–59
  Obelisk episode 50–54
  spatial historicity 41–42, 49–50, 59
  Waterworks Palace episode 54–56
Eloy Martínez, Tomás (ed.), *Panorama* (periodical) 137
ERP (Ejército Revolucionario del Pueblo) 135
*escrache* demonstrations 19, 20
Escuela Mecánica de la Armada (ESMA) [Navy Mechanics School] clandestine detention centre, Buenos Aires 17, 18, 100–02, 107, 115, 130
Eudeba publishing house 113
Eva Perón Foundation (Fundación de Ayuda Social María Eva Duarte de Perón) 144, 147 n. 9
*Evita Montonera* (periodical) 134, *142*

Falcón, Ada 111, 120
Falcón, Ramón 111
Faulkener, William 40
feasts and celebrations, carnivalesque 139–40, 140–43, 144–45
Featherstone, David 4
Feinmann, José Pablo 102
Fernández, Alberto 122 n. 1, 153
Fernández de Kirchner, Cristina 6, 7, 110, 152, 153
'fictionscape,' narrative framework 105
Fisher, Mark 42–43, 43–44, 61, 91
forgetting, discourse of 13, 16–17
Forsyth, Bill 42
Franco, Jean 46
Freitag, Florian 72
Frente de Todos, coalition government 122 n. 1, 153
Fuentes, Carlos 46
Fundación de Ayuda Social María Eva Duarte de Perón (Eva Perón Foundation) 144, 147 n. 9

Gálvez, Manuel 109
Gamerro, Carlos 130
  *Las islas* [The Islands] 128
  *El secreto y las voces* [An Open Secret] 128
  *El sueño de Señor Juez* [The Dream of Señor Juez] 147 n. 6
  *Un yuppie en la columna del Che Guevara* [A Yuppie in Che Guevara's Army] 128
Gamerro, Carlos, *La aventura de los bustos de Eva* 4, 6, 7, 126–28, 130, *143*
  bodily functions 132–33
  brothel episode 140–43

carnivalesque 139–40, 144–45
characters 131–35
grotesque architecture 138–39, 143–44
grotesque, elements of 131, 132–33, 134–35, 139, 145
horizontalism 127, 132, 135, 137, 144, 146–47
kidnappings 135–37
revolutionary Peronism 133–34
social class 131–32, 133–34
Garavelli, Clara 76
García, Charly 118, 121–22
Garibotto, Verónica 151–52
Gieco, León 118
Gociol, Judith 26
Goebel, Michael 109
Goldfinger, Ernő 42
Gordon, Avery 41, 44, 61
Gorelik, Adrián 44, 50, 73
Grass, Gunther 46
Great Britain, modernist architecture 42, 43, 51–52
grotesque realism 127, 128, 129–30
 aesthetics of Peronism 141–43
 Bakhtin, M. 129, 131, 134, 139, 140, 144
 bodily functions 132–33, 134
 capitalism 139, 143
 Gamerro's *Los bustos de Eva* 131, 132–33, 134–35, 139, 145
 horizontalism 129, 132, 135, 141, 142, 144
 naming in 131
 social class 131–32, 135
 topography/architecture 138–39, 143–44
Guevara, Ernesto 'Che' 131
Gutierrez, Juan 64 n. 63

Hartley, L. P. 98
Harvey, David 1, 5, 68, 75
Hatherley, Owen 41–42, 43, 51–52
hauntology 5, 43–44
 Benjamin, W. 42, 49–50
 Buenos Aires 44–49
 Derrida, J. 43
 Eloy Martínez's *El cantor de tango* 40–41, 44–50, 60–62
 Fisher, M. 42–43, 43–44
 Hatherley, O. 41–42, 43, 51–52
 Jameson, F. 43
 neoliberalism and 43
 utopianism 42, 43
H.I.J.O.S (Hijos por la identidad y la justicia contra el olvido y el silencio) (human rights organization) 3, 18, 19–21, 33–34, 35, 134
'historical event television' 105–06
historical materialism 12
historicity, context and overview 4, 151–53
 *Aparecidos* 14–16, 17
 *Argentinazo* 22–26
 definitions 11–13
 discourse of forgetting 13, 16–17

Jameson, F. 12–13, 16–17
*lavaca* media collective, *Mu* (periodical) 5, 25–35
Marx, K. 12
revitalization in 21st c. 3, 17–20
historicity, grotesque
 Gamerro's *Los bustos de Eva* 126–46
 '100 Evitas' march 146–47
 *see also* grotesque realism
historicity, material:
 Brodsky's 'El pañol' 100–04
 living history 6, 98, 105, 109, 122
 *Lo que el tiempo nos dejó* 104–22
historicity, spatial
 *Elefante blanco* 66–67, 75–77, 81–94
 Eloy Martínez's *El cantor de tango* 40–62
 *La multitud* 66, 69–75
 *see also* architecture and built environment; cognitive mapping; hauntology
Hobsbawm, Eric 11
Holquist, Michael 129
*La hora de los hornos* (dir. Fernado Solanas) 79
horizontalism (*horizontalidad*) 3, 4–5, 7–8, 11, 151–52
 *Argentinazo* 8–9, 129
 Arias's *Audición para una manifestación* 8–9
 and Cambiemos government 153
 citizenship, perception of 22
 definition and theories of 21–22
 *Elefante blanco* 76, 91–94
 Gamerro's *Los bustos de Eva* 127, 132, 135, 137, 144, 146–47
 and the grotesque 129, 132, 135, 141, 142, 144
 H.I.J.O.S. and 20–21
 language of 27
 *lavaca* collective and *Mu* (periodical) 26–27, 27–29, 35
 'living history' and 6, 105, 109, 122
 '100 Evitas' march 146–47
 Zibechi, R. 21–22, 27, 33
 *see also* Sitrin, Marina
Hueravilo, Emiliano 35
human rights community:
 Abuelas de Plaza de Mayo 19, 20, 107
 Centro de Estudios Legales y Sociales (CELS) 20
 hegemonic narratives of 127
 H.I.J.O.S (Hijos por la identidad y la justicia contra el olvido y el silencio) 3, 18, 19–21
 Kirchner administrations and 130
 Macri and 152
 Madres de Plaza de Mayo 19, 20, 115–18
 Memoria Abierta [Open Memory] 17–18
Huyssen, Andreas 41

immigration 64 n. 63, 112
Instituto Nacional de Revisionismo Histórico Argentino e Iberoamericano Manuel Dorrego 110–11

Interama/Parque de la Ciudad theme park, Buenos
    Aires 66, *69*, 69–70, *70*, 72, 74–75

James, Daniel 120
Jameson, Fredric 5, 12–13, 16–17, 43
Jauretche, Arturo 109
Jelin, Elizabeth 11
Jews and Judaism 57
Jitrik, Nóe 137
Justicialist movement *(Justicialismo)* (Peronist Party) 84,
    127, 143

Kaiser, Susana 16
Kapur, Jyotsna 87
kidnappings 135–37
Kirchner administrations 7, 18, 122 n. 1, 127, 130
Kirchner, Cristina Fernández de 6, 7, 110, 122 n. 1,
    152, 153
Kirchner, Néstor 17, 122 n. 1, 130
Klein, Naomi 23, 25
Kohan, Martín 127
Kohon, David José 79

La Boca district, Buenos Aires 83
Lamagna, Diego 25
late capitalism, *see* neoliberalism/late capitalism
*lavaca* media collective 5, 25–35
    article on *Argentinazo* 25–26
    and horizontalism 26–27
    *Mu* (periodical) 5, 7, 12, 27–35
Lessa, Francesca 19
Liberation Theology 85–87
Lichtenstein, Roy 31
Liniers district, Buenos Aires 57
living history, historiographic discourse 6, 98, 105,
    109, 122
Lomas de Mirador, Greater Buenos Aires 33
London 44
    Trellick and Balfron towers 42
López, Jorge Julio 27
López Levy, Marcela 23
López Rega, José 134
*Lo que el tiempo nos dejó* [What the Past Has Left Us]
    (TV mini-series) 6, 7, 98, *98*, 100, 111–22, *115*,
    *117*, *119*, *121*
    'La caza del ángel' [The Angel's Hunt] 111, 114–18
    genre 105–06, 107–08
    immigration 112
    'La ley primera' [The First Law] 111, 113–14, 120–21
    living history and 98, 105, 122
    Madres de Plaza de Mayo 115–18
    material historicity 104–05, 112, 113–14, 116–18,
        118–19, 120–21
    'Mi Mensaje' [My Message] 104, 111–12
    'Un mundo mejor' [A Better World] 111, 112
    music 118–19, 120–22

and neo-revisionism 109, 111
'Los niños que escriben en el cielo' [The Children
    Who Write in the Sky] 111, 118–20
Peronism 112
'Te quiero' [I Want You] 111, 120
University of Buenos Aires, state repression of
    113–14

Macri, Mauricio 111, 122 n. 1, 146, 152–53
Madres de Plaza de Mayo (human rights organization)
    19, 20, *115*, 115–18
Malvinas conflict 111, 118, 119
maps and mapping 67–69
    *see also* cognitive mapping
Márquez, Luis Alberto 25
Martínez Estrada, Ezequiel 46
Marx, Karl 12
Meades, Jonathan 42, 54
Memoria Abierta [Open Memory] (NGO) 17–18
memory sites and unofficial memorials 17–19
Menem, Carlos 16
micro-memory projects 18
Miessen, Markus 91
Mies van der Rohe, Ludwig 66
Miguez Bonino, José 86
Mitre, Bartolomé 109, 110
modernist architecture 42, 43, 50–51, 51–52
*Montecristo,* TV serial 107
Montoneros (guerrilla organization):
    Eloy Martínez's *El cantor de tango* 57
    *Evita Montonera* (periodical) 134, *142*
    Gamerro's *Los bustos de Eva* 126, 130, 133, 134, 140
    kidnappings 135–36, *136*
    Mugica, C. and 85
    Walsh, R. and 31, 140
Moran, Joe 104
Mouffe, Chantal 6, 76, 91–92, 93
*el Movimiento de Sacerdotes para el Tercer Mundo*
    [Movement of Priests for the Third World] 85
*Mu* (periodical) 5, 7, 12, 27–35, *28*, *30*, *32*, *34*
    Arruga issue 33
    blindfolded woman issue 33
    'fiolos' issue 27–29
    H.I.J.O.S. and 33–34, 35
    and historicity 29, 31, 33, 35
    horizontalism of 27–29, 35
    on neoliberalism 29
    on sex workers 29
    Walsh issue 31, 33
Les Muchachas Peronistas, collective 146
Mugica, Carlos 85
*La multitud* [The Crowd] (dir. Martín Oesterheld) 5, *68*,
    69, 69–75, *70*, 94
    business district 73–74
    shantytown 74, 81
    theme parks 66, 69–73, 80

*Mundo Grúa* (dir. Pablo Trapero) 80
Museo Evita, Buenos Aires *145*
music:
    Argentine national anthem 120–22
    Pedro y Pablo 118–19
    *rock nacional* 118, 121
    tango 120

naming, in grotesque genre 131
national anthem, Argentine 120–22
neoliberalism/late capitalism 87
    architecture and 52
    Argentine cinema and 79–80
    business districts and luxury developments 73–74
    and cognitive mapping 68
    and criminality 87–90
    and dictatorship 29, 31
    grotesque 139, 143
    hauntology and 43
    and historicity 12–13
        *Mu* (periodical) and 29
    normalization of crisis 1
    and politics 91–92
    theme parks 66
    urban alienation 68, 72–75
neo-revisionism, school of historical thought 109–11
    Instituto Nacional de Revisionismo Histórico Argentino e Iberoamericano Manuel Dorrego 110–11
New Argentine Cinema 76, 79–81
New Brutalism, architectural style 42
Ni una menos, feminist movement 153
'La noche de los bastones largos' [Night of the Long Sticks] 113–14
*Nunca más* report (CONADEP) 16, 100–01, 102

'Obediencia Debida' legislation 16, 31
Obelisk on Avenida 9 de Julio, Buenos Aires 50–51, *53*, 80
objectivity, historians and 108
O'Donnell, Mario 'Pacho' 109
Oesterheld, Martín, dir., *La Multitud* 5, 66, *68*, *69*, 69–75, *70*, 80, 81, 94
Onganía, Juan Carlos 111, 113, 114, 121
Onuch, Olga 25

Pacha (spokesperson of Les Muchaches Peronistas) 146
Page, Joanna 2, 79–80, 89
Page, Max 47
Palacio de las aguas corrientes [Waterworks Palace], Buenos Aires 54, *55*, *56*
Palacios, Alfredo 83, 84
*Panorama* (periodical) 137
Park Hill housing estate, Sheffield 42
Parque de la Ciudad/Interama theme park, Buenos Aires 66, *69*, 69–70, *70*, 72, 74–75

Pastoriza, Lila 101, 102
Paul VI, Pope 85
Pedro y Pablo, musical group 118–19
Perel, Jonathan 69
Perez, Mariana Eva 127
Perochena, Camila 110
Perón, Eva *142*, *145*
    capture of body of 136
    Eva Perón Foundation (Fundación de Ayuda Social María Eva Duarte de Perón) 144, 147 n. 9
    *Evita Montonera* (periodical) 134, *142*
    in Gamerro's *Los bustos de Eva* 126, 128, 140–41
    in *Lo que el tiempo nos dejó* 111–12
    Montoneros and 134, *142*
    murals depicting 153
    '100 Evitas' march 146–47
Perón, Isabel 126, 134, 135
Peronism, aesthetics of 141–43
Peronism, revolutionary 127, 133–34
Peronist Party (Justicialist movement/*Justicialismo*) 84, 127, 143
Perón, Juan 84, 132, 136
Petrella, Ivan 85
Piccinelli, Mariana 120
Piglia, Ricardo 5, 46, 59, 67
Pigna, Felipe 108–09, 111
    and Instituto Nacional de Revisionismo Histórico 110
    on Madres de Plaza de Mayo 117
    on Malvinas conflict 119
    on 'La noche de los bastones largos' [Night of the Long Sticks] 114
    on *el Proceso* 119
    on tango 120
*piqueteros* (activist groups) 3, 21, 92, 129
*Pizza, Birra, Faso* (dir. Caetano and Stagnaro) 80
Podalsky, Laura 48, 49
*política afectiva* 27, 29
popular history 108–09
postmodernism 12
Prebisch, Alberto 50, 51
*el Proceso* [Process of National Reorganization, 1976–1983] 15, 16
    *afectados* 20
    Club Atlético, clandestine prison 58, *58*
    CONADEP (Comisión Nacional para la Desaparición de Personas) *Nunca más* report 16, 100–01, 102
    'dirty war,' term 36 n. 17
    Escuela Mecánica de la Armada (ESMA) [Navy Mechanics School] clandestine detention centre, Buenos Aires 17, 18, 100–02, 107, 115, 130
    Pigna on 119
    sites of repression 17–19
    'two demons' theory 16, 19, 152
    *see also desaparecidos* ('disappeared' persons)

Puerto Madero, Buenos Aires 72, *73*, 73–74, 77
Puerto Nuevo (dir. Soffici and Amadori) 77–79, *78*
Puerto Nuevo, Buenos Aires 77–78
'Punto Final' legislation 16

Radowitzky, Simón 111, 112
Radway, Janice 60
*Revolución libertadora* [Liberating Revolution] 84, 136
Rio de Janeiro, *favelas* 77
Riva, Gastón *24*, 25
Rock, David 133
*rock nacional* music genre 118–19, *119*, 120, 121
*Rodrigazo* uprising 22
Rojas, Patricia 26
Rolnik, Suely 27, 29
Roman Catholic Church 85
    Liberation Theology 85–87
Romero, Luis Alberto 111, 113
Rosas, Juan Manuel de 48
Rosemberg, Diego 26
Rothenberg, Molly Ann 2
Rúa, Fernando de la 2, 23, 60
Ruarte Britos, Tatiana 107

Sábato, Ernesto 16
Sábato, Hilda 111
Samuel, Raphael 6, 98, 105, 109
Sánchez, Sonia 29
Santa Cruz church, Buenos Aires 115
San Telmo district, Buenos Aires *18*
Santoro, Daniel 141
Sarlo, Beatriz 7–8, 117, 130, 136–37
Sarmiento, Domingo Faustino:
    *Civilización y barbarie* [Civilization and Barbarism] 48, 109
Scorer, James 72, 77
Second Vatican Council 85
Semán, Ernesto 127
sex workers 29
Shaviro, Steven 81
Sheffield:
    Castle Market 51–52
    Park Hill housing estate 42
'silencio es salud' placard on Obelisk 52, *53*, 54
Silvestri, Graciela 50
Sinclair, Iain 44
Sitrin, Marina:
    definitions of horizontalism 5, 21, 27, 91–92, 144
    H.I.J.O.S. and horizontalism 20
    horizontalism and *Argentinazo* 129
slums/shanty towns, *see villas miseria* (shanty towns)
social class 26, 131, 133–34, 135
Soffici, Mario 77
Solanas, Fernando 79
Sommers, Doris 109
Sosa, Cecilia 17, 20

'space of agonism' 76
spectrality, *see* hauntology
Spinetta, Luis 118
Stagnaro, Bruno 80
'structures of feeling' 153
    *Aparecidos* 17
    *Elefante blanco* 66, 95
    Gamerro's *Los bustos de Eva* 131, 147
    *Lo que el tiempo nos dejó* 7, 122
    *Mu* (periodical) 27, 35
    Williams, R. 2, 3, 13, 130, 151
suburbs in cinema 5, 80–81
Svampa, Maristella 2, 22

Tanfuri, Manfredo 44
tango 120
Telefe Argentina 6, 104, 107
*telenovela* genre 106–07, 109
television:
    *Algo habrán hecho por la historia argentina* [They Must Have Done Something for Argentine History], historical docudrama 109
    *Años Rebeldes* [Rebel Years], telenovela 106–07
    'Argentina's Dirty War', documentary 102
    docudrama genre 106
    'historical event television' 105–06
    *Montecristo*, serial 107
    and *el Proceso* 107
    *telenovela* genre 106–07, 109
    *Televisión por la Identitdad*, serial 107
    *see also Lo que el tiempo nos dejó* [What the Past Has Left Us] (TV mini-series)
Thatcher, Margaret 1
theme parks and leisure parks:
    Ciudad Deportiva de La Boca *71*, 72
    Interama/Parque de la Ciudad 66, *69*, 69–70, *70*, 71, 72, 74–75
    theme park, concept 72
torture porn 14
Torre Espacial, Villa Lugano 69–70, 72, 74–75, *75*, 80
Trapero, Pablo 81, 88
    *El Bonaerense* 80
    *Carancho* 80
    *Mundo Grúa* 80
    *see also Elefante blanco* [White Elephant] (dir. Pablo Trapero)
Trellick Tower, London 42
Triple A (Alianza Anticomunista Argentina), death squad 134, 135
'two demons' theory 16, 19, 152
2001 Crisis, Argentina, *see Argentinazo* (2001 Crisis, Argentina)

University of Buenos Aires 113–14
    Eudeba publishing house 113
Urraca, Beatriz 80

utopianism:
    failed utopias  41, 42, 82–84
    hauntology and  43, 44
    historicity and  61, 62
    and horizontalism  94
    Liberation Theology and  86–87
    modernism and  41, 42, 51–52

Vasena metalworks, Buenos Aires  58
Vezzetti, Hugo  16, 85
Videla, Jorge Rafael  15
Vila, Pablo  118, 119
Villa 20:  74
Villa 31, Buenos Aires  76, 85
Villa Desocupación (later Puerto Nuevo), Buenos Aires  78
Villa Esperanza (later Puerto Nuevo), Buenos Aires  78
Villa Lugano, Buenos Aires  5, 74
    Ciudad Deportiva  71, 72
    Ciudad Oculta  5–6, 75–76, 81–82, 83–84, 84–87, 88
    Interama/Parque de la Ciudad  66, 69–70, 70, 71, 72, 74–75
    Torre Espacial  69–70, 72, 74–75, 75, 80
    Villa 20:  74
Villa Rodrigo Bueno, Buenos Aires  76, 77
*villas miseria* (shanty towns)  5–6, 66, 74, 75–76, 77–79
    *curas villeros*  85, 88
    see also *Elefante blanco* [White Elephant] (dir. Pablo Trapero)
violence, normalization of  127, 135, 137

Wagner, Keith  87
Walsh, Rodolfo  26, 31, 33, 140
Waterworks Palace [Palacio de las aguas corrientes], Buenos Aires  54, 55, 56
Williams, Raymond:
    on culture  3, 4, 7
    on historicity  13
    'structure of feeling'  2, 3, 13, 130, 151
Wilson, Jason  47
Wolfreys, Julian  44
Wylde, Christopher  1–2

Zibechi, Raúl  21–22, 27, 33

www.ingramcontent.com/pod-product-compliance
Lightning Source LLC
Chambersburg PA
CBHW050454110426
42743CB00017B/3355